Baseball in Omaha

BASEBALL IN OMAHA

Devon M. Niebling and Thomas Hyde

ARCADIA
PUBLISHING

ISBN 978-0-7385-3276-9

Published by Arcadia Publishing,
Charleston, South Carolina

Printed in the United States of America

Library of Congress Catalog Card Number: 2004110242

For all general information contact Arcadia Publishing at:
Telephone 843-853-2070
Fax 843-853-0044
E-mail sales@arcadiapublishing.com
For customer service and orders:
Toll-Free 1-888-313-2665

Visit us on the Internet at www.arcadiapublishing.com

Contents

Acknowledgments		6
Introduction		7
1.	League Park: Hub of Early Omaha Baseball	9
2.	Sandlot Rivalries and Local Heroes	25
3.	College World Series: National Scene, Local Tradition	45
4.	Omaha Builds a Ballpark: Rosenblatt and Community	55
5.	And the Band Played . . . Cardinals, Dodgers, and Polka	77
6.	Trader Jack Came to Omaha	97
Special Thanks		128

ACKNOWLEDGMENTS

I would like to dedicate this book to my parents Ralph and Mary Jean Hyde, my wife Deborah, and children Rebecca and Laura. I cannot forget my grandfather, George Lechner, who I fondly remember talking about baseball with and listening to on the radio. Also, I must mention the Lechner family: Mike Suydan, Dejuan Cribbs, and Mike Kelly at MAT. I cannot fail to mention Rich Herold and Pep Riha, the Nebraska Oldtimers Association, Joann Meyer, and Rita at the Douglas County Historical Society and Museum, where my interest in baseball began. Especially, I must thank Joann Meyer, Rita Jerins, Don Snoddy, and Elizabeth Krecek for facilitating my research there. Also, my best friend, Tad Deja (who really got me involved in baseball history and statistical analysis); one day when you are not scared you'll actually run our all-time fantasy baseball league.

Also, to all the Negro Leaguers who played in Omaha and elsewhere, your greatest is not forgotten.

Once again, my parents, wife Deb, and children Rebecca and Laura. I cannot forget my grandparents or my uncle. Wherever you are, I wish you could be here to enjoy this.

I also wish to thank the Durham Western Heritage Museum, Omaha World-Herald, the Omaha Bee, and the NCAA.

Finally, to Mr. Tyrus Raymond Cobb, the greatest ballplayer in the world of all time. Wherever you are, God bless you.

–Thomas Hyde

For a small book, the list of thanks runs long and deep. For research assistance and encouragement along the way, thank you to Les Valentine, Bob Nash, Gary Anderson, Janelle Lindberg, Kathryn Morrissey, Carol Foreman, Kim Mickelsen, Keely Rennie, Doug Stewart, Kevin McNabb, Sandy Wilson, Don Preister, Michael Daily, and Dan Worth. Thanks to the Omaha World Herald's Mike Kelly for coffee and conversation. For stories and a love of Omaha and baseball, thank you and much gratitude to Gary Domet, Sam Piccolo, Lou Marcuzzo, Jesse Cuevas, Brian and Jana Donohoe, Pat O'Donnell, and Steve Hayes. Thanks to Tim Hantula, Jim Fields, and Paul Lugo for technical assistance and good humor. A special thanks to my mother and sister for staying close; Andy Meeks, Jane O'Brien, Michele Miller, Jen McWilliams, Kaz Ikeda, and Chinnapat Wirachakul for asking about the book; Nora Hantula for inquiring about photos, and Will and Sadie for vigilance. Finally, thank you to Gary Kastrick of Project Omaha at South High School, Mr. Kastrick's students, and the South High front office staff; thank you for the conversations, material, and opportunity to work at South High.

For Dad, who would have done the legwork for this project.

–Devon Niebling

INTRODUCTION

Omaha became an incorporated municipality on February 2, 1857. Coming together on the west bank of the Missouri River, Omaha grew into a town along the practical gridlines of the surveyor's map. Dirt-packed streets led away from the riverbank, straight, serious paths into the heart of the early business district. Paths opened to the squares and rectangles of frame and brick buildings.

Then came the maze of tracks, the railroad lines in and out and around Union Station, narrowing at 10th Street, only to broaden and stretch up and out to the sky and into the vast plain, halving the horizon. With the trains came livestock for the stockyards and packing plants; South Omaha had four major players: Armour in 1897, Cudahy in 1897, Dold slightly later, and Swift, the first, in 1855. The Livestock Exchange rose up, casting the symmetrical maze of yard pens in shadow. Krug, Metz, and Storz added breweries, and the town blocks continued to fill.

Writing in 1938 for the Federal Writers' Project, Maria Donohoe noted the location of Bohemian Town or Little Bohemia in the vicinity bound by 10th Street on the east, 16th Street on the west, Pierce Street on the north, and Center Street on the south. Czechs began arriving in 1868, with many initially finding jobs in the smelting works or packing plants. Vaclav Stepanek built the first dance hall at 13th and William, a building later converted into St. Wenceslaus, the first Bohemian Catholic Church. Edward Rosewater, publisher of the *Omaha Bee* arrived in Omaha in 1863.

Sicilians began arriving in 1905 at a time when the railroads needed maintenance crews and shop workers. Packing plants and stockyards continued to expand.

John Gondola, Genoa native and "maker and repairer of boots and shoes," is known to have been in Omaha as early as 1857 when he was listed as a leading merchant. As far as is known, Gondola was the first permanent Omaha settler of Italian origin. Little Italy was defined on the east by the Missouri River, on the north by Marcy Street, extending westward to 20th or 24th and Poppleton.

Immigrants from Poland settled north and northeast of the stockyards at 41st and J Street or 32nd and K Street, with the Irish also on the north end, immediately west and southwest of the Yards at 36th and Q Street.

The blocks settled and churches went up. Sokol Halls and centers for community festivals and music were popular for each section of the growing city.

In time the blocks eased, and the lines gave way to diamonds, the wooden benches, dirt, and scrubby grass diamonds of the community sandlots. The rough, makeshift diamonds of ballparks that became as important to the life of the city as the train tracks, yard pens, and livestock exchange rates. Brown Park at 18th and S Street. Fontenelle Park at 42nd. Miller Park at 24th and Kansas, and Riverview Park at 10th and Deer Park. Union Pacific and the Stockyards, Cudahys, Armour, and other companies sponsored teams and the teams multiplied enough to require leagues. The *Omaha Bee* records company picnics and long afternoon games of baseball.

When Thomas J. Hickey's American Association baseball league came together in the fall of 1901, Omaha was to be one of the eight charter cities, but before the initial season began, committee members decided Omaha was too far removed geographically from the other cities in the league. Louisville, Kentucky, was contracted as a replacement.

In the early throes of the national Depression, Omaha was a city on the Western League of Colored Baseball Club barnstorming tour, a tour that in the 1920s included Oklahoma City, Tulsa, Topeka, Wichita, Kansas City, and St. Joseph. J.L. Wilkinson fought the Depression malaise by drawing fans with his portable lighting system, a lighting system Wilkinson commissioned the Giant Manufacturing Company of Omaha to build. The system cost between fifty and one-hundred thousand dollars and included an elaborate, innovative network of telescoping poles for lights suspended 50 feet above the playing field. Poles were fastened to truck beds and raised by means of derricks. A 250-horsepower motor powered a generator that fueled the system.

A mainstay of the Western League beginning in 1885, Omaha was left without a playing field after the grandstand of Western League Park at 15th and Vinton burned in August 1936. Depression conditions made it impossible to rebuild the park, and Omaha dropped out of the pro ball leagues for more than a decade. The *Omaha World Herald* carried an article about the "alarming cost of baseballs" at this time:

It is no trick at all, for instance, to spend two hundred dollars in a season for these most essential little pellets. Bill Williams, who managed the Saunders System club to a Metropolitan league and city championship last year, said the bill for balls was 210.00.

It isn't that all these balls are worn out, knocked cock-eyed or driven out of the park on long drives. Most teams on Sunday lose from four to a dozen during a game because the kids in the crowd run off with the fouls.

At Fontenelle Park, the teams have lots of trouble over stolen balls because of the large crowds. The mascots and kids kept around the team have difficulty breaking through the crowd in time to see who stuck the ball in his pocket.

Yet baseball continued to be played.

Ruth and Gehrig came to town in the 1920s, and a fellow named Rosenblatt envisioned a new stadium on the hill overlooking the Missouri. The semi-pro, amateur, and school leagues thrived in the 1930s and pro ball came back in the 1940s.

The Western League, American Association, and Pacific Coast League. Omaha Municipal Stadium to Johnny Rosenblatt Stadium. Wood tiers to multi-million dollar seats beneath a state-of-the art press box. The American Legion Little World Series to the College World Series.

Continuity. Baseball is about continuity. An *Omaha World-Herald* editorial celebrating the 50th anniversary of the College World Series in Omaha speaks to Omaha's relationship with the greater social and cultural institution of baseball:

It's about more than the games, though. It's about friendships, some spanning decades, that form in the stands and grow from one CWS to the next. It's about good food and drink, about relaxing and enjoying a city that has come to fit the series like a comfortable old shoe.

Growing out and beyond the grand old lines of the railroad tracks, livestock pens, and neighborhoods, the ball diamonds and the promise of Saturdays spent playing from dawn to dusk kept the spirit of community, of diamonds and circles. Baseball was a common language for immigrants, a form of leisure and story shared by neighborhoods and generations.

ONE

League Park
Hub of Early Omaha Baseball

Not long after statehood, Omaha's first experience with organized baseball was on November 10, 1869, when a group of locals lost to the Cincinnati Reds, 65-1, at the Douglas County Fairgrounds in front of a crowd of 2,000.

About ten years later, the Northwestern League, the first minor league west of the Eastern Seaboard, was formed by Ted Sullivan. Omaha played its first professional league game as a result of this league on May 8, 1879, against Dubuque, and lost, 6-3. But the league was disbanded on July 7.

Omaha became a member of the Western League in 1885 but disbanded on June 4 and the franchise transferred to Keokuk. However, the league closed a week later. After having no team in 1886, it played its games on 20th and Lake Street, which was a good site because it was easily accessible to horse cars and trams. Omaha finished that season 36-65 and in sixth place of eight teams. In 1888, Ed Parmalee filed an injunction against the team because of the bad language and the frequent baseballs hitting his home. The injunction was denied when it was discovered that other homeowners had no similar complaints against the park. The 1889 season brought a pennant to Omaha, but the following year the team slid back into mediocrity, and in 1891, on July 12, it disbanded. A reorganized Omaha team played until September 15, when lack of team finances and low attendance at home games forced the team to fold before the final few games of the season. Even though Omaha was having a better year in terms of winning and finances, lack of finances still caused the league to fold by July 17.

Omaha spent 1893 without a league, but became part of the league again in 1894. Unfortunately, money was still a problem, as it would be in 1895 and 1896. It tried to field a team again in 1898 but disbanded in midseason.

In the fall of 1899, the Western League was reformed and Omaha became a member. That spring, William Rourke and Col. Buchanan Keith were co-managers and co-owners of the team. Omaha's team would play its games at Nonpareil Park on 13th and Vinton, the home of Omaha's professional teams until 1936, originally designed by Isaac Hascall. A grandstand and bleachers were erected to hold 3,600 fans. However, after personal differences in the running of the club, Rourke bought out Keith's share and managed the team on his own.

In 1904, Omaha took its first pennant under Rourke. Omaha was last place in April, but by June had pulled within six games of Denver. They finished the season winning 17 of their last 18 games (including 15 in a row), and took home the Western League flag. Mordecai "Three Finger" Brown and Jack Pfeister anchored the pitching staff, with Brown leading the league in winning percentage and Pfeister leading in strikeouts as well as pitching a no-hitter. Another pennant came to Omaha in 1907, and James Austin lead the league in steals that year.

A full renovation of the park was begun in the fall of 1910 and finished in time for the 1911 season. It included increased seating and parking. However, Pa Rourke resigned as manager and acted only as president of the franchise after 1914. Rourke named Marty Krug as the new manager.

The team won the pennant in 1916 under Krug; many believe this was Rourke's best team! During the war, to counter the drain on resources due to contributions to the war effort at home and the lack of players to replace those going to Europe, the Chamber of Commerce had to help the team's finances. Rourke even introduced twilight baseball to accommodate working people. In July 1918, league play was nevertheless suspended due to the Great War and financial losses.

In 1921, the Rourke era ended as Barney Finch Burch bought the team. He had the team renamed the Buffaloes after a contest in the Omaha Bee. He managed the team in 1924, but after that the fortunes of the team lessened. It was an era of out of control salaries and losing teams. Fan support waned and so did the finances of Burch's teams.

To help make money, Burch decided, after seeing it in Des Moines, to install lights at League Park. Burch hoped to break the record of 11,800 for a single game, but only 7,000 came to watch baseball under the lights. In 1931, a windstorm knocked down a light tower and destroyed the right field fence. Unfortunately, Burch had no insurance. With the mounting financial losses, Burch could barely keep a team in 1932 and had to sell players just to keep the team running. Finally, the league brought a bankruptcy suit against Barney Burch, and Francis "Pug" Griffin managed the team in 1933. Later that year, on December 27, the team's assets were auctioned off.

Mrs. Branconier of St. Louis bought the team in 1934, and Frank Wetzel ran the team through her. By the end of July, she became the team's sole owner. However, the Omaha franchise was later taken away from her for not paying player salaries and disregarding creditors.

Joe McDermott managed and ran the team in 1935, but Mrs. Branconier would not let the team play at League Park as she was still sole owner of it, so the team played in Council Bluffs.

Larry Harlan, a Lincoln insurance man, bought the team in 1936. On July 19, the wind caused $3,000 in damage, destroying three light poles. Games were played in Lincoln until repairs were made. On August 13, Satchel Paige's All-Stars played the House of David team. After the game, at 12:15 p.m., a fire started. The loss to the park was estimated at $45,000.00 and John Ostronic, the park owner, had only $4,000 in insurance. For the rest of the season the team played in Council Bluffs and Omaha would not see professional baseball until the 1950s.

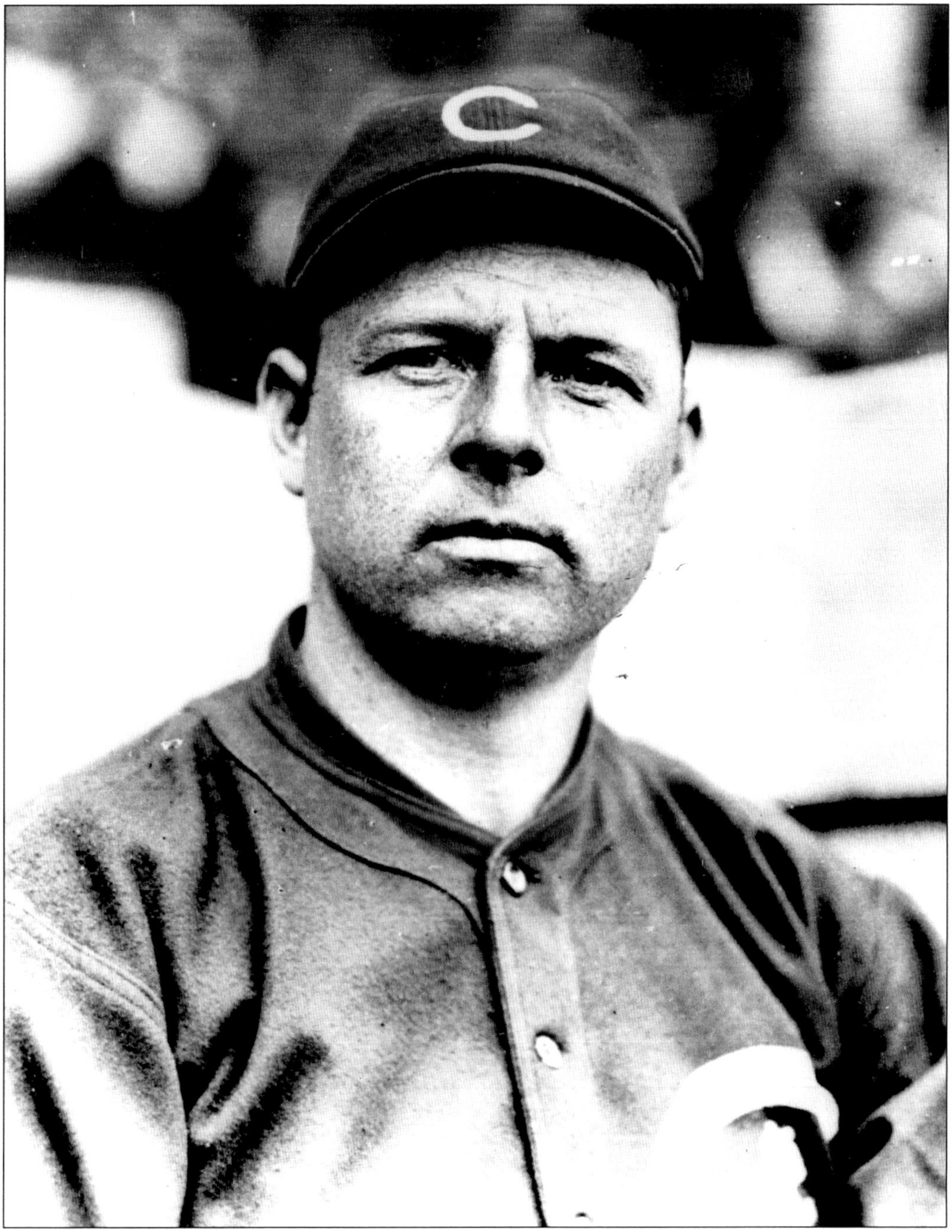

Mordecai "Three-Fingered" Brown was a part of Pa Rourke's pennant winning team of 1904. Brown went on to win two World Series rings with the 1907 and 1908 Chicago Cubs. Brown also played for the Reds and St. Louis in the National League, and Brooklyn and Chicago of the Federal League. Brown was elected to the Hall of Fame in 1949. (Courtesy of the National Baseball Hall of Fame, Cooperstown, New York.)

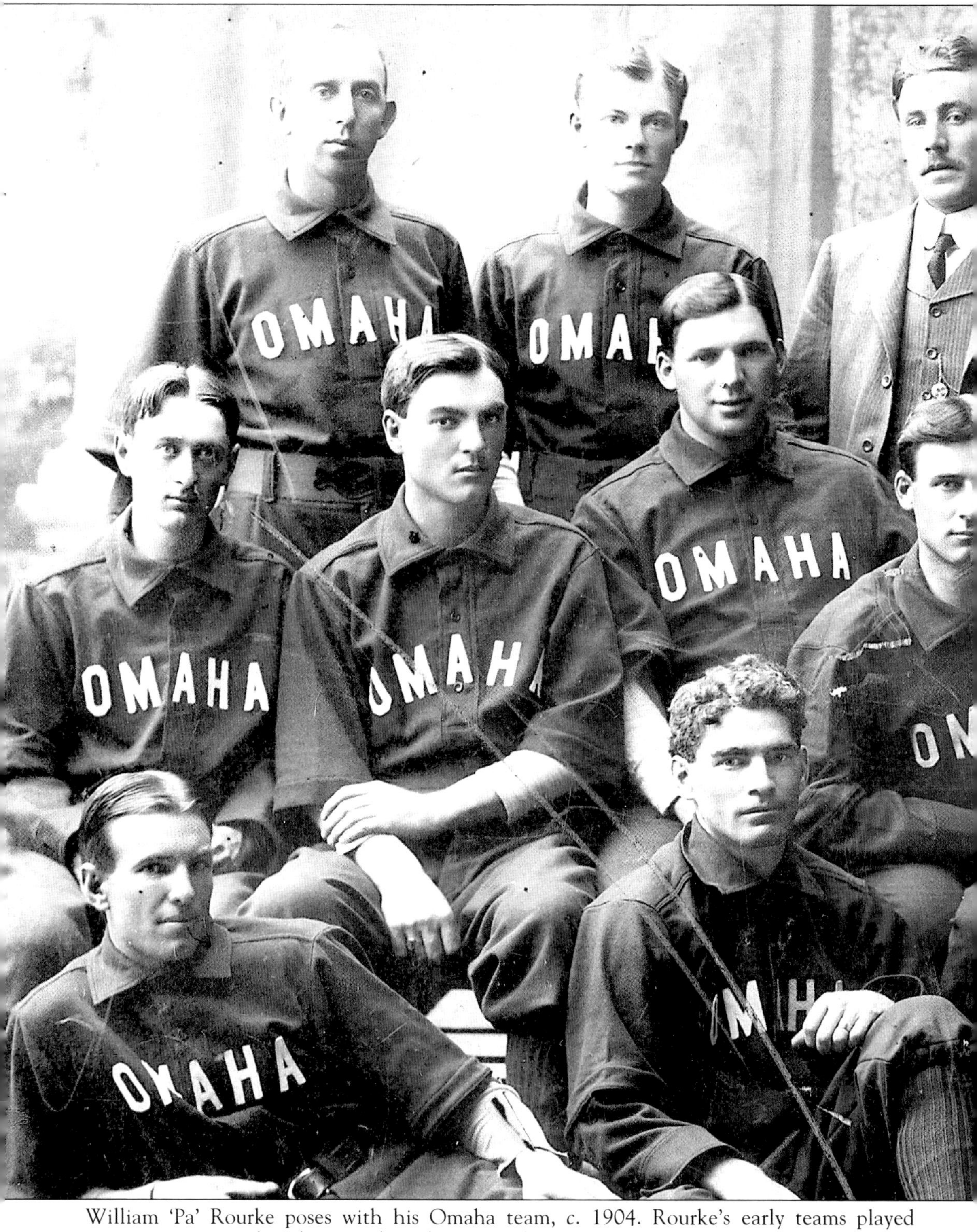

William 'Pa' Rourke poses with his Omaha team, *c.* 1904. Rourke's early teams played games at Nonpareil Park on 13th and Vinton. (Courtesy National Baseball Hall of Fame,

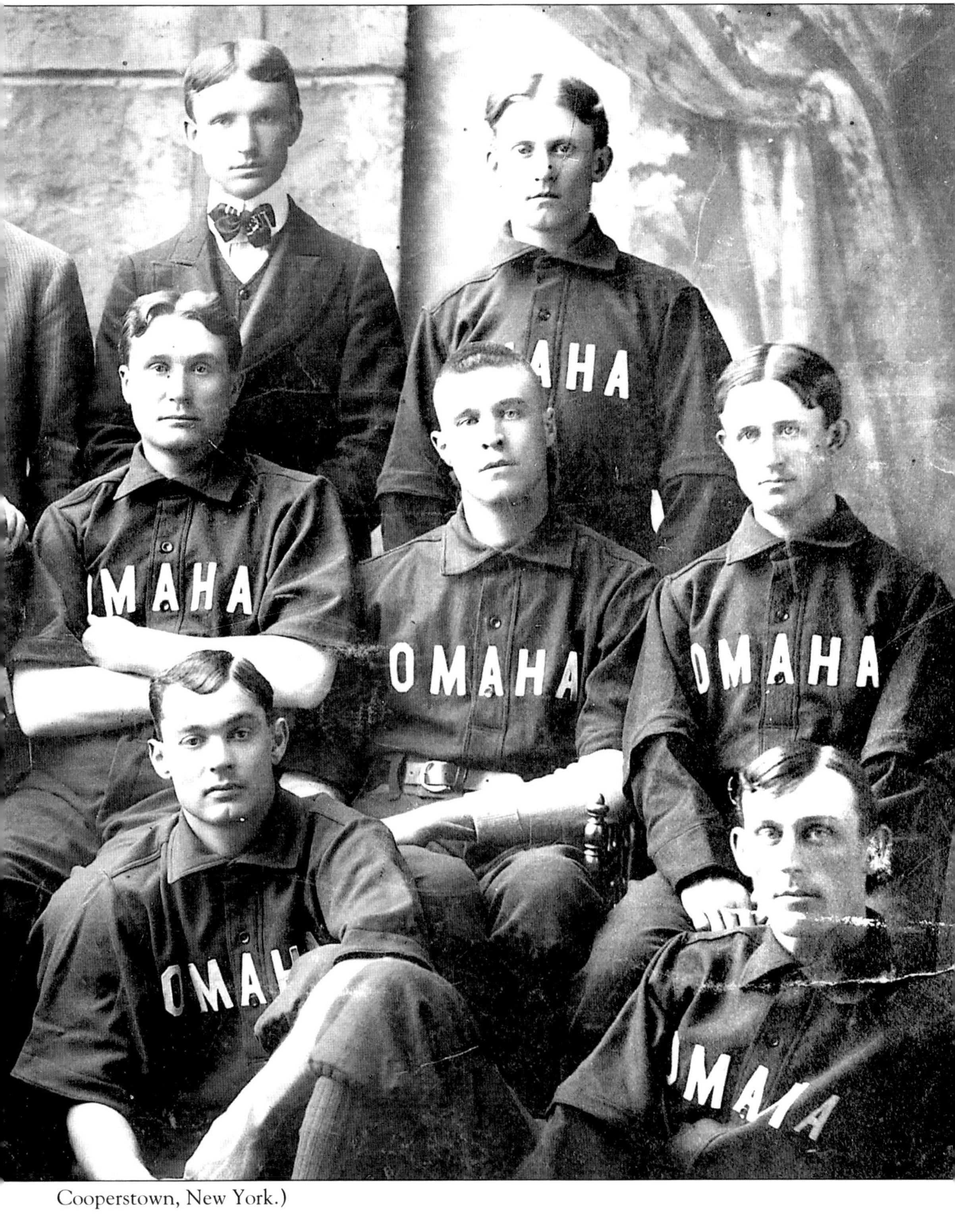

Cooperstown, New York.)

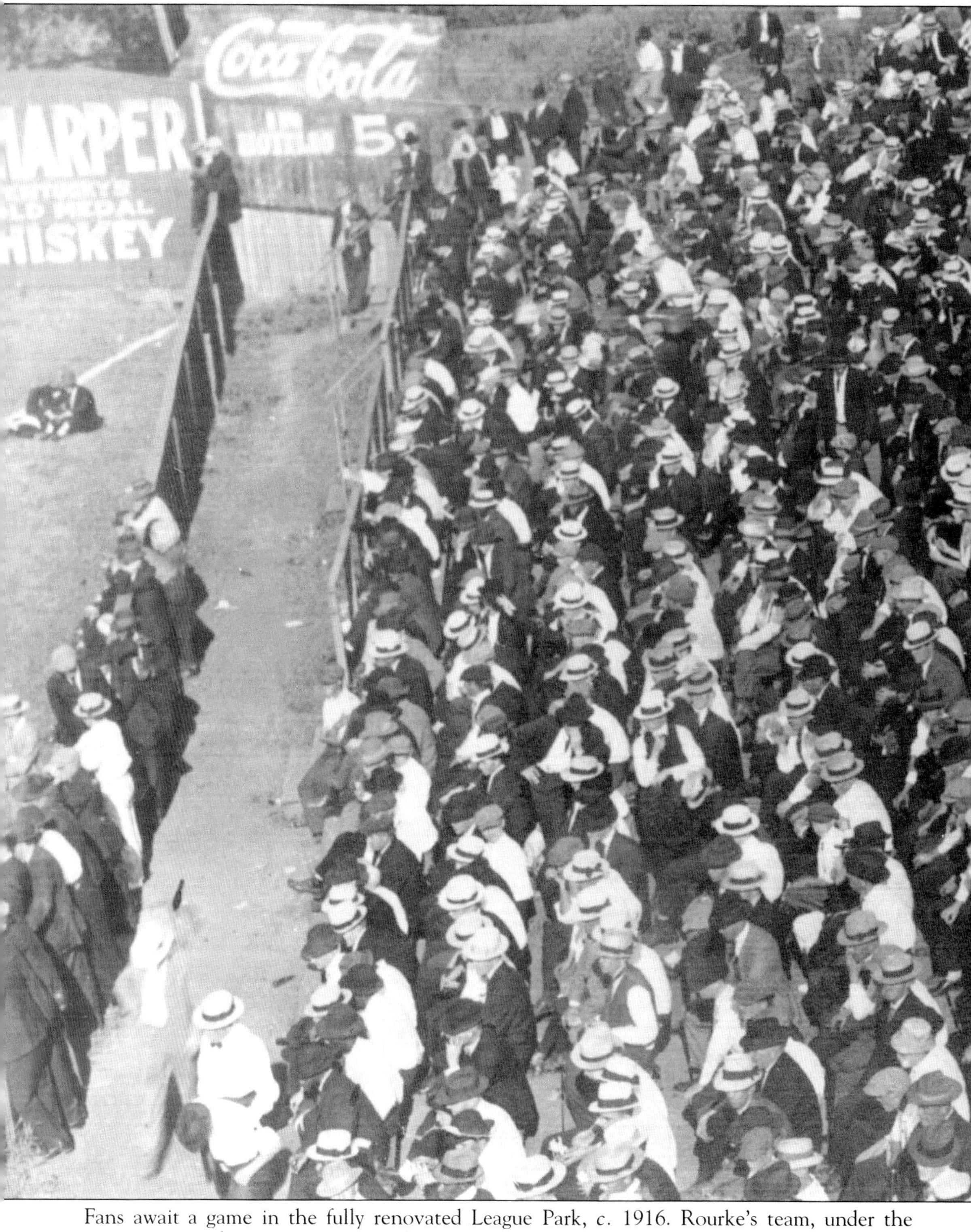

Fans await a game in the fully renovated League Park, *c.* 1916. Rourke's team, under the management of Marty Krug, won the Western League pennant in 1916. (Courtesy of the

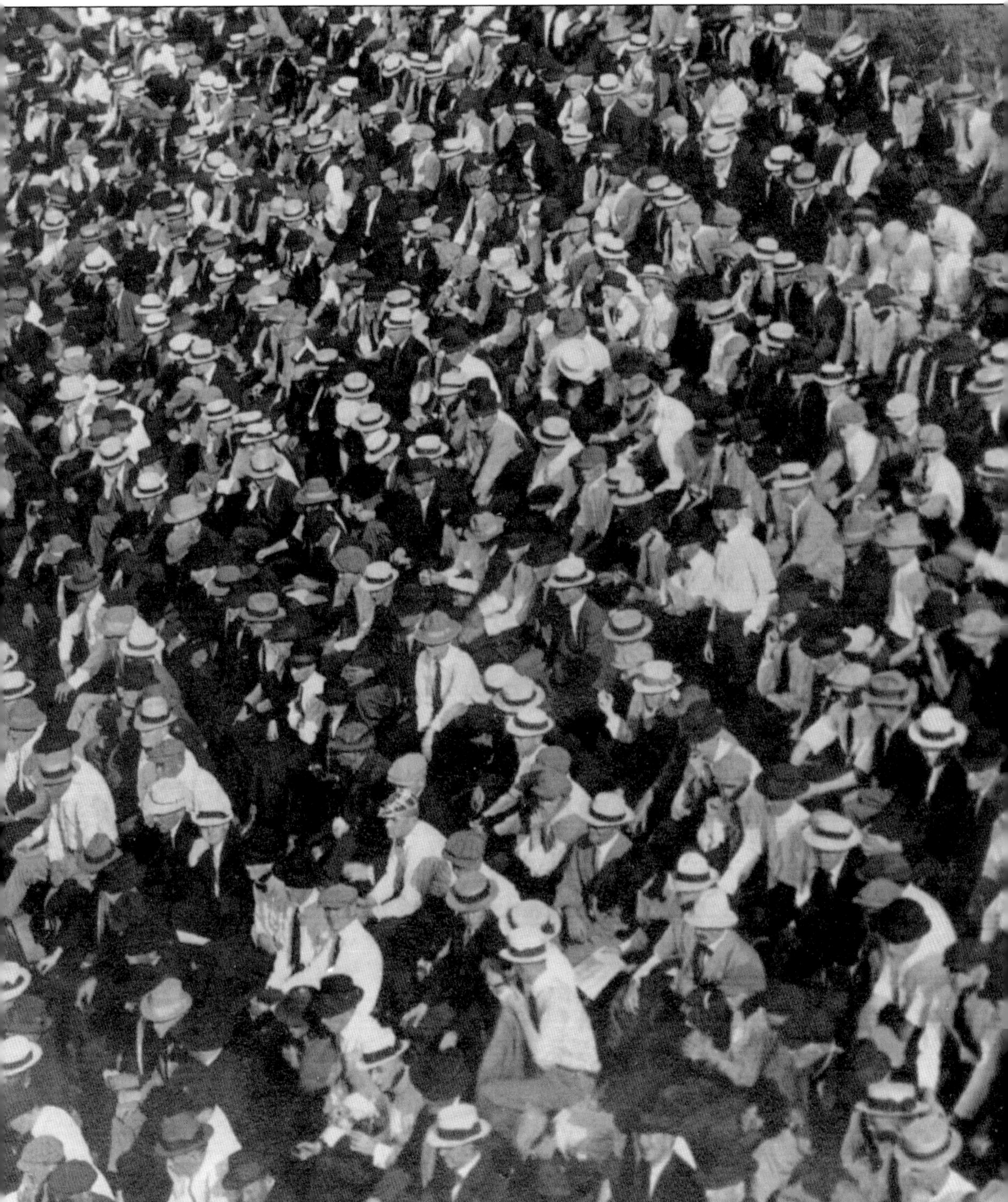

Durham Western Heritage Museum).

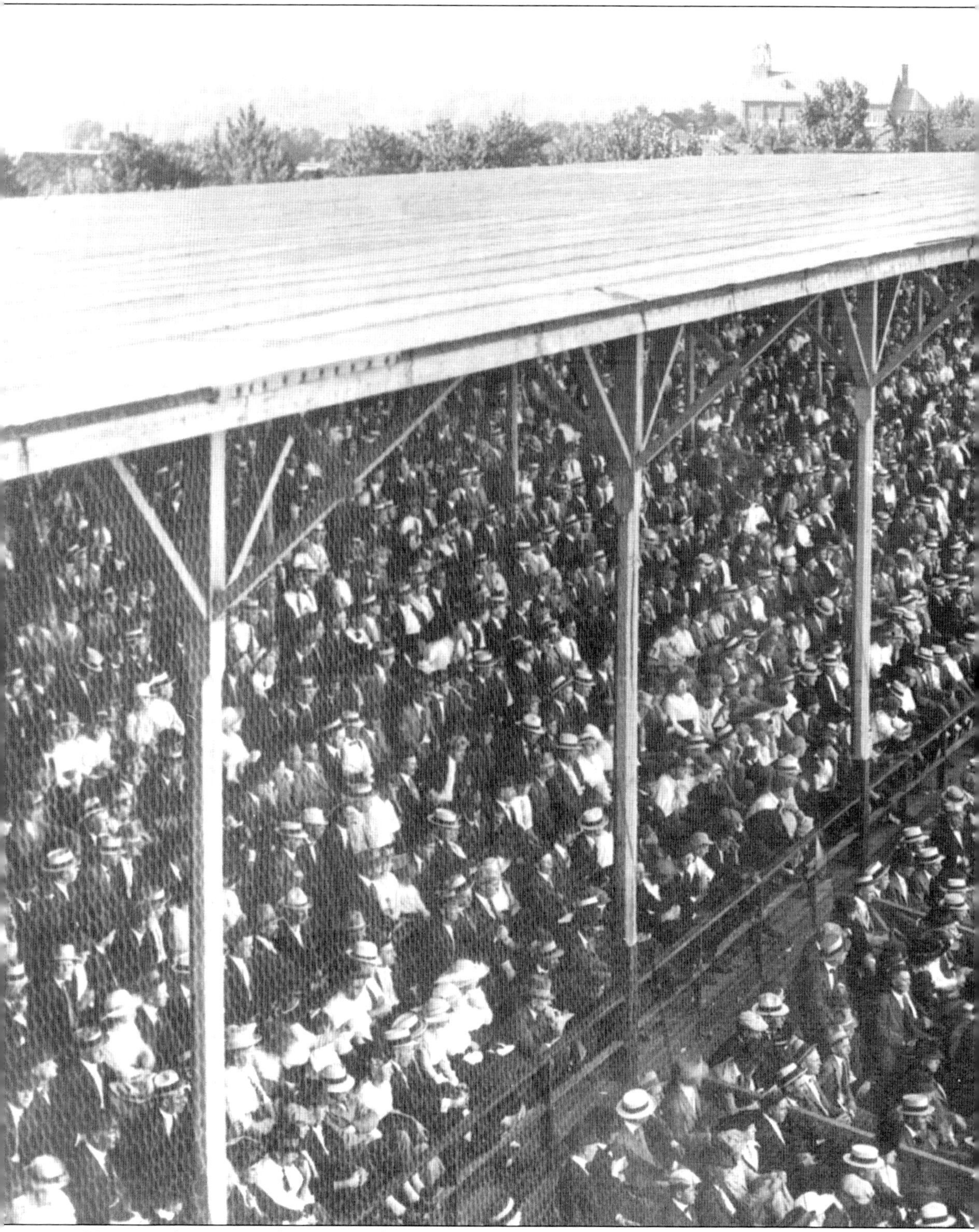

Here is a closer view of League Park's grandstands. Note St. Joseph Hospital beyond the outfield

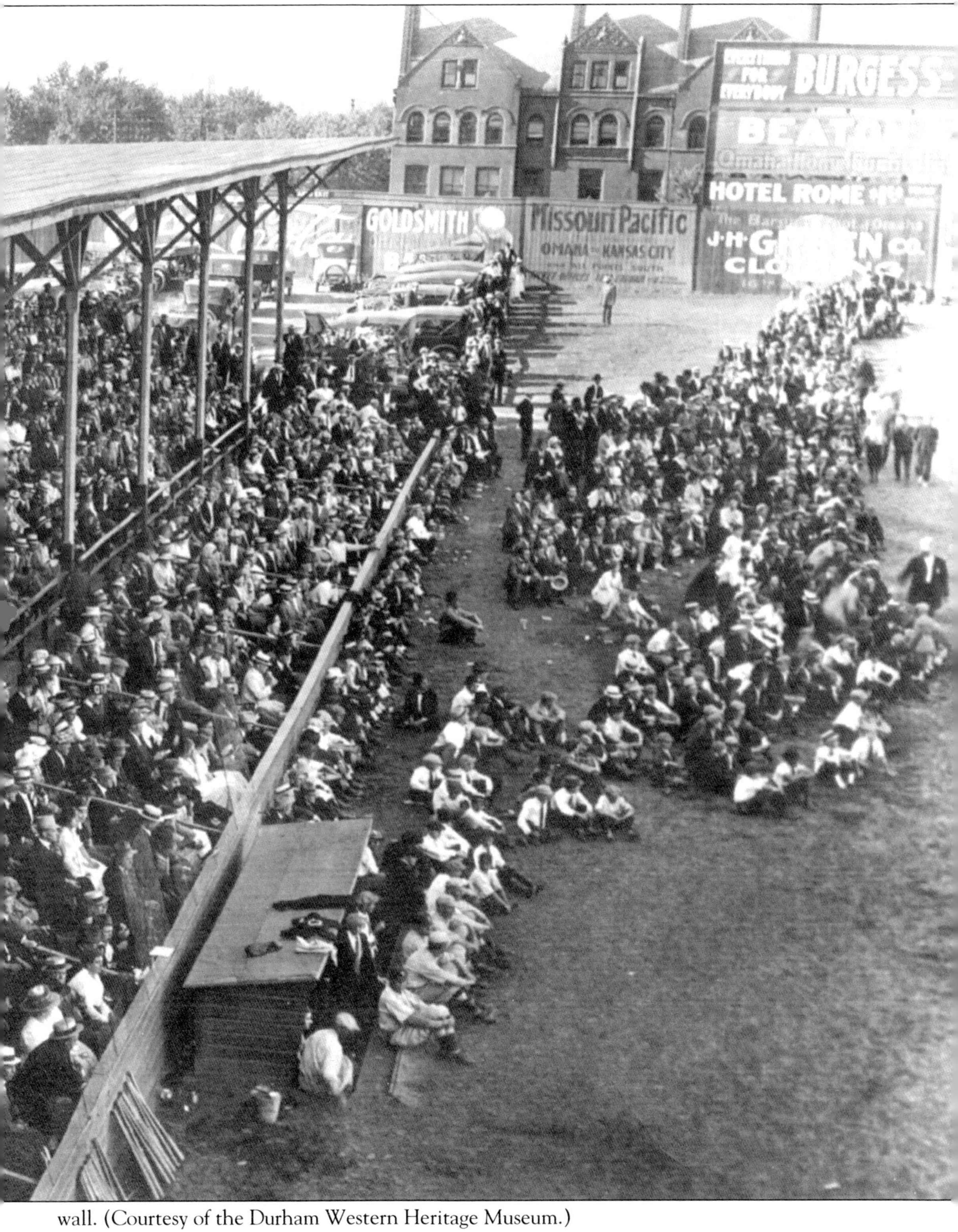

wall. (Courtesy of the Durham Western Heritage Museum.)

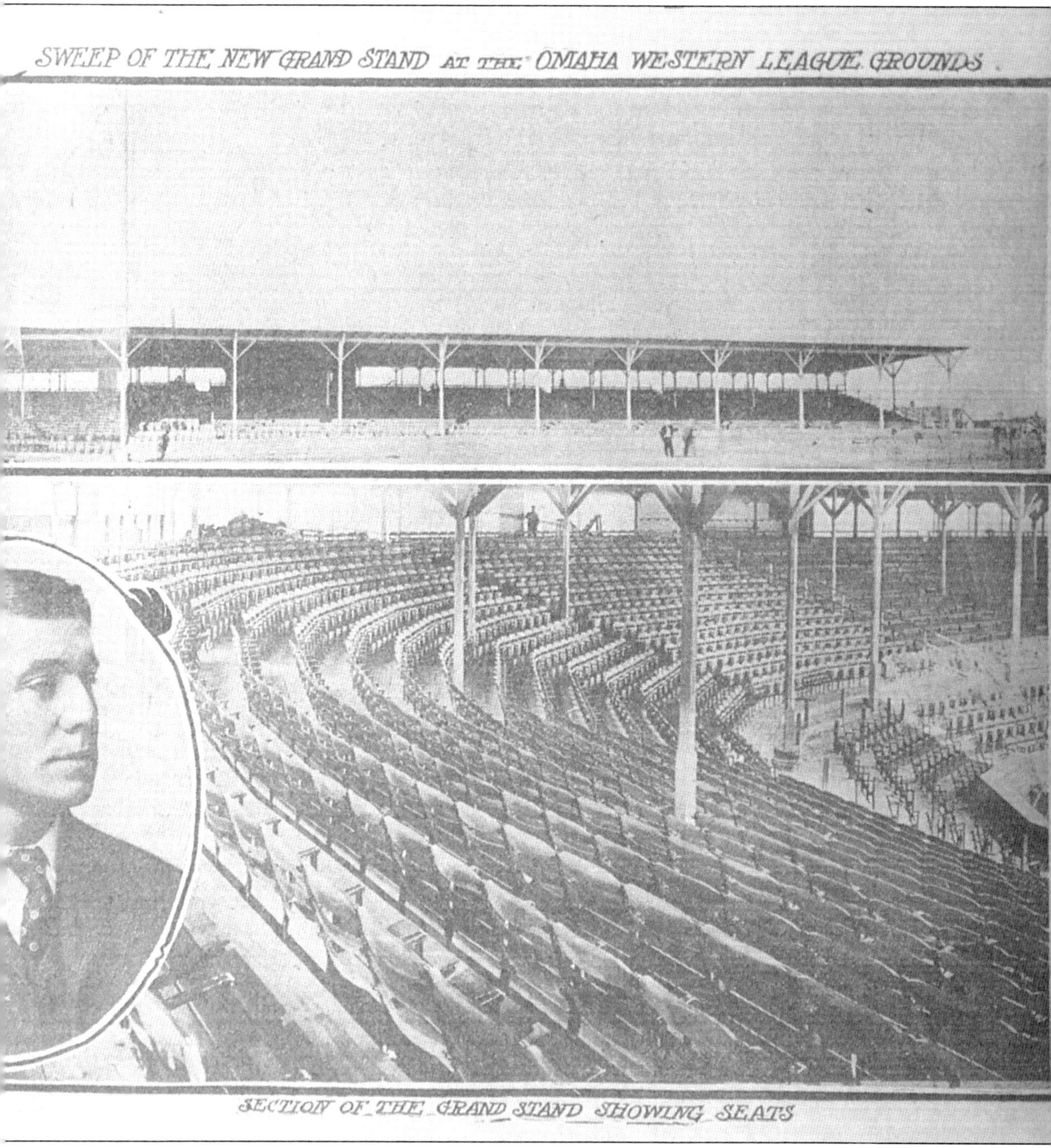

Pa Rourke remodeled the stadium for the 1911 season, a season in which the Omaha Rourkes finished behind the Denver Grizzlies, St. Joseph Drummers, Wichita Jobbers/Pueblo Indians, and Sioux City Packers, but well ahead of the Lincoln Railsplitters, Topeka Kaws, and Des Moines Boosters. (Courtesy of the Douglas County Historical Society, Omaha, Nebraska.)

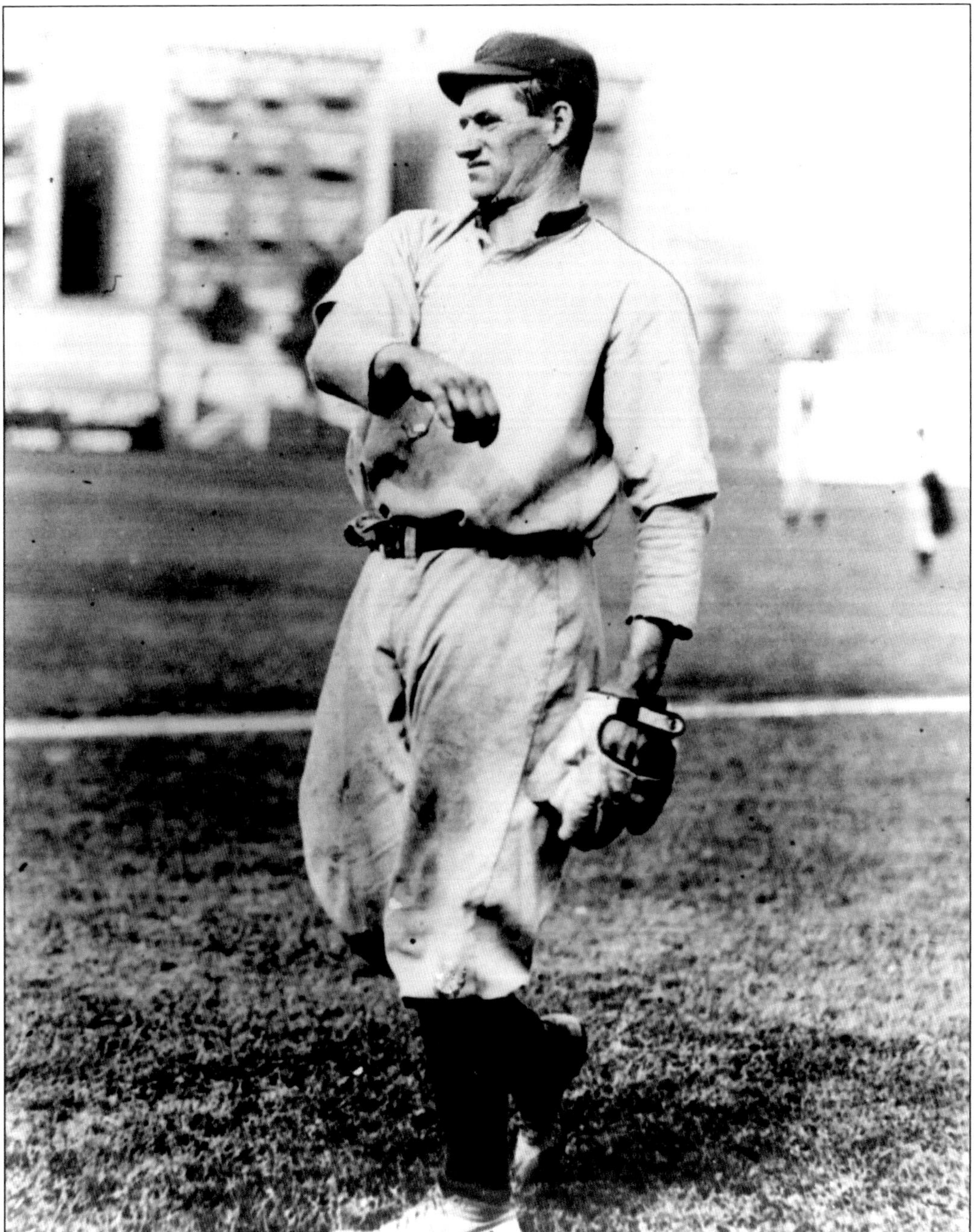

Jimmy "Pepper" Austin, a third baseman under Pa Rourke and famous for his photo with a sliding Ty Cobb, led the Western League in steals in 1907. (Courtesy of the National Baseball Hall of Fame, Cooperstown, New York.)

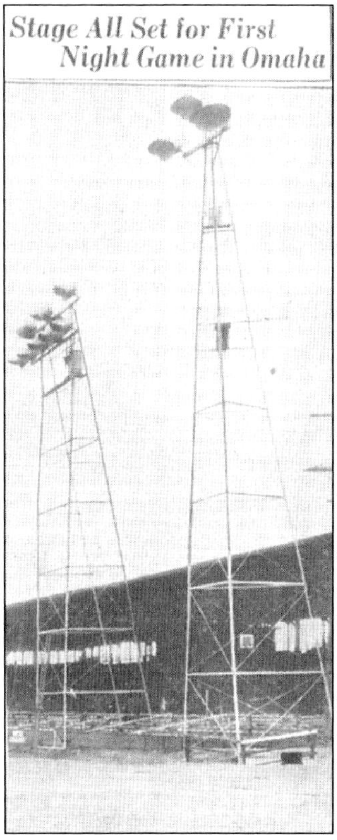

Light towers were constructed in 1930 after Barney Burch saw a night game in Des Moines. Burch had hoped the lights would help ticket sales, but due to lackluster teams, the lights only put him further in debt. (Courtesy of the Douglas County Historical Society, Omaha, Nebraska.)

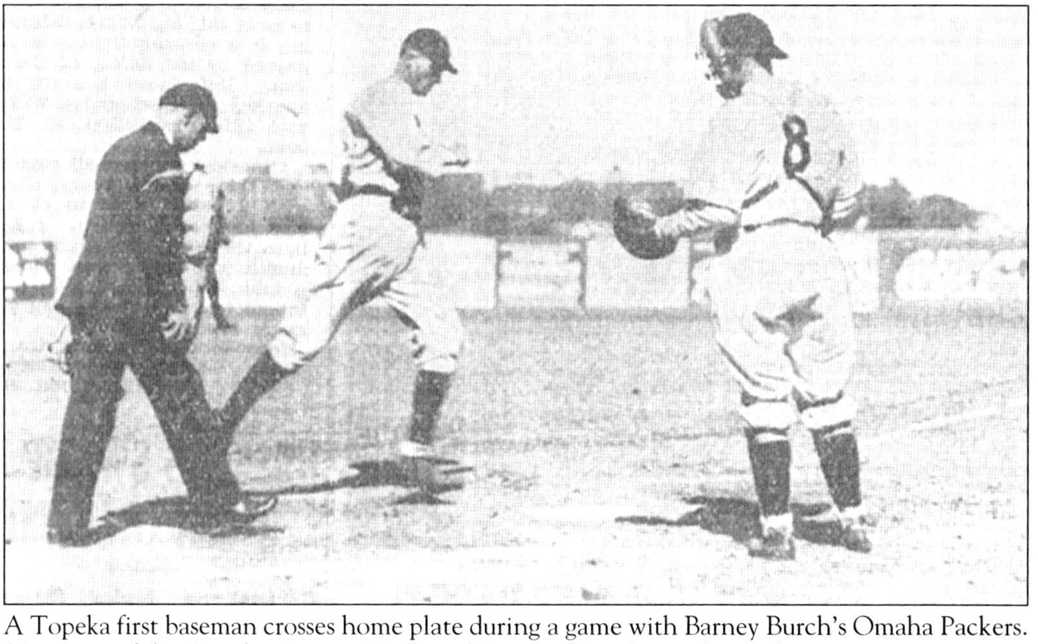

A Topeka first baseman crosses home plate during a game with Barney Burch's Omaha Packers. (Courtesy of the Douglas County Historical Society, Omaha, Nebraska.)

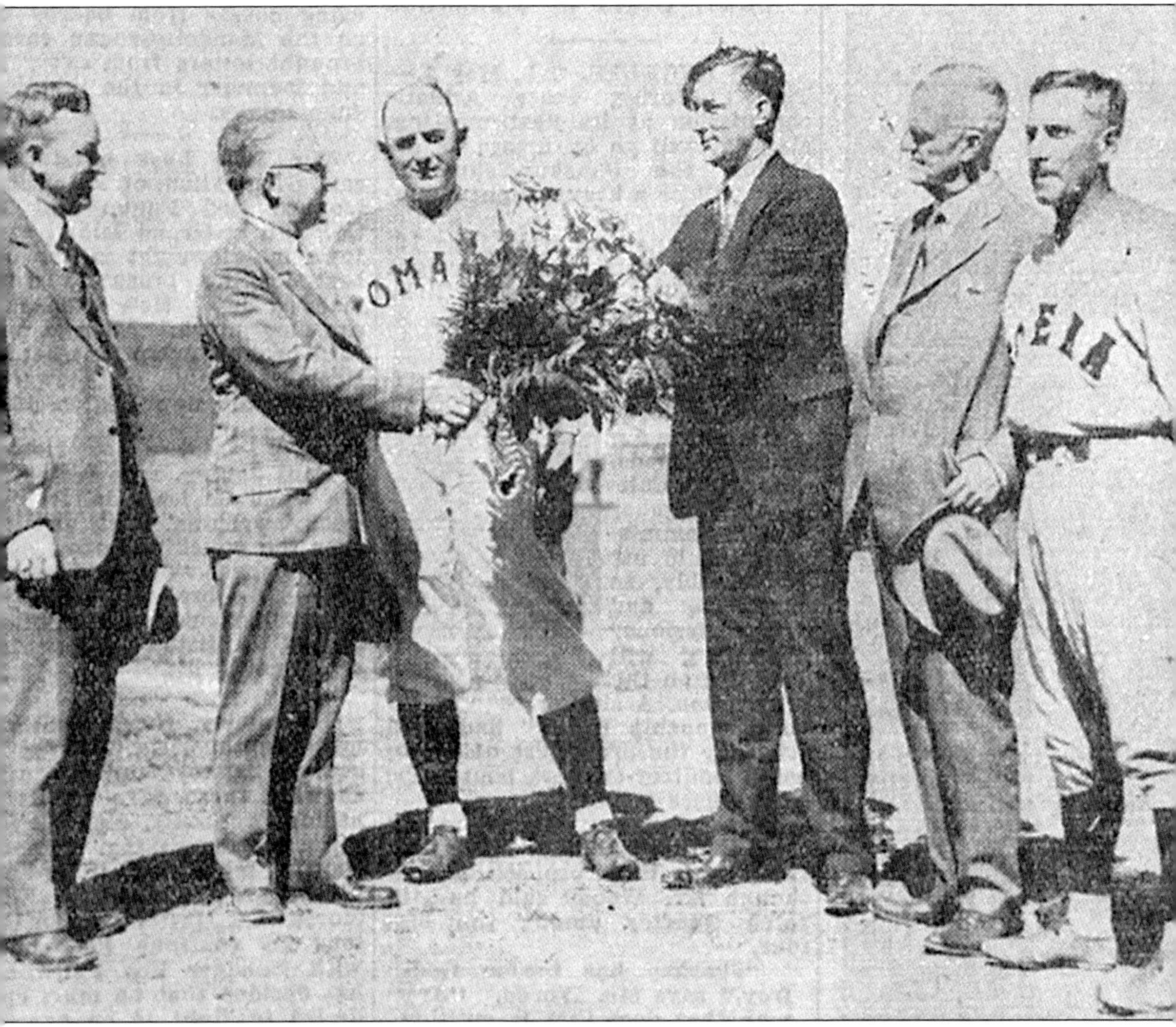

Barney Burch presents an award from the Elks on May 5, 1930. Pictured, from left to right, are: Walter Nelson (Elks secretary), Harry Jones, Spencer Abbott (Omaha manager), Barney Burch, Mayor Metcalfe, and Topeka manager Betzel. (Courtesy of the Douglas County Historical Society, Omaha, Nebraska.)

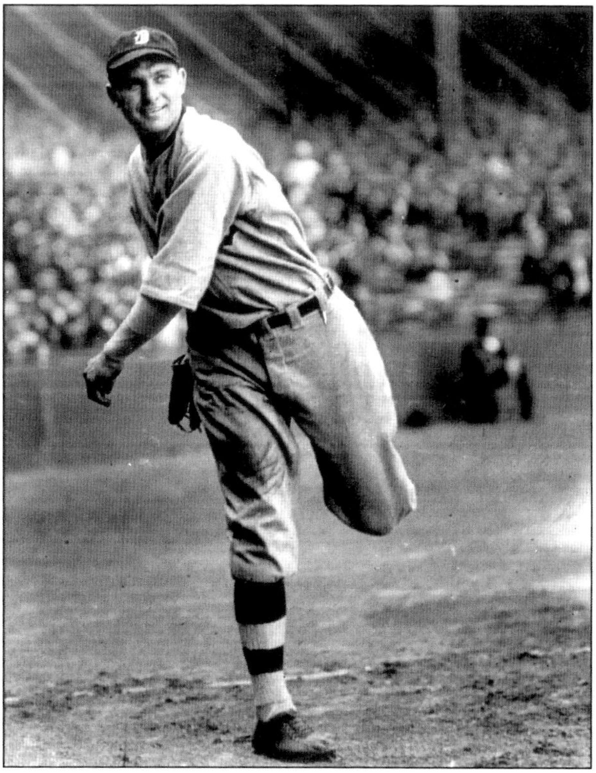

Former Omaha player Heinie Manush played 17 years with the Tigers, Browns, Senators, Red Sox, Robins, and Tigers and was elected to the Hall of Fame in 1964. (Courtesy of the National Baseball Hall of Fame, Cooperstown, New York.)

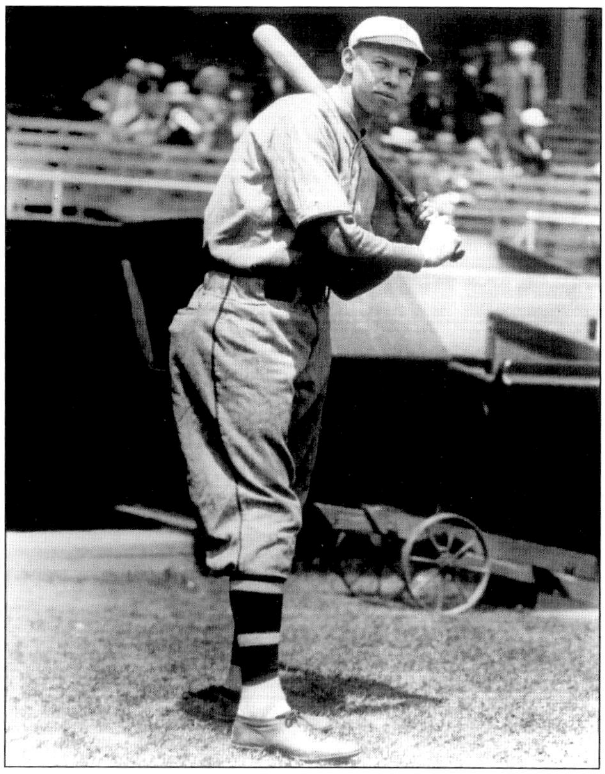

Babe Herman, who played for Barney Burch, became a consistent presence in the major leagues, playing for Brooklyn, Cincinnati, and Detroit, among other teams. Dazzy Vance dubbed Herman the "Headless Horseman of Ebbets Field". (Courtesy National Baseball Hall of Fame, Cooperstown, New York).

Daniel Tipple, a player of the Burch era, had no-hitters in 1922 and a 23-8 record. Tipple also led the Western League with a .793 winning percentage. He played for the New York Yankees in 1915. (Courtesy of the National Baseball Hall of Fame, Cooperstown, New York.)

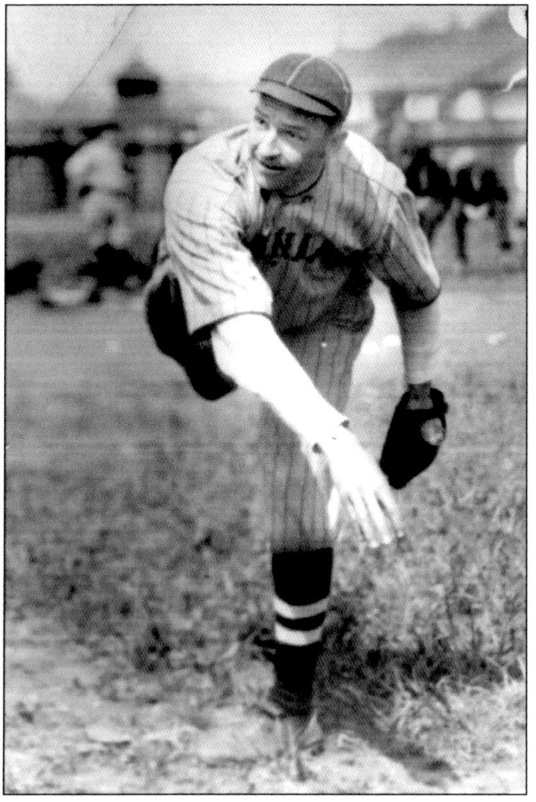

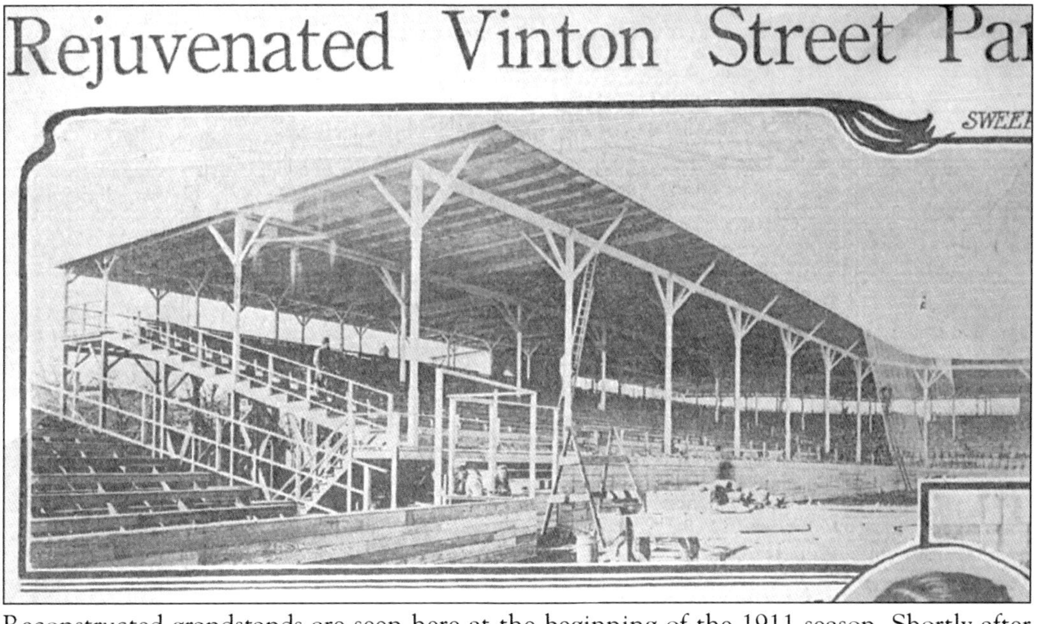

Reconstructed grandstands are seen here at the beginning of the 1911 season. Shortly after this, Cobb's Tigers came to town but did not play exhibition games with Omaha due to inclement weather. (Courtesy of the Collections of the Douglas County Historical Society, Omaha, Nebraska.)

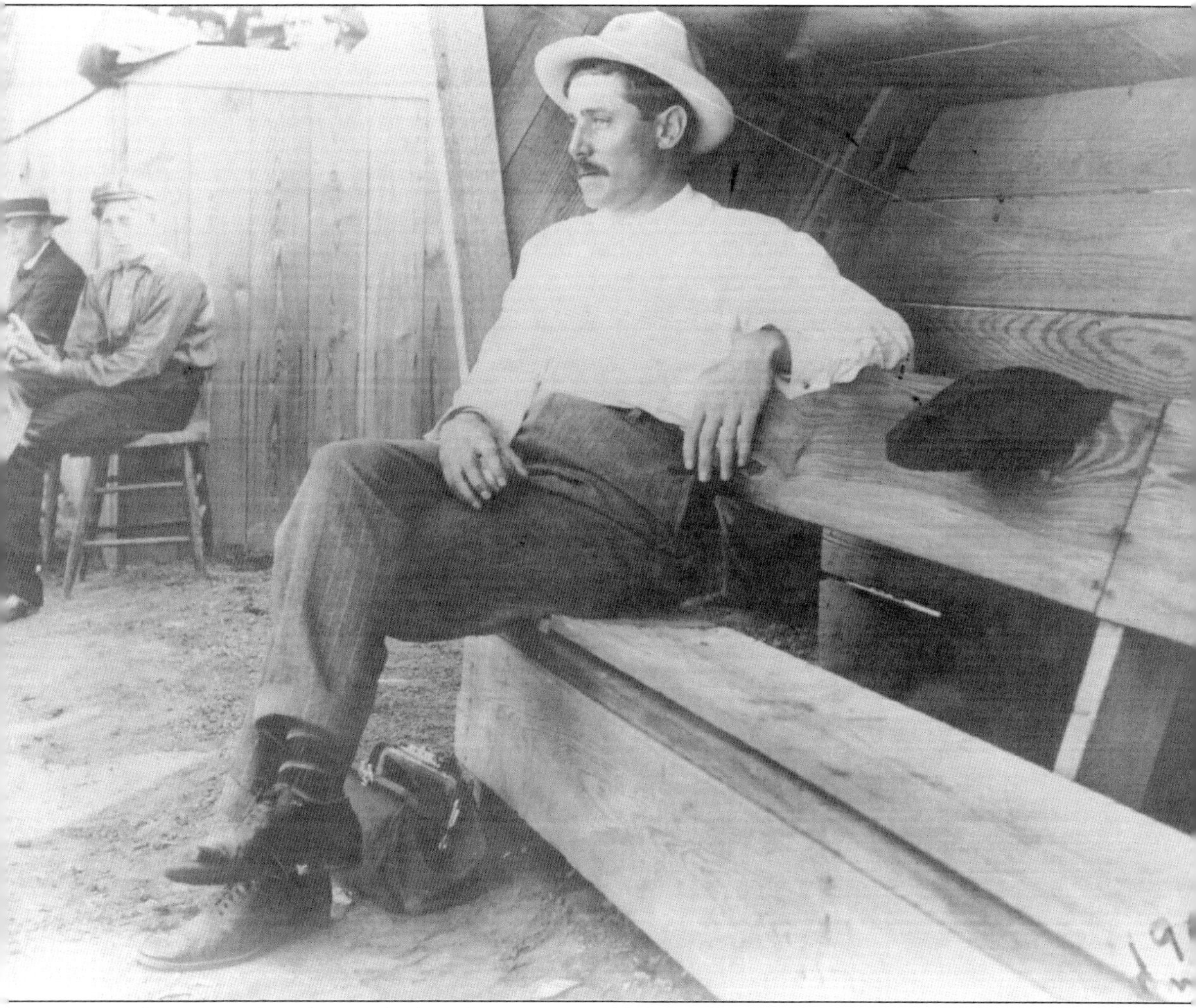

William "Pa" Rourke on the bench in League Park. Rourke came to Omaha in 1887 as a third baseman. He organized the Nebraska State League in 1899 and ran the Omaha team for 21 years. (Courtesy of the Durham Western Heritage Museum).

Two

Sandlot Rivalries and Local Heroes

Hanging from the wall of Louie M's in the Vinton Street Corridor, not so many blocks from the site of League Park, is a photo of Mondo Marcuzzo with the Bank of Italy Team. In the 1920s and 1930s, the battery of Marcuzzo and Leo Pezdirtz was in demand by Omaha's amateur and semi-pro sandlot teams. The "hired guns" traveled everywhere, in and out of Omaha and Iowa, taking batters to task at the plate.

Marcuzzo and Pezdirtz both played for the St. Philomena CYO team. St. Philomena's, originally at 9th and Harney, moved in 1908 to South 10th, where it was the designated Omaha cathedral. In 1958 the church was renamed St. Frances Cabrini, and St. Cecilia's Parish became Omaha's designated cathedral. Mondo Marcuzzo's mother, Josephine, was the first female restaurateur in Omaha, operating the Italian Gardens. Mondo helped out in the restaurant while also working for Pabst Blue Ribbon Distributing, later owning his own bar, Mondo's Steamliner Bar.

Lou Marcuzzo remembers being a kid, waking early on summer mornings, grabbing his ball, glove, and swim suit, hopping his bike, and taking off for an entire day at Riverview Park, overlooking the Missouri River.

In the 1920s and 1930s, Omaha led the country in butter production, was the second largest livestock market in the world, and one of the largest grain markets. Railroad lines crisscrossed at Union Station, leading to and from the rest of the country. The Pacific Railroad Act, signed into law by Abraham Lincoln on July 1, 1862, provided for the construction of a transcontinental railroad straight through the Nebraska Territory. For Omaha, which had been granted a city charter in 1857, the Pacific Railroad Act meant people and jobs, and where there were new jobs and people, there was the right atmosphere for sandlot baseball.

Neighborhoods were tight in 1920s, 30s, 40s, and 50s Omaha. Even earlier, "before there was any board of directors to worry about ball players rushing an umpire, there were the Vinton Vags, the Brown Packers, the Coronas and Victors around Riverview Park, and the Sheeley town gang...Sheeley town, named for the old Sheeley packing plant and Joe Sheeley, the owner, was the district between Dorcas and Martha Streets on 26th." (Robert Phipps, *OWH*) Sandlot lore was the language spoken then and local legends were Frank "Frunt" Konicki, Eddie Bogats, and Ted Stolinski, "the man with the fiddler's twist." Stolinski was a fiddler and a pitcher; his pretzel windup on the mound was called a "fiddler's twist."

A June 1, 1926 *Omaha World Herald* account of a game between the Burlingtons and Stock Yards reflects a certain skepticism:

> *They (Burlingtons) played good baseball for 4 innings and just as the fans were ridding themselves of their pregame notion of them being a collection of section hands and passenger brakemen, their hurler, Maney West, blew up. At this point the home aggregation of horsehide chasers started working on them and collected 7 runs in the next 2 innings and 7 more in the 8th, winning 15-7. Grover's wildness and Russell's home run in the fourth inning accounted for the Railroaders' runs. The Yards started their scoring ceremonies in the fifth, batting around in this frame and again in the eighth when they belted West and two of his hurling henchmen, Masters and Braniff, for seven runs.*

Another typical headline notes the Auditors of Miscellaneous Accounts and the Nebraska Division set to play for third place in the Union Pacific League at either Brown Park or Carter Lake club.

Baseball was a binding force, a level playing field for high school rivalries between the Packers of South High, Creighton Prep, Boystown, Central, Tech, and Holy Name at Brown Park. In the summer, the Thirteenth Street Merchants hashed it out with Mainelli Construction, the Eighteenth Infantry Marines, Brandeis, and Carter Lake. At various times, the city grids offered as many ballparks per block as churches.

On the semi-pro, amateur side of things, it was not unusual to wear the colors of two or three teams. In 1929, Marin Olson played for the Union Stockyards (a Sunday team), the Northwestern Bells (a Saturday team), and the W. Electrics (a twilight team).

Early 1930s baseball coach Leo "Zip" Lowry kept the city high school baseball championship at South High with teams of veterans including Bernard "Bunny" Donohoe, "a lad who eats, sleeps, and lives his baseball." In addition to the Packers, Donohoe pitched for the Two Hundred Club. Brian Donohoe has the 1933 championship baseball, autographed by his father, Elias Dahir, Vince Zezulak, Mike Dukich, and others from that championship season.

At a 1945 intramural baseball game at the naval air station in Jacksonville, Florida, former Packer Don Meier pitched against Ted Williams. A pitcher for South, Meier was serving as an aviation machinist for the Navy. Williams was a Marine Corps pilot. The future Hall of Famer went hitless in three at-bats against Meier, who went on to pitch professionally for one season with the Class D Appleton (WI) Papermakers and Columbus (OH) of the Pioneer Night League.

The *South Omaha Sun's* Floyd Hayes wrote in his 1937 "Sports Scraps" column of Eddie Stanek, "spark plug of the Cudahy team," "ball-playing idol of Brown Park," "the cream of the crop, the Dizzy Dean of the Omaha diamonds," and the one "all South Omaha believes will make good in pro baseball." Stanek later signed with the Detroit Tigers.

Softball was played at Falstaff Park where Hayes wrote of the School of Romance section of the park where girls sat on the narrow board bleachers, talking with the Metro Package Delivery boys. Girls played softball, with teams sponsored by Malashock Jewelry, Russell Sports, Metz Beer, and Safeway Cabs. Girls also played baseball, with the 1929 grade school championship Gould Dietz cup shared by teams from Edward Rosewater School and Hawthorne.

In text-packed columns, the *Omaha World-Herald* covered it all, every day; Robert Phipps, Don Lee, and Maurice Shadle tracked the AAA Midget Leagues, CYO Leagues, high school leagues, semi-pro leagues, and summer American Legion ball, drawing connections between teams of note such as the 1948 Legion Champ Metz, a team that went all the way to the "Little World Series" in Indianapolis, to the first Omaha team to do so, the 1939 McDevitts under Skip Palrang.

In 1939, the McDevitts won the district championship by winning 14 games in Omaha, taking the Eastern Championship of Nebraska in York, and eventually taking the Western Championship in Stockton, California, with wins against Topeka, Kansas, and Los Angeles.

The McDevitts won three out of four games against a Berwyn, Illinois team to win the National title (and a trip to New York to see the Worlds Fair and the first two games of the World Series).

Cornie Collin coached championship football, basketball, and baseball at South High for 30 years. Losses for the American Legion Metz team (with 11 city crowns to their credit by the 1950s) made headlines such as a 1958 liner "Jim Karabatsos Guides Club Past Collin's Nine," with the lead paragraph reading, "Jim Karabatsos finally beat Cornie Collin in a baseball game. The big moment arrived Wednesday evening at Brown Park." Karabatsos' Budweisers, with Steve Rosenblatt in the line-up, took the game, 10-9, from the Metzes.

In 1956, Collin was in his 19th season at the helm of the Metz squad. Collin-coached teams had won or shared 11 city titles in 18 years, garnered 4 state and regional titles, including a second round 1948 finish in the Little World Series.

For decades, in the waning, long days of summer, Omaha had the annual North-South game, Collin-Orcutt, Metro League tourneys. Neighborhoods gathered to cheer on Cudahy's against Lincoln's Arcade Garage, or the Omaha Jobbers of the Italian League played for steak dinners at Johnny's Café. The Deckers and McFaydens challenged the Metz hold on the American Legion, with the seasonal epics recorded in the evening paper. Kids played pick-up games on the rare occasions when there was an empty field.

Yesterday afternoon an exciting and well-conditioned game of baseball was played at the end of the street car track in North Omaha, between the Excelsior club, composed of the B & M railroad boys, and the Gladiator club, composed of the painters. The players, together with a large number of spectators, went out in the street cars making a jolly trip of it.

–Wilbur Harris, *Omaha Bee*, July 1876

Baseball was a community game in Omaha: a connection, from one neighborhood park. . . one summer. . . one generation, to the next.

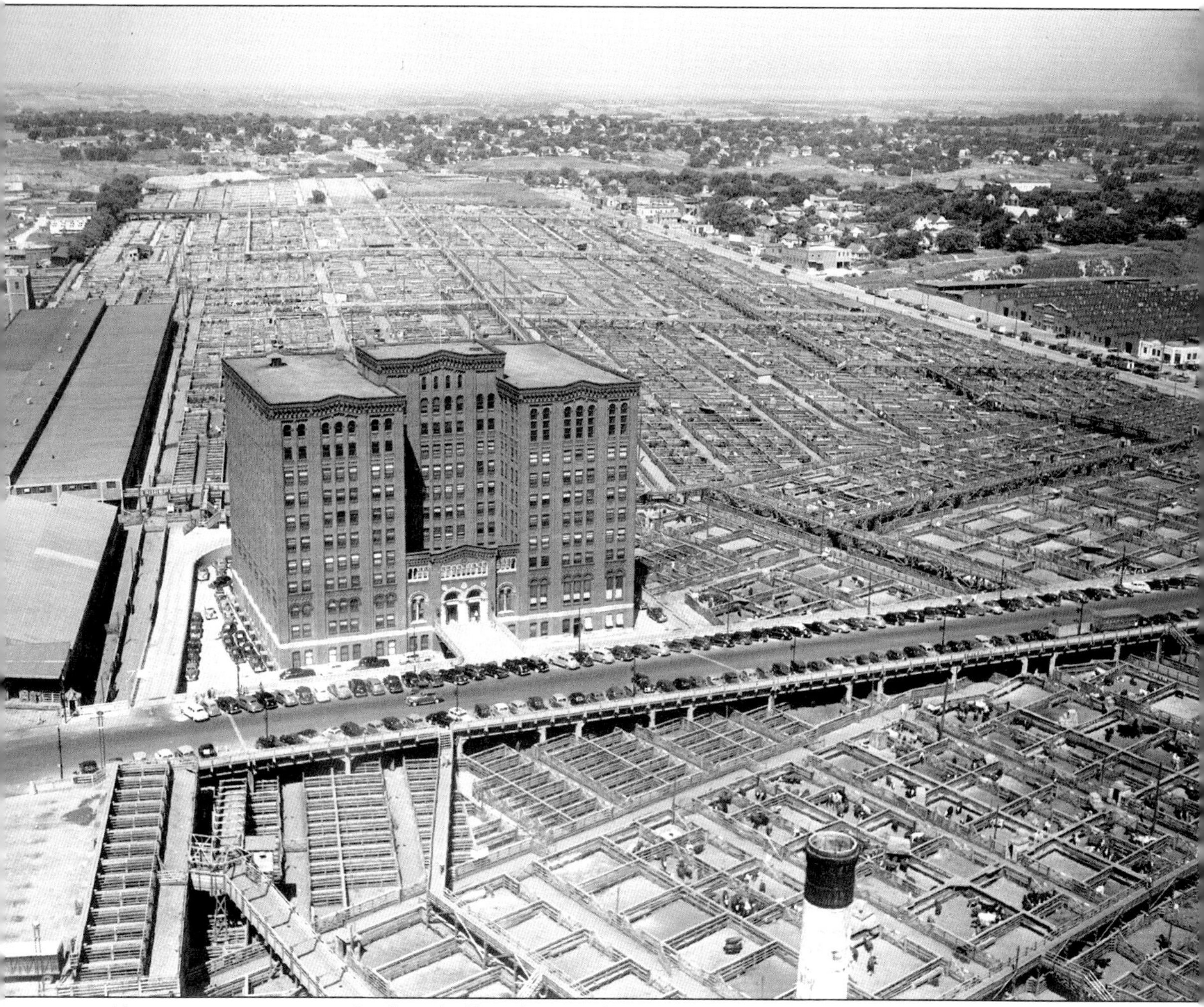

Above is a view of the hallmark Stockyards. (Courtesy of the Durham Western Heritage Museum.)

Opposite page: Pictured are *(top)* the Union Pacific Enginemen, Fontenelle Park, 1926 and *(bottom)* the Gold Coast, Fontenelle Park, 1929. Union Pacific teams were many, with league picnics often held at Elmwood Park. At the time these photos were taken, the Omaha Amateur Standings noted three leagues. The Twilight League included teams such as the Nebraska Tires, Northwestern Bells, Western Weighers, and Liggett Drugs. The Commercial Twilight League had Roberts Dairy, Fairmont Creamery, Peters National, and Peter Pan. Omaha Prints, Burlingtons, Murphy-Did-Its, Edholm Shermans, Carter Lake Club, Saunders Drive-its, and Russell Sports, among others, made up the Metropolitan League. A Sunday School League included the South Side Church, Pearl Memorial, Hanscom Park Wildcats, North Side Christian, and St. Barnabas. Indeed, the 1920s and 1930s were ripe for baseball at the amateur and semi-pro level. (Courtesy of the Union Pacific Railroad Museum.)

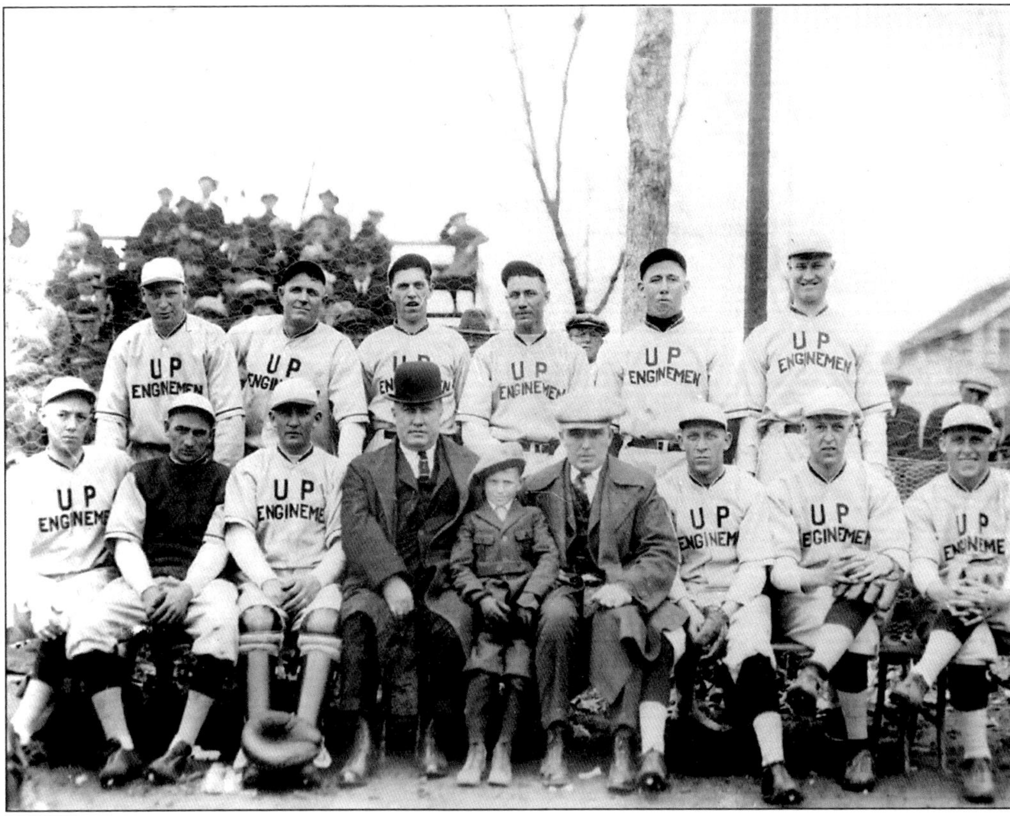
U P
ENGINEMEN

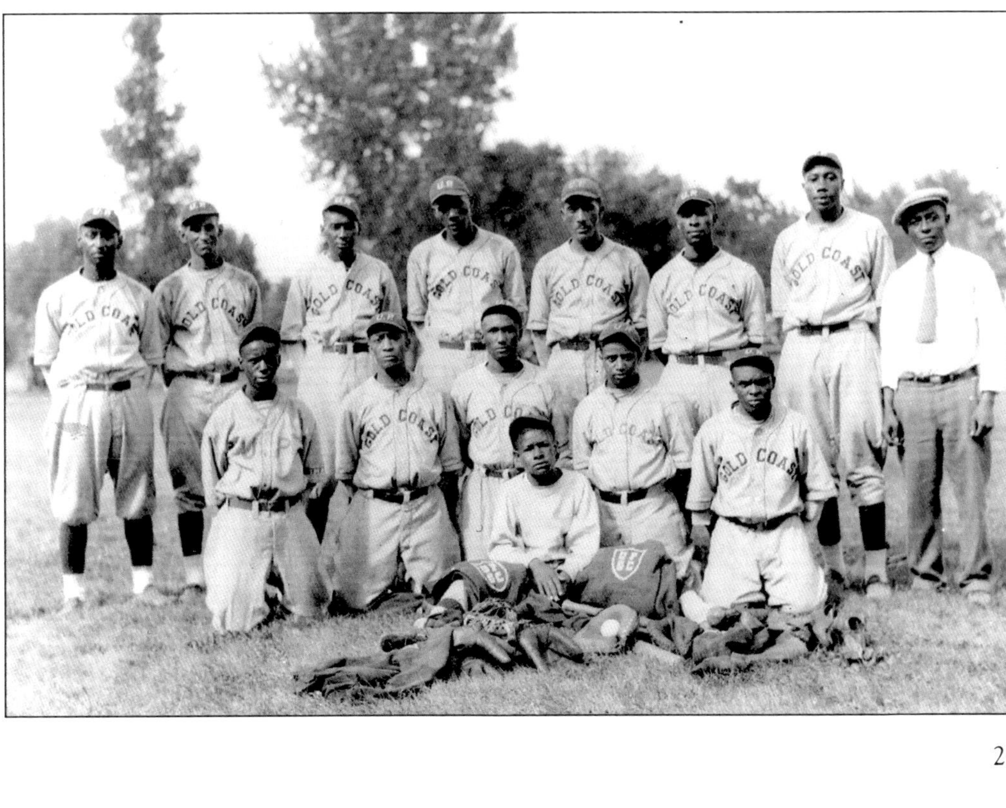
GOLD COAST

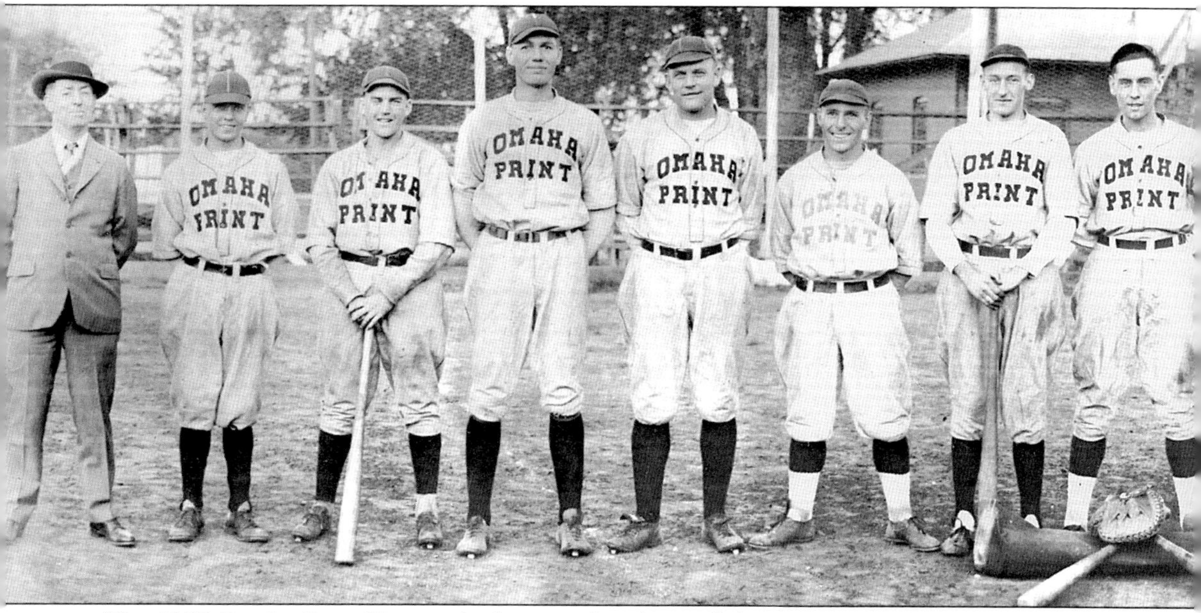

The 1927 Omaha Print Team, which once played an exhibition game with Ruth and Gehrig, represented a tradition of strong baseball in the Metropolitan League that included such teams as the Murphy Did-Its, Saunders System, the Burlingtons, Carter Lake Club, Russell Sports, and Schneider Electric. Teams played their games at Fontenelle Park, Miller Park, and East Elmwood. In this photo, Francis O'Donnell is pictured twice, owing to the photo being shot in

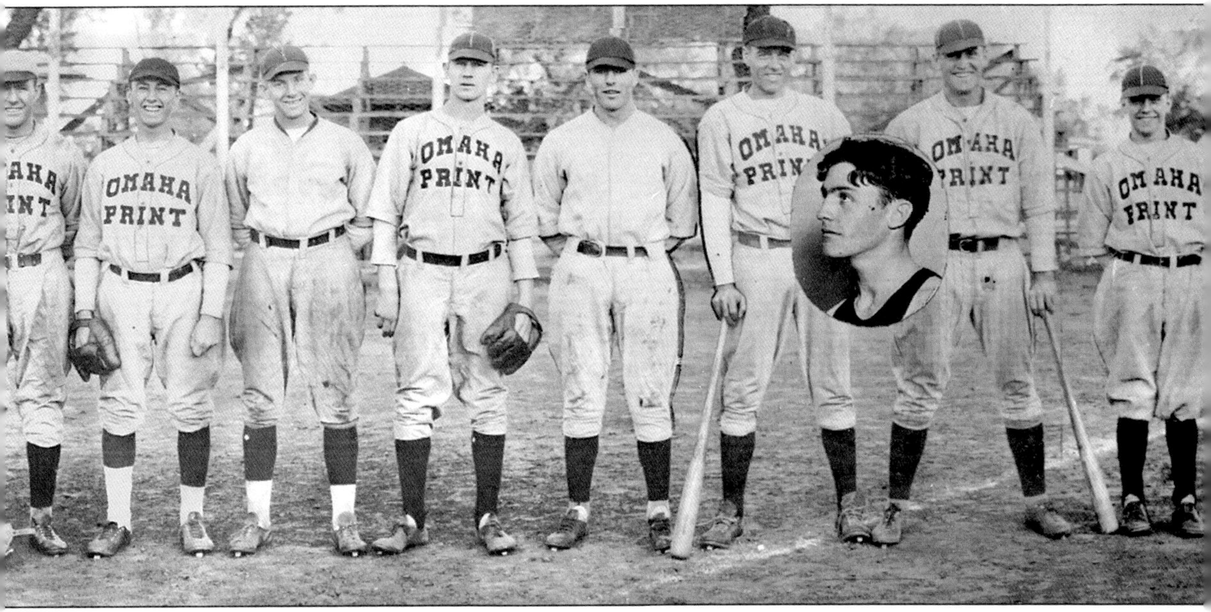

two frames. Transactions for the storied Omaha Prints often made the newspaper. A 1926 blurb noted that Eddie Minikus, "veteran of many a sandlot campaign, signed Friday to play second base for Stubby Mack and the Omaha Prints. He played on the old Luxus team and last year performed for Ed Kelley's Corn States Serums. The Prints released Ralph Mailliard." (Courtesy of Steve Hayes, Omaha Print.)

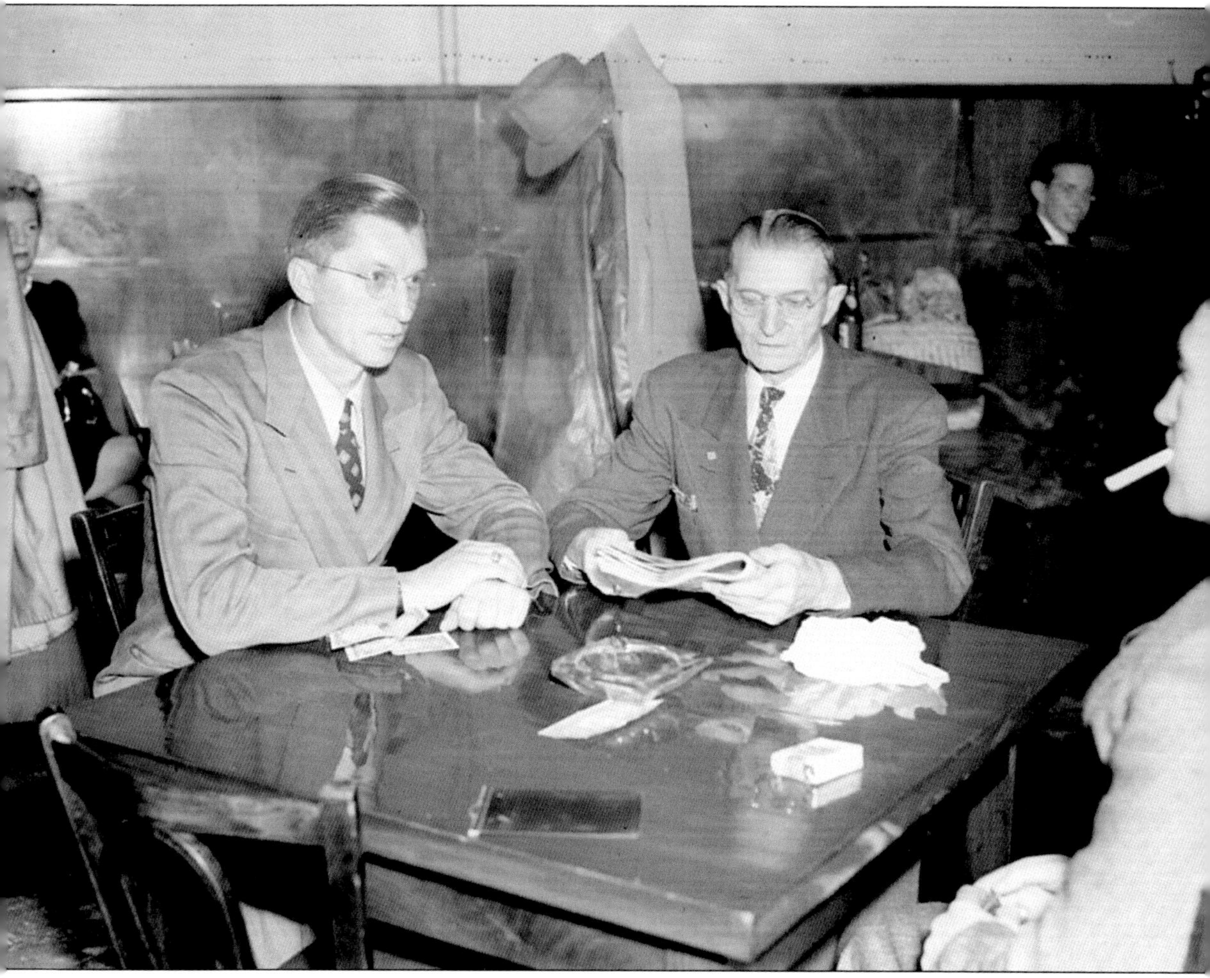

Mel "Chief" Harder, a Beemer, Nebraska native, and graduate of Tech High, pitched for 20 years in the major leagues. Only Bob Feller had more wins than Harder's 233 in a Cleveland Indian uniform. Harder came back many times for exhibition play in Omaha. (Courtesy of the Durham Western Heritage Museum.)

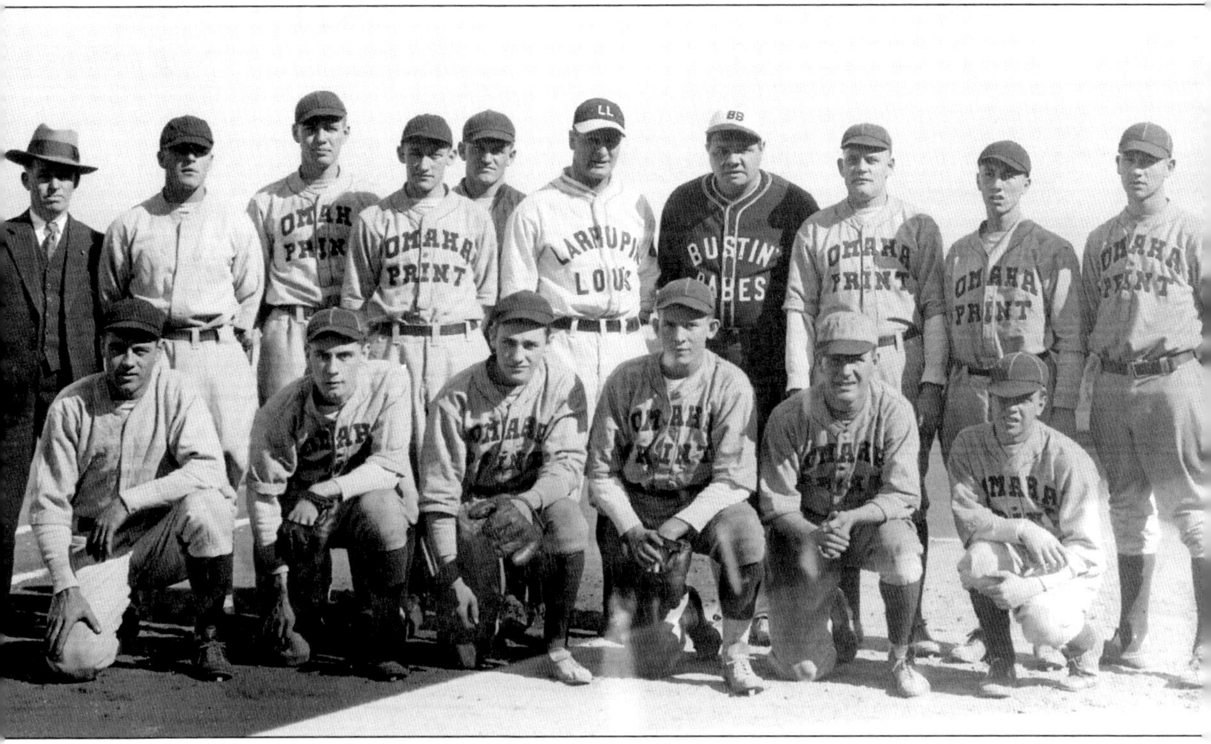

Pictured here with baseball legends Babe Ruth and Lou Gehrig, from left to right, are as follows: (front row) Shorty Guinnotte, Carl Vachal, Willie Worthing, Jimmy Carey, Kinky Spellman, and Frances O'Donnell; (back row) Clint Miller (manager), Johnny Monaghan, Fred Melcher, Bill Bloom, Joe Prerost, Lou Gehrig, Babe Ruth, John Rosenblatt, and Tony Simones. Players for the Brown Parks included John Gardner, Emil Urban, Harold Hunter, Ed Minikus, Benny Simpson, Chuck Dunne, Maynard Daley, Bill Farley, Dode Hubatka, Ollie Bloemer, and Leo Pezdirtz.

Gehrig, newly crowned American League MVP, and Ruth, basking in his 60-homerun season for the Yankees, came to town in 1927, arriving in the morning at the 10th Street train station. They came at the invitation of promoters Jake Isaacson and Johnny "Dynamo" Dennison to participate in an exhibition game between the Omaha Brown Parks and Omaha Prints; Gehrig played with the Prints, while Ruth teamed up with the Brown Parks. Eighteen-year-old recent South High graduate Otto Matulka pitched batting practice to Ruth, serving up a fastball Ruth reportedly drove to the far reaches, landing atop a tie factory. Bill Bloom's pitches to Gehrig were met with a similar reception of quick hellos and blinding, 400-foot good-byes out of Barney Burch's Western League Park at Fifteenth and Vinton.

With the antics and two epic homeruns of Ruth, the Brown Parks won the game, 9-5. Ruth and Gehrig received diamond stickpins as gifts, with Ruth also presented with a fresh egg, the 170th laid by his namesake, a hen known as the Babe Ruth of Poultry. Per various accounts of the presentation, the egg was inscribed, "From the Queen of Eggs to the King of Swat." (Photo courtesy Steve Hayes, Omaha Print.)

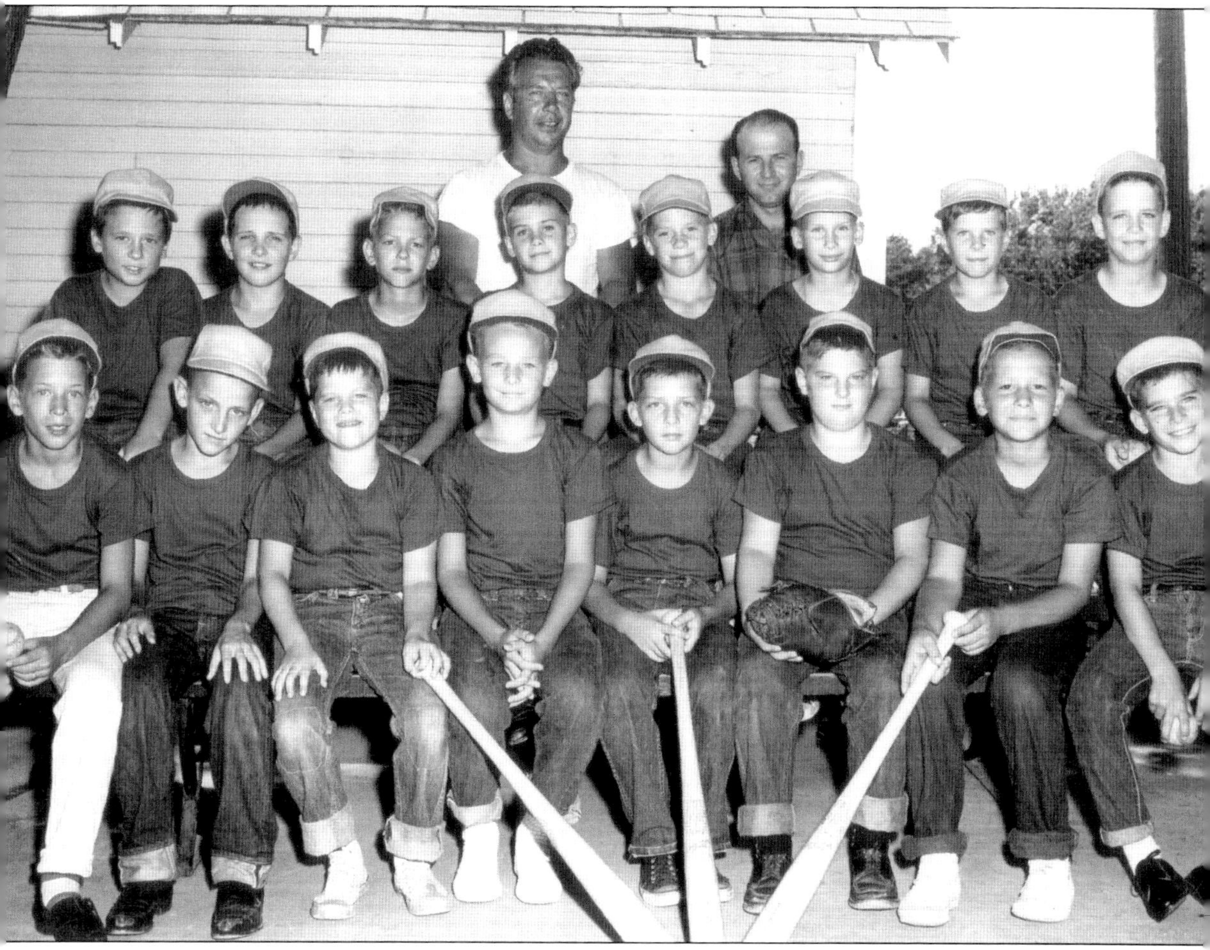

The Goldenrod Team, from left to right, are as follows: (front row) Larry Conatella, Gary Kastrick, Ray Churchich, Jim Chiurej, Joey Waszak, Mark Crisman, Rick Swierczek, and Billy Jadlowski; (middle row) Frank Sobczyk, Mark Stuczynski, Mike Jadlowski, Mike Nowak, John Miodowski, John Szalewski, John Churchich, and Ray Beatterman; (back row) Ray Churchich and Ray Conatella. Even as professional baseball in early 1960s Omaha was fading into a period of dormancy, the grassroots spirit of the game lived in places like the basement of Joe Swatak's house, behind Swatak's Grocery on the corner of 42nd and Hillsdale. With his Goldenrod Club, Swatak brought the neighborhood boys together for ballgames and to listen to local legends such as Bob Gibson. Thirty-five cents a month covered food and equipment fees. Games were played at Riverview Park, where Gary Kastrick remembers a field on a hill looking over the Missouri River, into Iowa. And he recalls discovering Mountain Dew in the basement club, tossing back bottles of the sweet yellow elixir, talking baseball with his friends. (Courtesy of Gary Kastrick.)

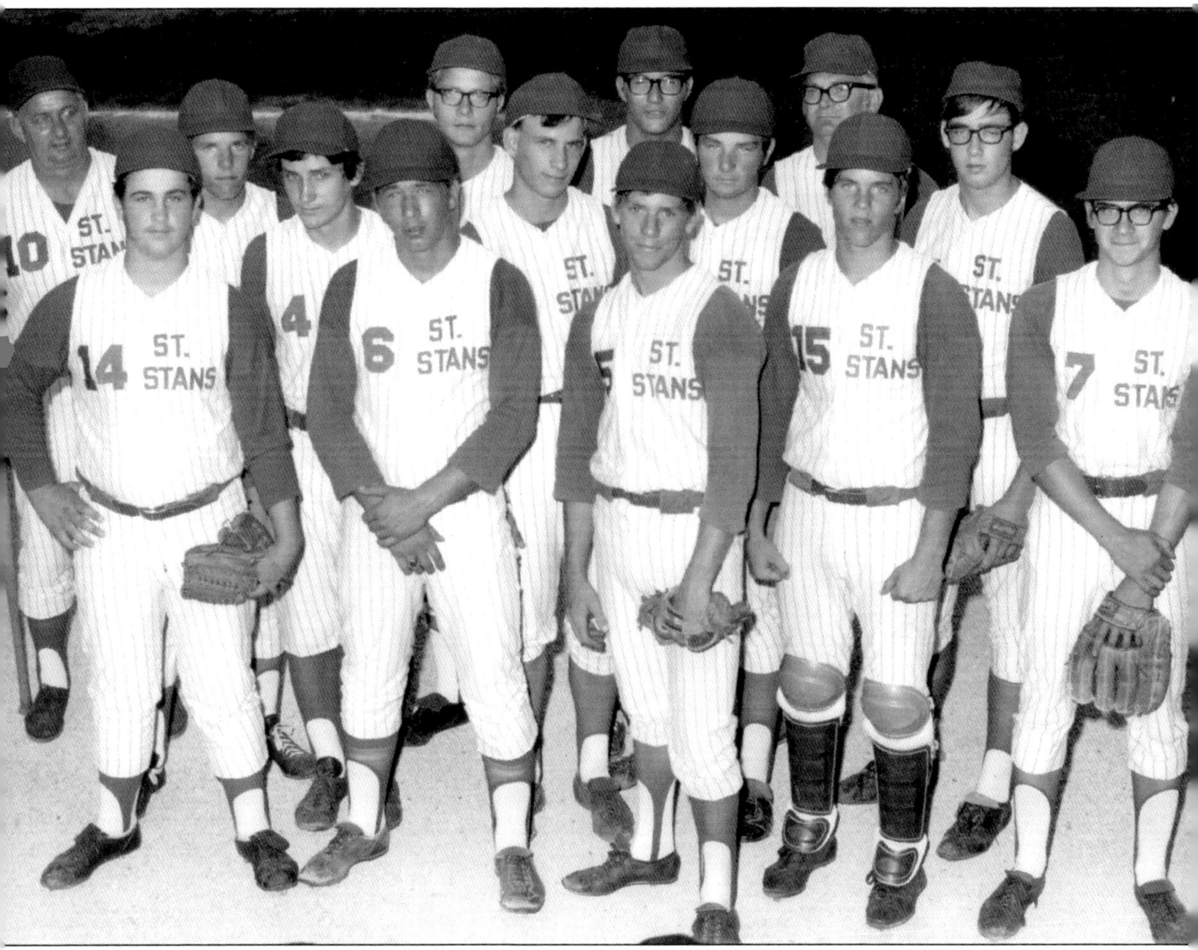

Pictured here for the 1970 St. Stanislaus Team, from left to right, are as follows: (front row) Tom McLaughlin, Larry Conatella, John Miodowski, Ray Churchich, and Mike Nowak; (middle row) Bob Cherek, John Churchich, Gary Kastrick, Ed Szczepaniak, Jim Chiurej, and Tom Szczepaniak; (back row) Steve Heiman, Danny Foral, and John Szalewski.

Rosenblatt Stadium was the setting for the 1970 Catholic Youth Organization (CYO) Championship, with St. Adalbert taking the Class B title from St. Robert with a 7-0 shutout pitched by Don Eckley who allowed only four hits, while collecting three singles.

The stuff of drama was in the Class A series between CYO "Giants" St. Stanislaus and St. Frances Cabrini, with a 3-1 win by St. Stanislaus forcing another playoff game. Gary Kastrick pitched a five-hitter as St. Stan's staved off a bases-loaded seventh-inning threat by St. Frances Cabrini. Pitching for St. Frances, Nino Vacanti allowed only two hits in the close game. The final play-off game took place on Saturday night, July 25, at Rosenblatt, with Cabrini breaking out in a seven-run seventh inning to take the Class A Tournament Championship, 9-1. Until the seventh, pitchers Jerry Vinci of Cabrini and Dan Foral of Stanislaus kept the score close. Having pitched the night before, Gary Kastrick played right field for Stanislaus, contributing two hits. Following the game, eight players from the championship game teams were honored for sportsmanship. Nino Vacanti and Tony Beard were recognized from St. Frances Cabrini; Gary Kastrick and Ed Szczepaniak from St. Stanislaus. From the Class B pairing, Don Klein and Don Eckley were recognized from St. Adalbert, and Denny Berigan and Tim Hautzinger from St. Robert. (Courtesy of Gary Kastrick.)

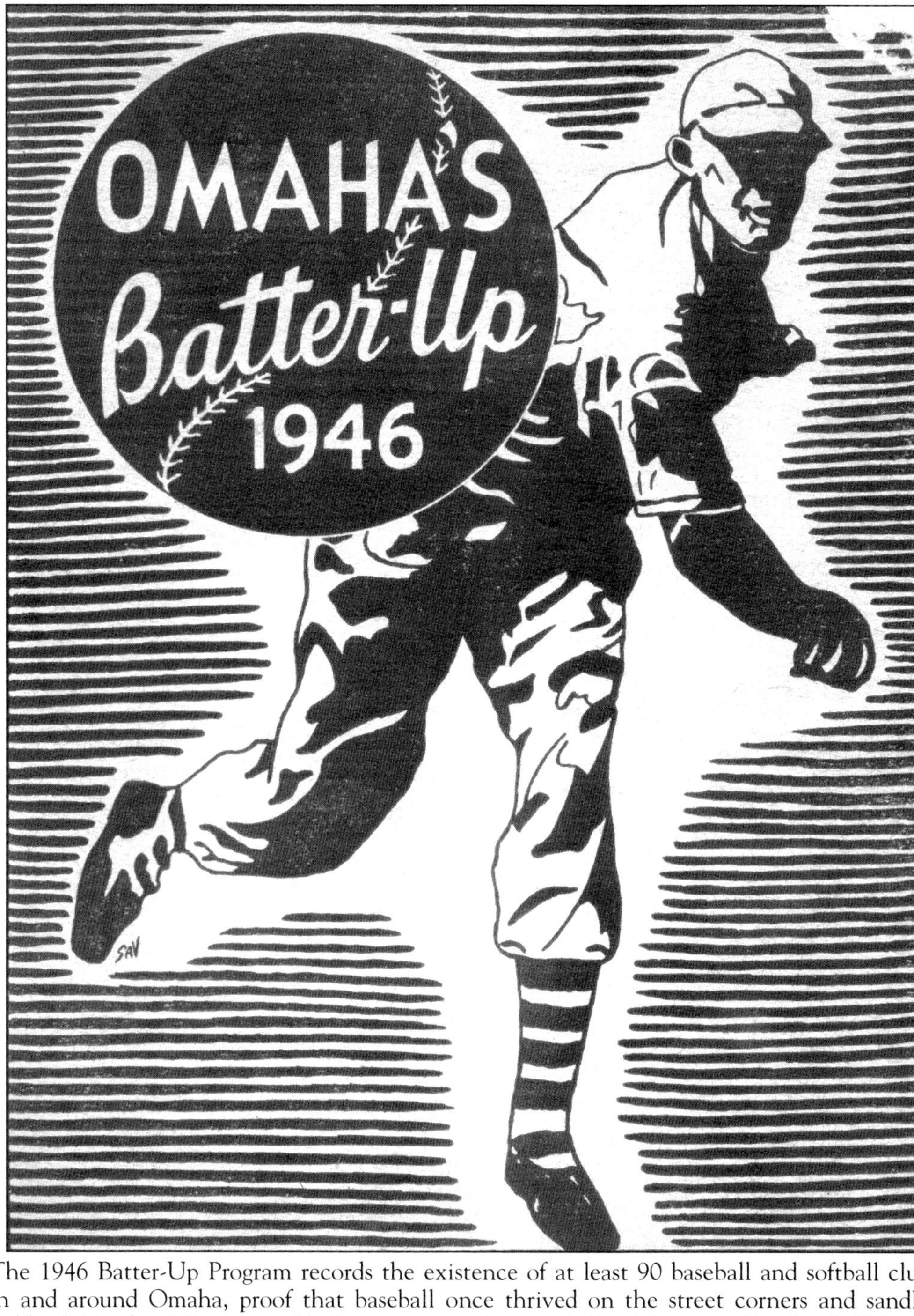

The 1946 Batter-Up Program records the existence of at least 90 baseball and softball clubs in and around Omaha, proof that baseball once thrived on the street corners and sandlot fields of Omaha. Likewise, softball was gaining in popularity. The Semi-Pro Baseball Board in 1946 included Corky Kremke, George Venous, Charles Cook, Murray Woodling, and Max Zimmerman. Fr. Robert Hupp was director of the Catholic Youth Organization (CYO) league. A girls' softball league included teams sponsored by Jeep Bar, Phil Besler's, St. Francis, and the Union Pacific Steamliners. (Courtesy of Gary Kastrick, Project Omaha.)

Holy Angels

(C. Y. O. League)

L to R Back Row

RAY MOHATT
BOB CASEY
BOB KREBS
TOM WHYTE
BERNICE SCANLAN
BILL JOHNSON
LAWRENCE MICHEELS
WALT SPELLMAN
BILL BROWN

L to R Front Row

JIM McCASLIN
WALTER REYNEK
JACKMcCASLIN
DICK McCASLIN
PAT McCASLIN
GENE ELLERMAN
JACK LEE
LEO SOMMER

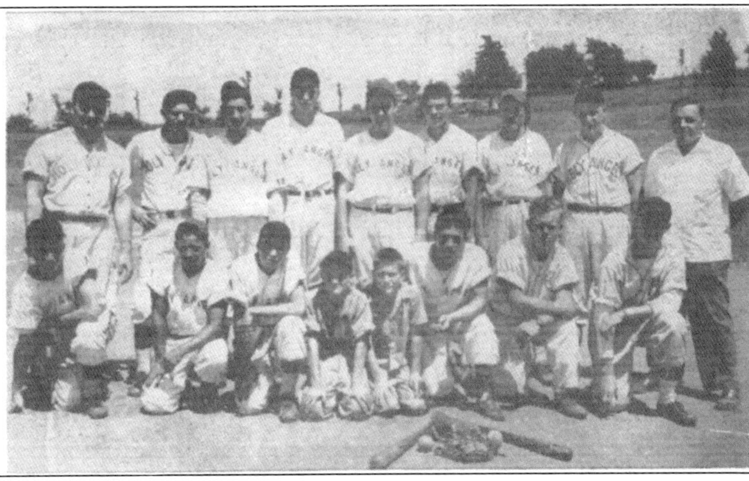

In 1946, teams from Holy Angels (top) and Guadelupe (bottom) parishes competed against teams from St. Peter and Paul, St. John, St. Bernard, Cathedral, Holy Angels, Our Lady of Lourdes, Sacred Heart, Boys Town, and Holy Cross. Parishes fielded teams of adults in the Omaha amateur baseball class, including teams from Holy Angels, Our Lady of Lourdes, St. Francis, St. Ann, Assumption, St. Bernard, Immaculate Conception, and St. Mary. The Reverend Francis Barta was one of the original organizers of the CYO leagues in 1938, serving two terms as director. Others responsible for the organization and initial growth of CYO included the Right Reverend James O'Brien of St. Peter, The Right Reverend Floyd Fischer, and the Reverend Bernard Connelly. CYO Annual North-South All-Star games were played at Brown Park, with the Reverend Robert Gass once ordering the starting time strictly at 7:30pm because of the "natural delay in completing a game of this nature in less than two to three hours." (Courtesy of Gary Kastrick, Project Omaha.)

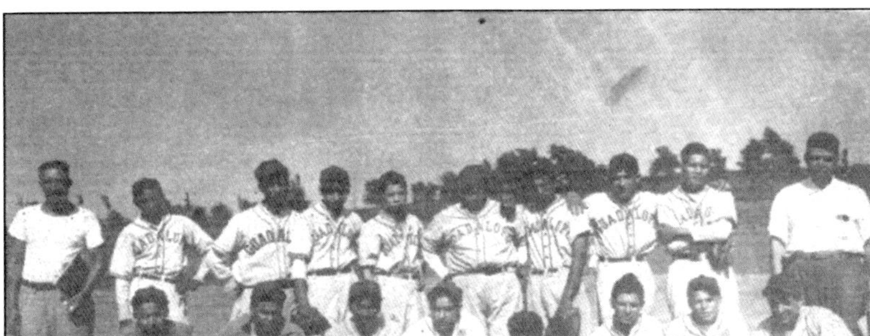

Guadalupe

(C. Y. O. League)

L to R Back Row

C. VALBERDE
. MARTINEZ
E. PLAZA
A. VELA
A. REYES
R. VELASQUEZ
S. DELGADO
L. LLAMA
M. PENISKA
J. RAMIREZ

L to R Front Row

M. GONZALES
A. CARRILLO
C. MARTINEZ
A. CASTRO
R. MARTINEZ
F. MARTINEZ
E. REYES
F. GOMEZ

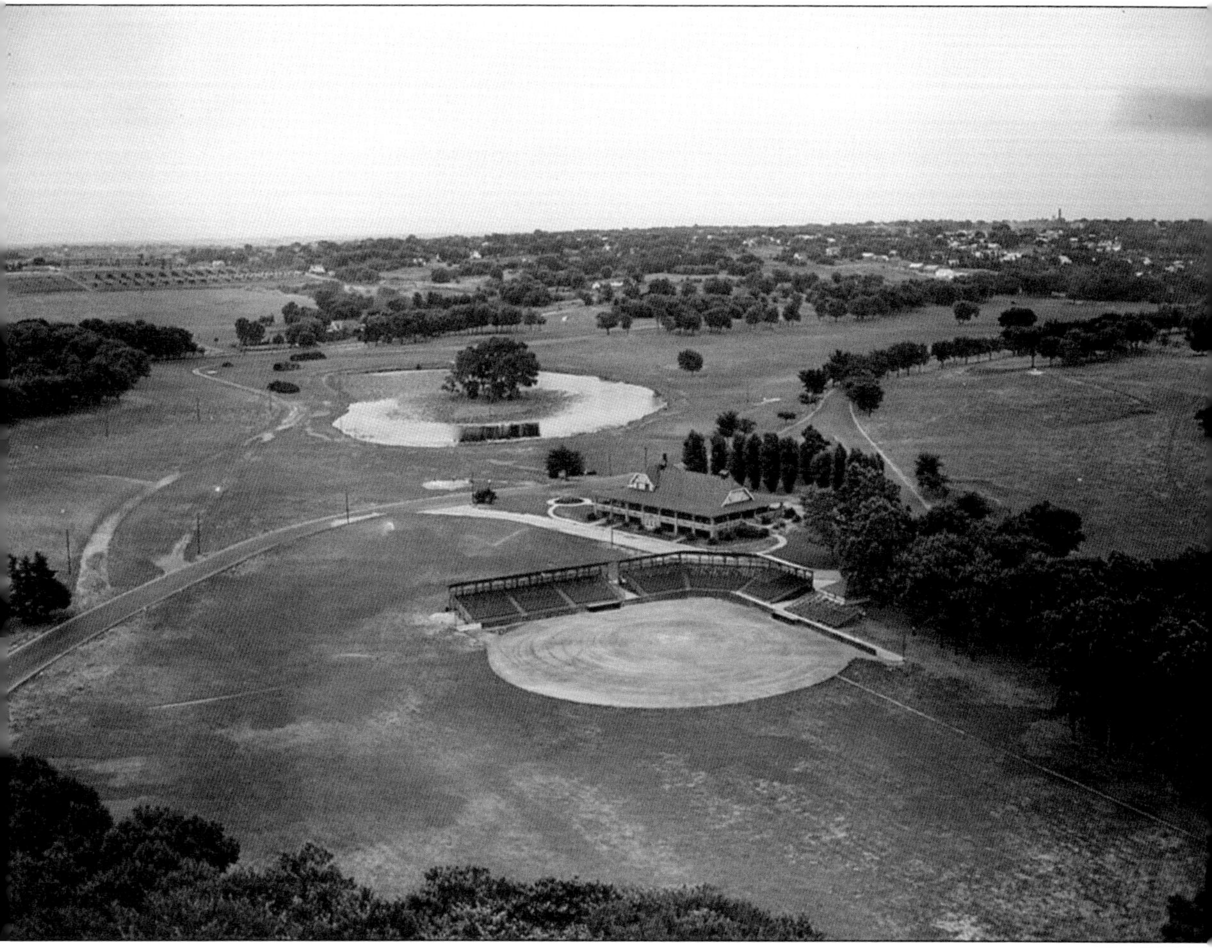

The City of Omaha bought the site of Fontenelle Park, 110 acres at 42nd and Ames, seen here c. 1947, for approximately $90,000 in 1893. The purchase coincided with the acquisition of Riverview Park on property so rolling that, "the land could not support a table on four legs." Riverview Park offered grand vistas of the Missouri River, views appreciated by many generations of sandlot ballplayers and neighborhood kids playing pick-up games on Saturday mornings. In 1964, around the time Municipal Stadium was renamed for John Rosenblatt, Riverview Park was leased to the Omaha Zoological Society as the anticipated site of the Henry Doorly Zoo. Fontenelle Park and Riverview Park were popular ball-playing spots in a city full of ballparks, including Benson Park, Brown Park, Carter Lake, Christie Heights, Athletic Park, Columbus Park, 22nd and Paul Streets Park, Clearview, Old Pulaski Park, and Burdette. Fontenelle Park made headlines during John Rosenblatt's quest for a Triple A franchise for Omaha. Fontenelle Park was suggested as a possible site for the Class A Western League Cardinals (in anticipation of a Triple A club). (Courtesy of the Durham Western Heritage Museum.)

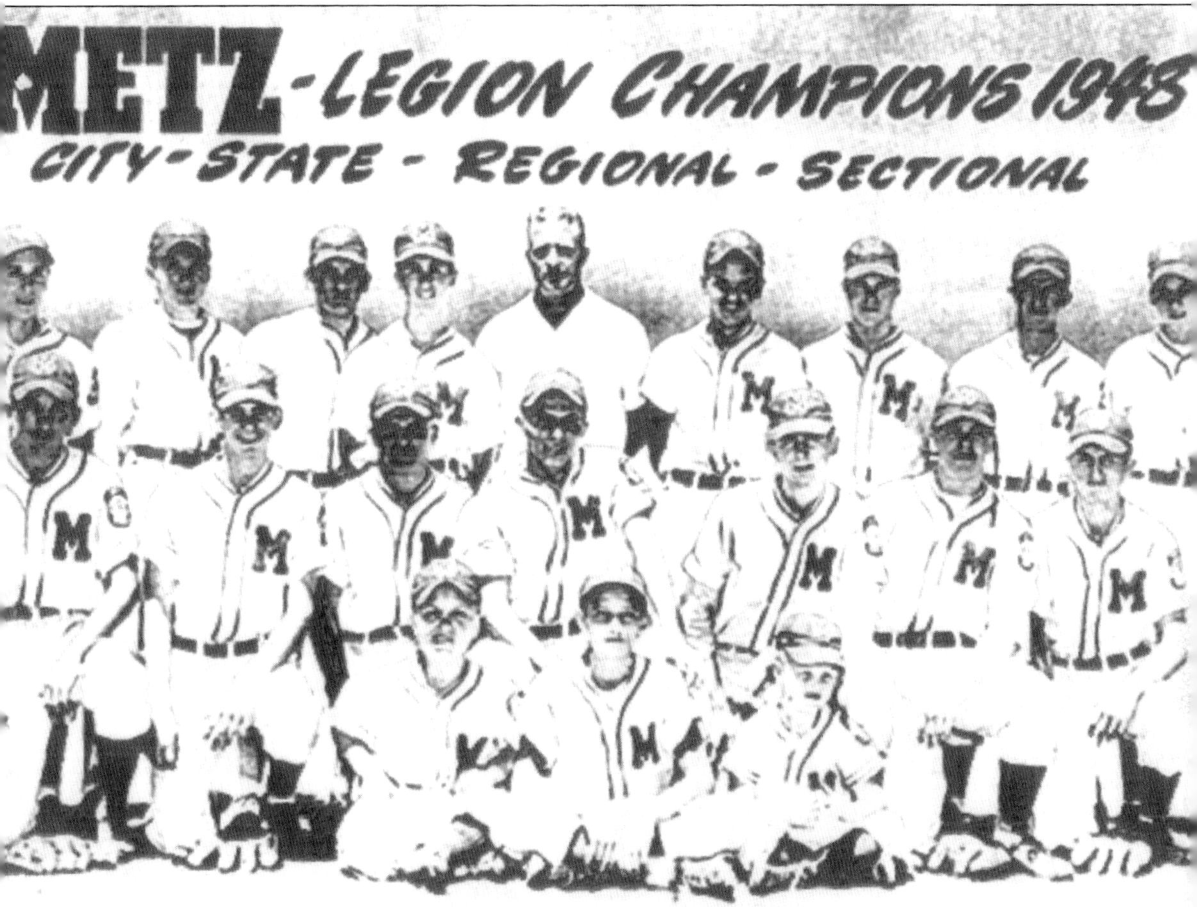

Pictured here is the 1948 Metz Legion Championship team. Cornie Collins led the perennial championship Metz nine on a grand summer adventure in 1948, a season in which the Omaha American Legion was divided into the American League and National League. Most games were played at Fontenelle Park. This team, including Don Hunter, Steve Marinkovich, Ben Letak, Steve Cavlovic, Jim Gorup, Bill Falt, Ray Mladovich, Joe Stanek, Don Zeski, and Ed Benak, was largely intact after a state and sectional winning 1947 season. By late August, the Metzes retained their State American Legion Junior Baseball Championship in a 6-1 win over the Omaha McFaydens in Grand Island. Steve Cavlovic, Metz catcher, cracked a bases-loaded double in the fourth inning and the Metzes never looked back, earning a spot in the Regional Legion Tournament in Hastings. On Duncan Field in Hastings, the Metzes took their second straight sectional American Legion junior baseball championship, with an 11-2 victory over Heaston-Thomas of Albuquerque. Joe Stanek pitched a four-hitter, striking out 15, while Don Hunter hit a pair of triples in as many times at bat to lead the offense. The win carried the Metz team to Lewiston, Idaho, for the Western Regional Legion Tournament, which the Metz team won with a 14-5 win over Yakima. The win meant that the Metz team would be the first Omaha team since 1939 to participate in the American Legion "Little World Series" in Indianapolis. Cornie Collins' team was four hours late to Indianapolis, having missed their train connection in Chicago. Once in Indianapolis, the team had to wait through a rain delay before playing a team from Trenton, New Jersey, a game the Metzes lost 8-3; the *Omaha World-Herald* reported that Zeski was wild, allowing 4 runs in the first 2 innings. The Metzes were sent packing the following day in a 4-3 loss to Jacksonville, Florida. (Courtesy of Gary Kastrick, Project Omaha.)

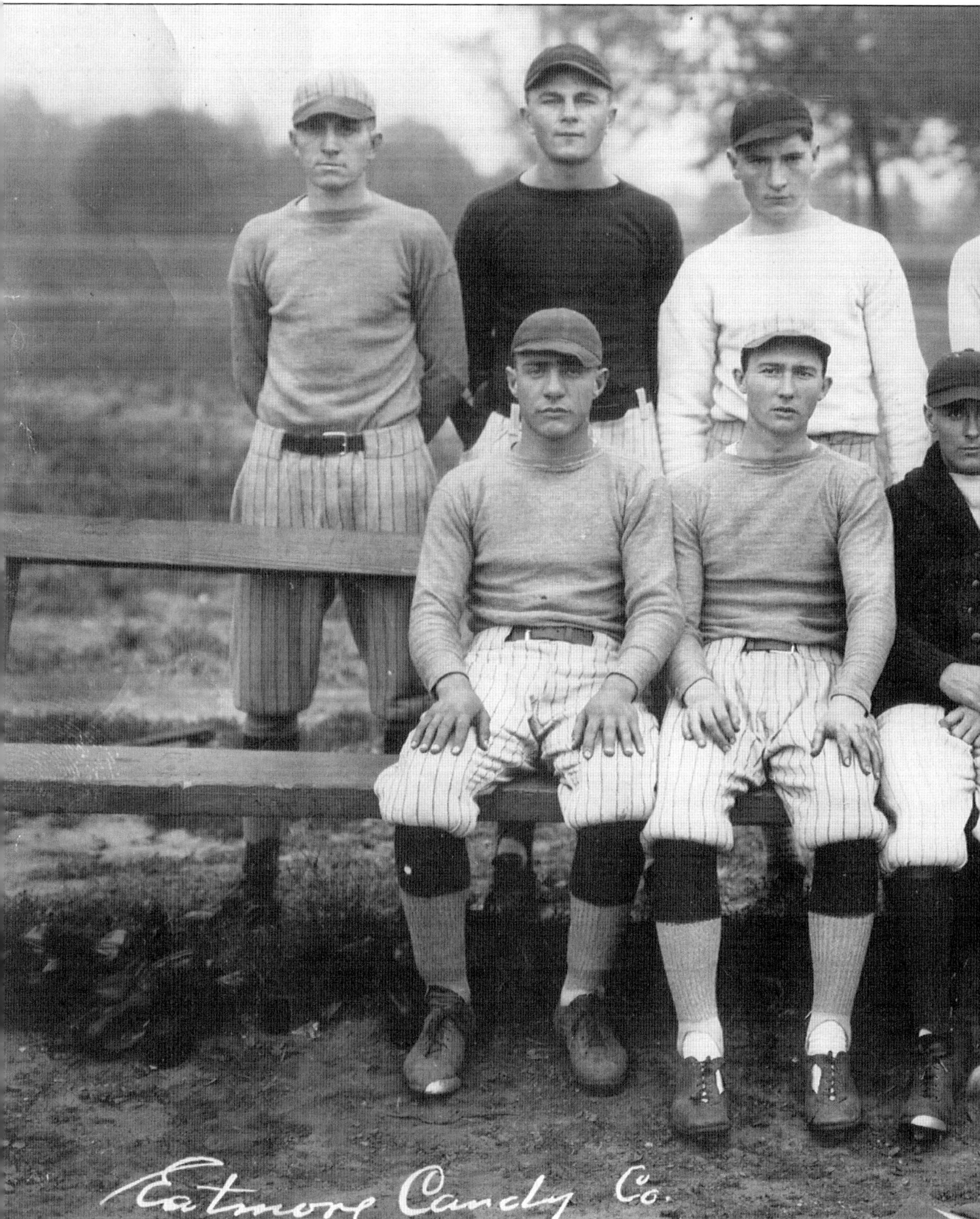

Eatmore Candy Team, Intercity Champions (with a win over a team from St. Louis) in 1923 . In the front row, from left to right, are Mondo Marcuzzo, J. Tuhy, Chuck Brown, George Krebs,

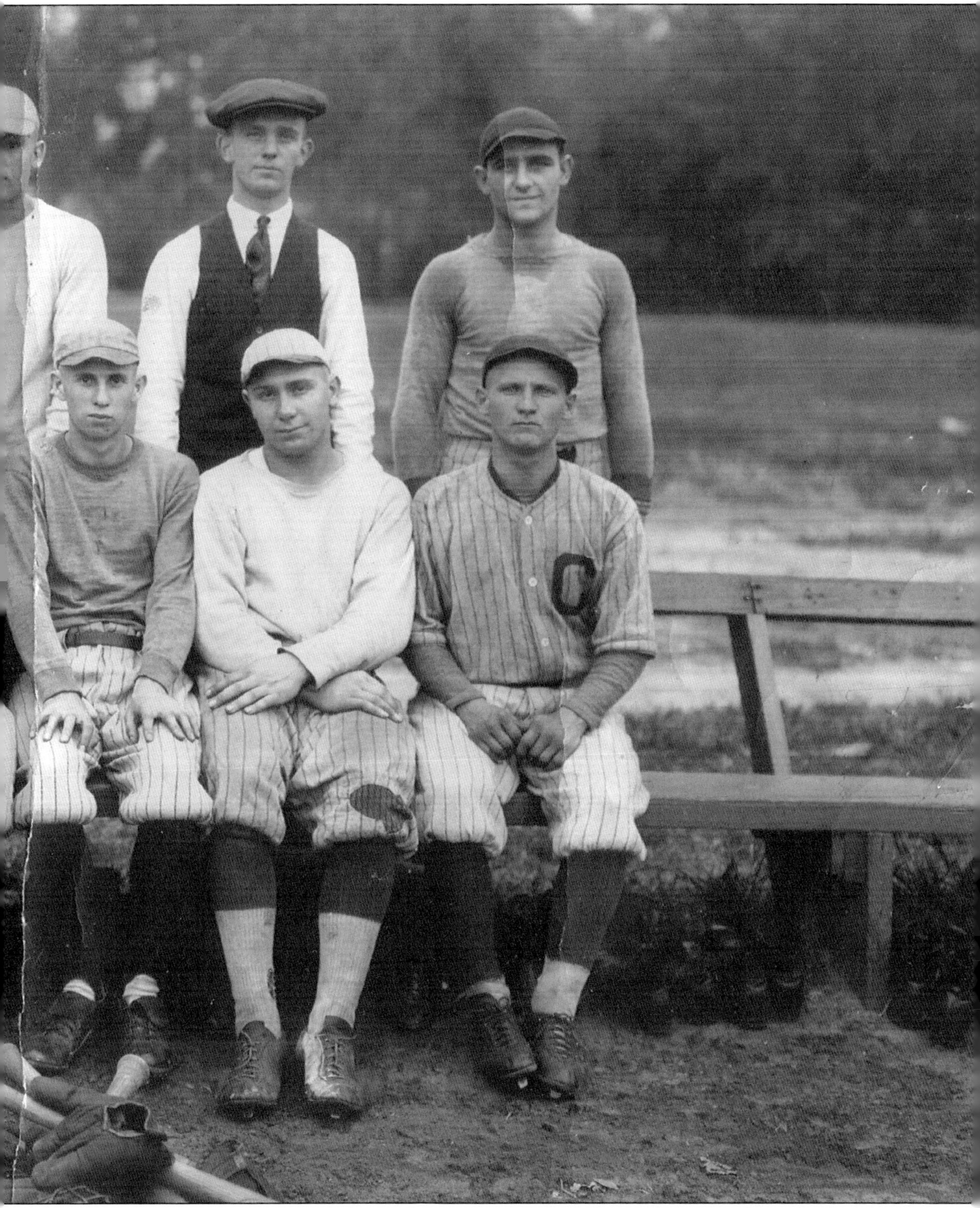

Vince Satrapa, and Anton Vodicka. In the back row, from left to right, are Red Howland, Louis Semerad, G. Gurnant, Frank Tesar, Henry Victor, and John Satrapa. (Courtesy Ray Vodicka)

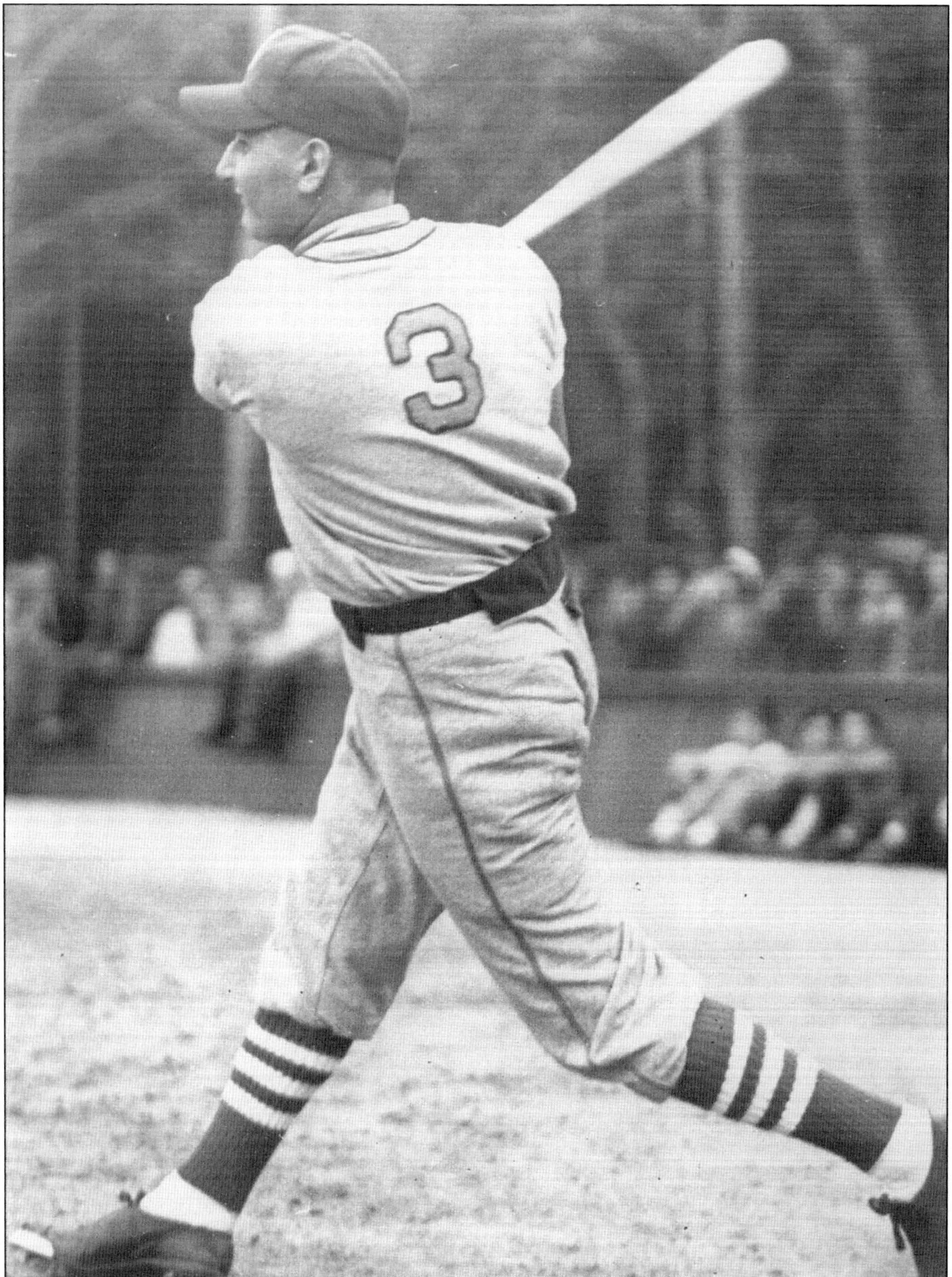

Bill Danze, member of the Roberts Dairy Legion team, was selected to play in Esquire magazine's second annual All-American Boys' Ball Game at Ebbet's Field. Danze pitched six innings for Manager Ty Cobb in the game held August 28, 1945. Danze also pitched for the Braves farm club in Leavenworth, Kansas. (Courtesy of Michael Danze).

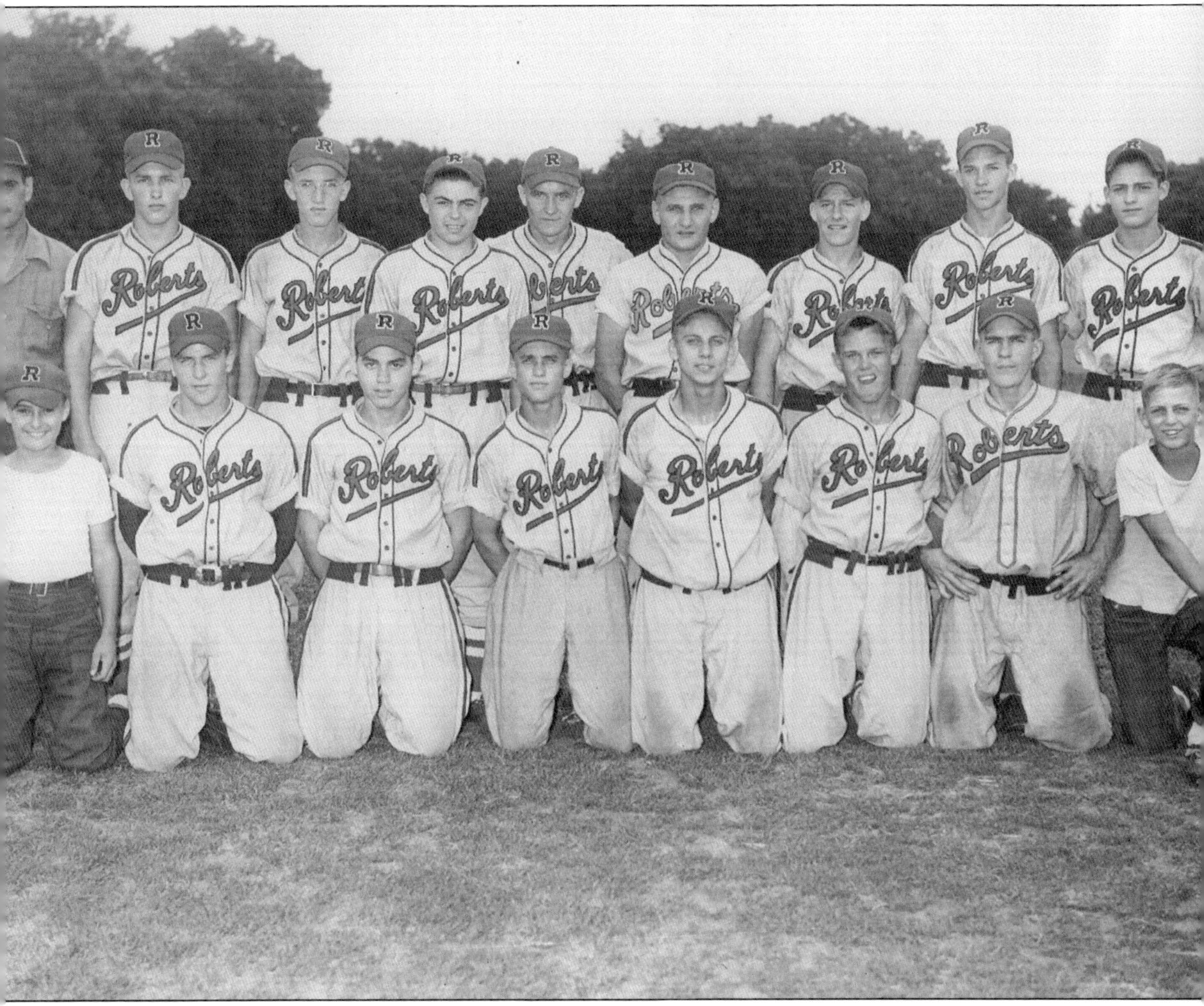

Roberts Dairy Team, 1944 City Champions, are picture as follows, left to right: (front row) Bob Moscrey, (mascot), Wayne Armer, Al Sortino, Bob Sweet, Neal Rowe, Don Jellsey, Don Penney, and Dave Ellis; (back row) Ted Moscrey (manager), Frank Watkins, Norman Steffen, Alan Pascale, John Kendall, Bill Danze, Jack Urban, and Don Baty. After winning the City Championship, the Roberts Dairy team lost to the Omaha Metzes in the state playoffs. (Courtesy of Michael Danze)

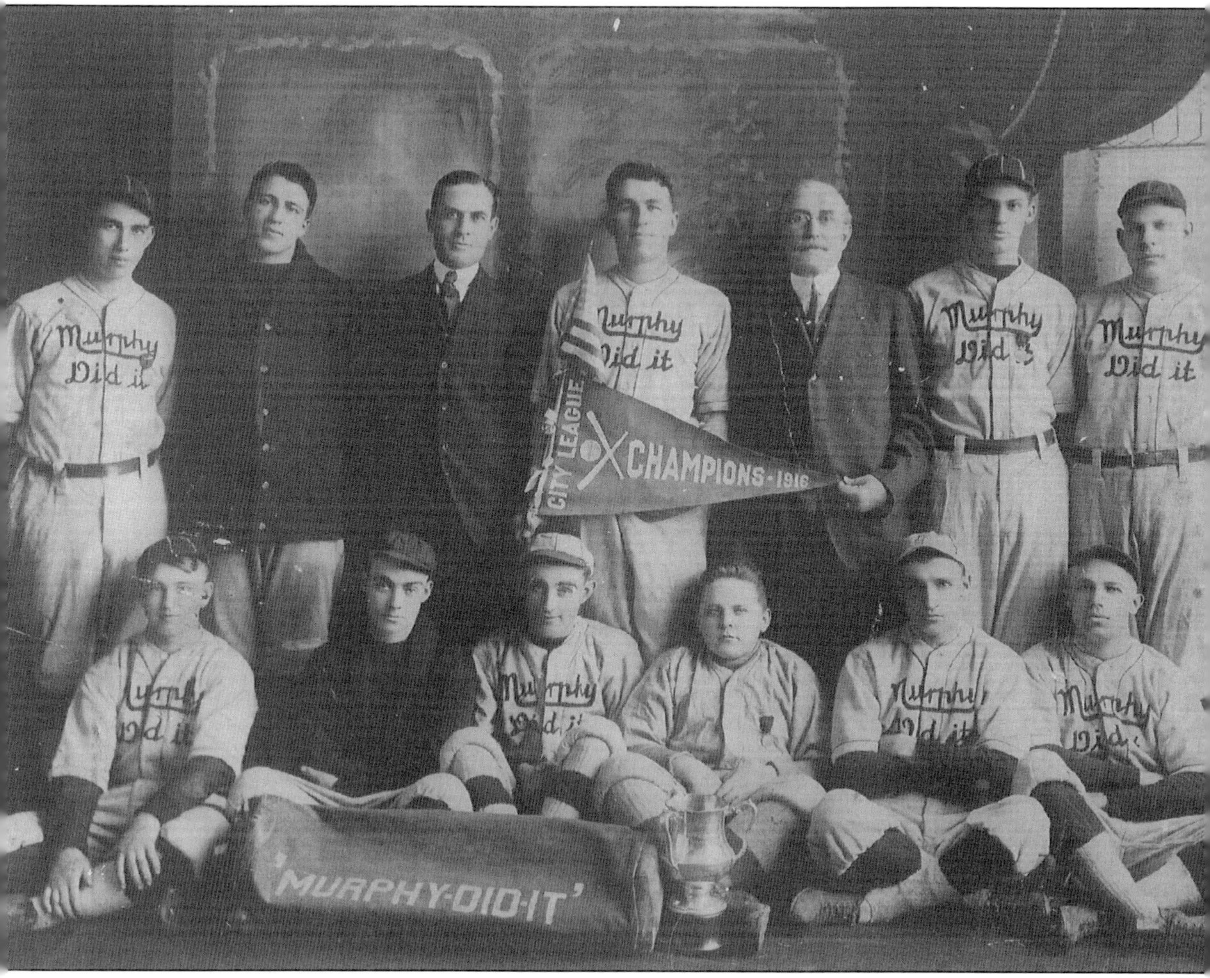

On September 3, 1916, the Murphy Did Its won the Class B City Championship 28-2 over McCarthy's. McCarthy's went on to win the Southern League, while the Murphys took the City League. (Courtesy Bain Family).

THREE

College World Series

National Scene, Local Tradition

The biggest event of the year for Omaha and college baseball fans, the College World Series, which spells the start of summer in Omaha, has been an institution here since 1950. From tailgating to Dingerville, this is college baseball at its best. Before it came to Omaha, the series was held in Kalamazoo, Michigan, and Wichita, Kansas. Weathering format changes, stadium renovation, and the like, the College World Series in Omaha remains a constant.

The where and when of college baseball's first game is a disputed point among historians. Jurist Oliver Wendell Holmes claimed that he played baseball at Harvard before he graduated in 1829. There are reports of the formation of the first college team at Harvard in 1865, followed not long after by Yale and Tufts. Many historians identify the first college game as the July 1, 1859 match between Amherst and Williams. The root of all these conflicting claims is the fact that there were so many different versions of the game we call baseball: it is really hard to find a definite starting point.

We do know that it isn't until 1945 that college baseball organized on a national level. That year, college baseball coaches formed the American Association of College Coaches. A year later an East-West All Star game was played at Fenway Park in Boston. The problem with such all star games was that much of the emphasis of the game was on individuals and not teams. In 1947, the first national championship was played in Kalamazoo, Michigan on the campus of Western Michigan University and California beat Yale in a best two of three series. The Yale teams of 1947 and 1948 had future 41st President George Bush on the roster, losing the CWS to California and then USC. A first baseman, Bush was a good fielder but an average hitter.

Wichita, Kansas held the 1949 series and the format changed to a four-team double-elimination tournament, won by the Texas Longhorns.

However, with a new Municipal Stadium, Omaha was able to draw the College World Series in 1950. In its move to Omaha, the series changed its competition format to an eight-team double-elimination tournament. By the time Texas won the championship and became the first team to win back-to-back national baseball championships, there was already talk about Los Angeles holding the series. The first years of the tournament it was known as the "Collegiate World Series," "Collegiate Baseball Championship," or the "NCAA Baseball Championship."

The series has had its share of notable visitors over the years, such as Branch Rickey, Kevin Costner, Tommy Lasorda, Bob Feller, Tony Gwynn, Mickey Cochrane, Warren Spahn, and Billy Martin. Players in the CWS who would later have fame in the majors were Roger Clemens, Barry Bonds, Reggie Jackson, Dave Winfield, and Robin Ventura.

Much like other attempts at baseball in Omaha, the CWS met with some financial problems during the early years and the Chamber of Commerce helped with funding.

Aluminum bats and designated hitters were first allowed in the NCAA in 1974. This was also the year that the series final was finally streaked. It was June 15, 1974 and Dan Krzemien stepped up to the plate in the seventh inning. Of course, Krzemien wasn't on the lineup. He wasn't even on a team. He had nothing on as he stood at the plate but his sneakers, socks, and a polka-dot hat. Twenty-two at the time, Krzemien exited the men's bathroom, worked his way through the stands, down the center aisle, behind home plate, then ran. Finally, he made it out to right field to attempt his escape, where he was caught by the police.

Locally, Creighton entered the CWS in 1991, but failed to win, ending the tournament with a 2-2 record. Nebraska entered the series in 2001 and 2002, but also failed to win, even with the huge number of fans who came out to support their Huskers.

Records at the CWS are like hopes, always falling. In 2003, no less than 20 records were broken during the session. The session attendance record was set on June 14, at 26, 327. It was also in 2003 that a best of three series was added. At the end of the 2003 CWS, many wondered if Omaha would host the CWS again as rumors swelled with talk of the Royals wanting a smaller park.

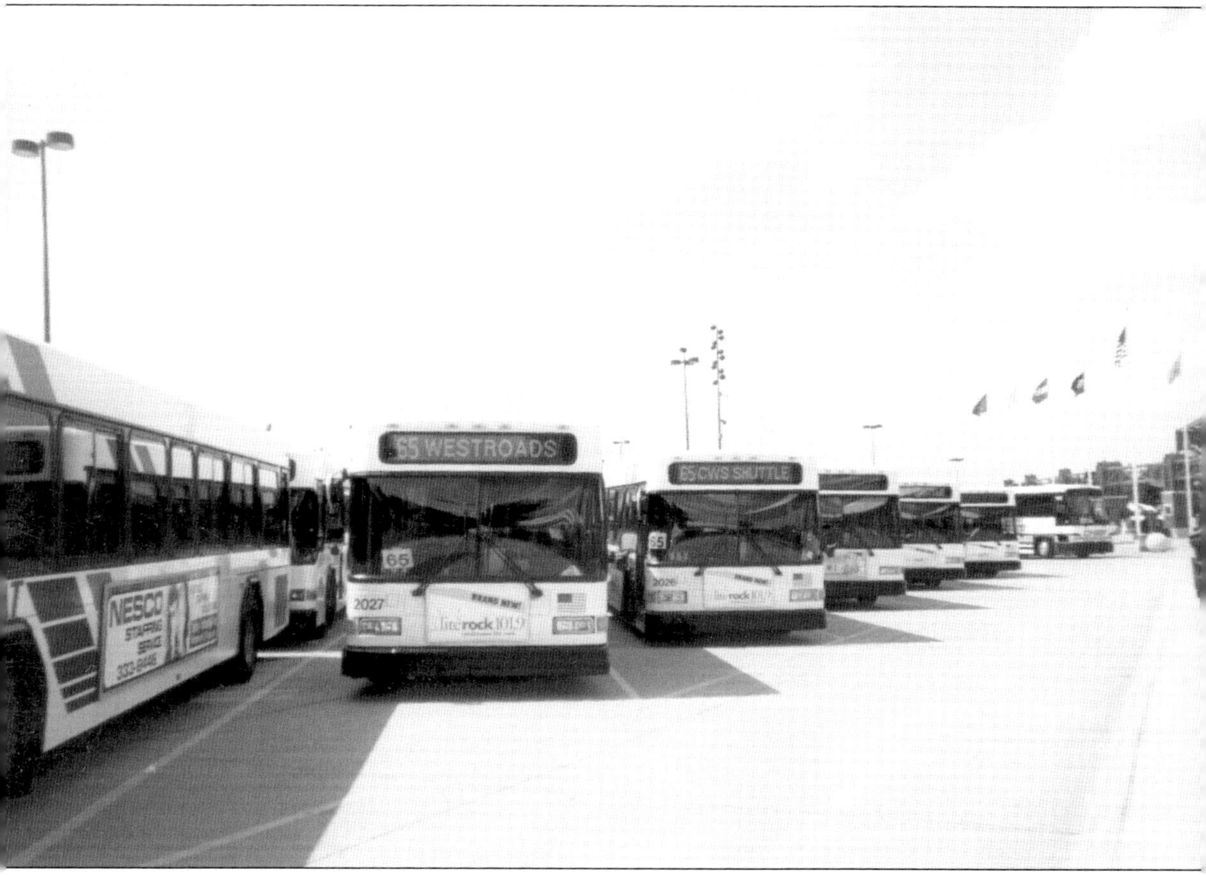

Metro Area Transit buses stand ready to shuttle College World Series fans at Rosenblatt in 2001. (Courtesy of Victor Slape.)

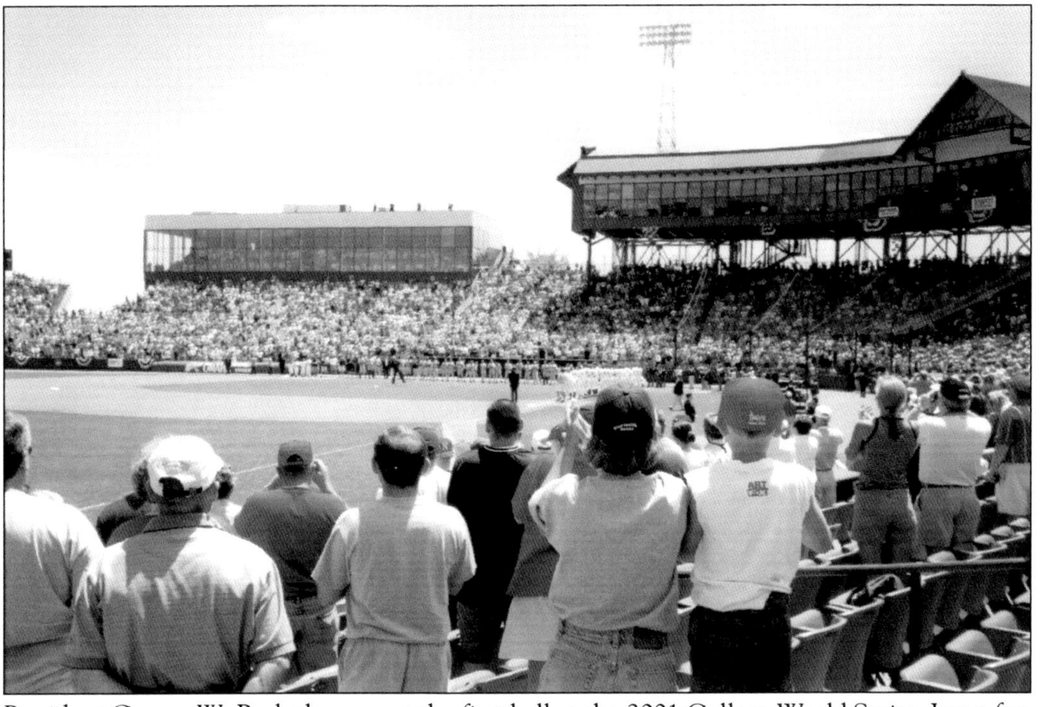

President George W. Bush throws out the first ball at the 2001 College World Series. Just a few months later, on September 11, 2001, he would return to Omaha. (Courtesy of Sally Collins)

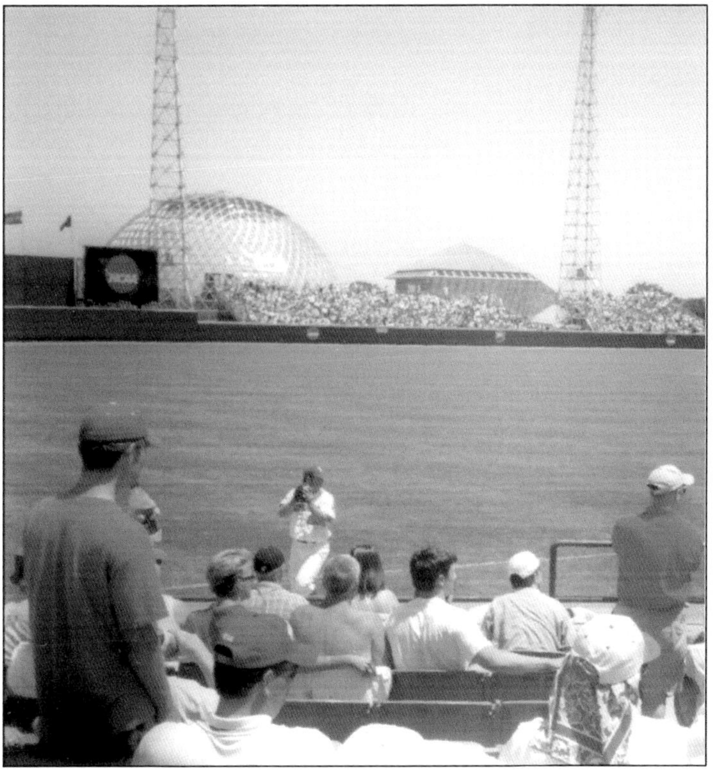

Shane Komine of the Nebraska Cornhuskers warms up before a College World Series game. His Huskers would not win a single game. (Courtesy of Sally Collins)

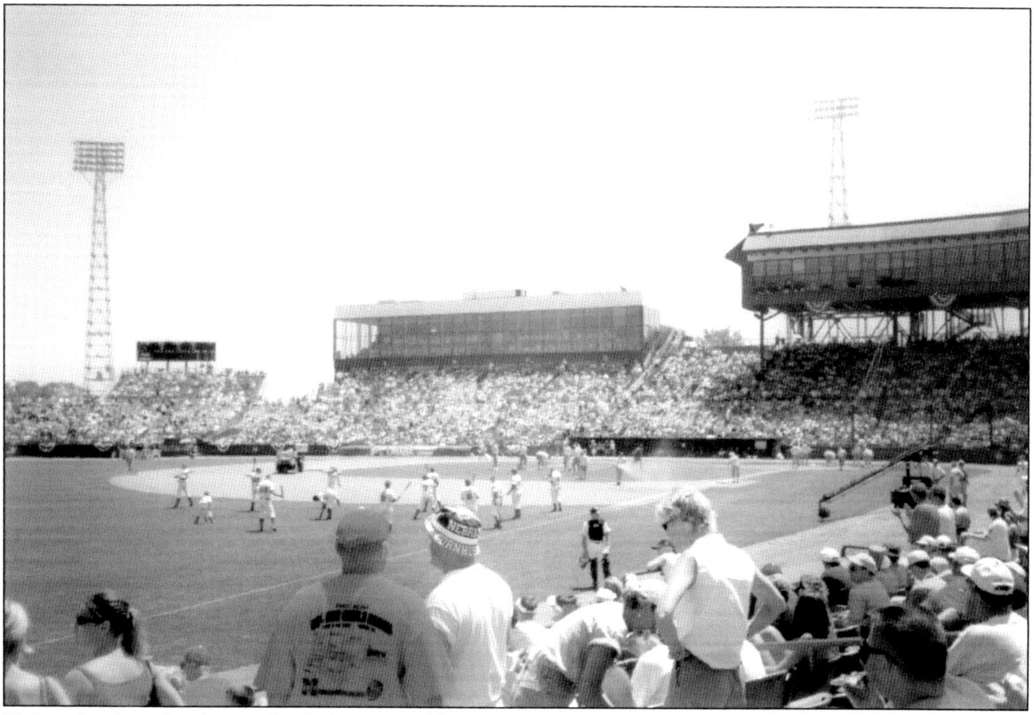

Nebraska Cornhuskers take fielding and batting practice before a College World Series game as groundskeepers prepare the field. (Photo courtesy Sally Collins.)

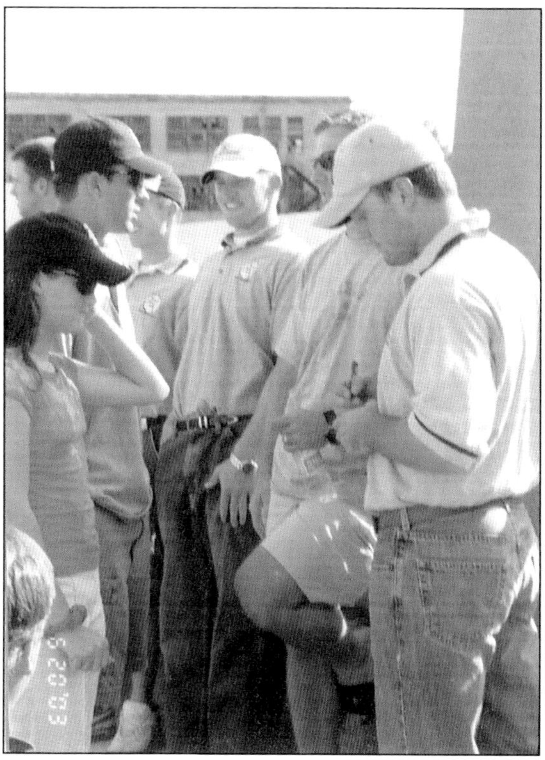

Rice players sign autographs during the CWS Fanfest at the Durham Western Heritage Museum on June 30, 2003. (Courtesy of Nathan Jamison.)

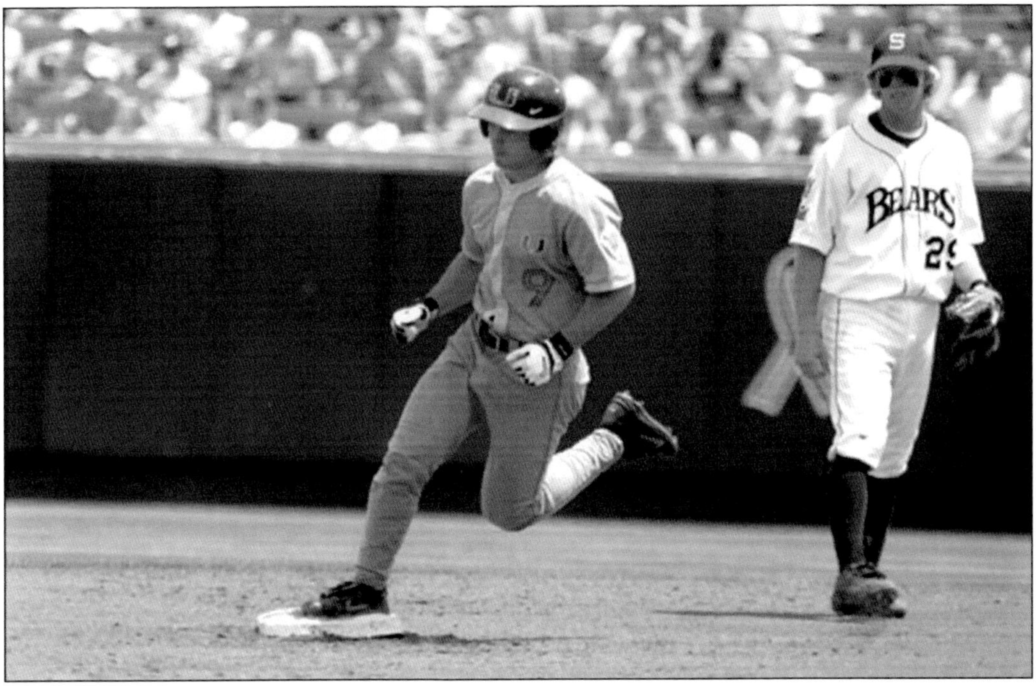

With a 7-5 win over the Southwest Missouri State Bears, the Miami Hurricanes eliminated the Bears from their first appearance in a College World Series. The 2003 CWS marked the Hurricanes 20th appearance. (Courtesy of Mark Johnson Photography.)

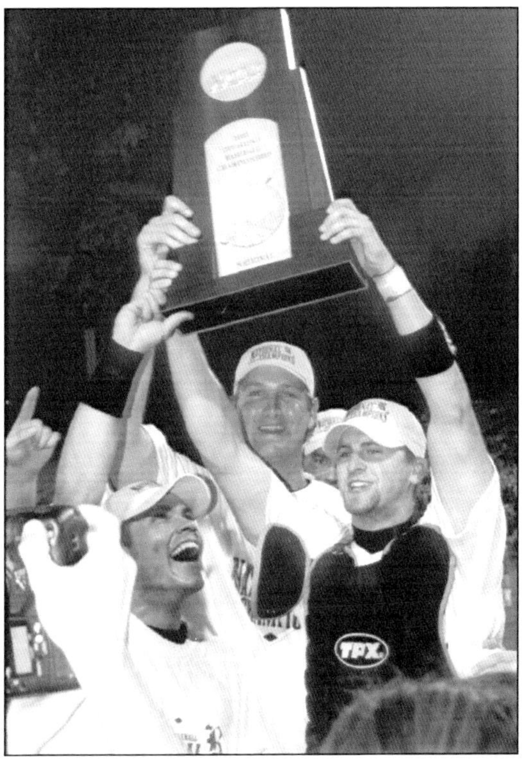

Pictured are the 2003 College World Series Champions, Rice University. (Courtesy of Mark Johnson Photography.)

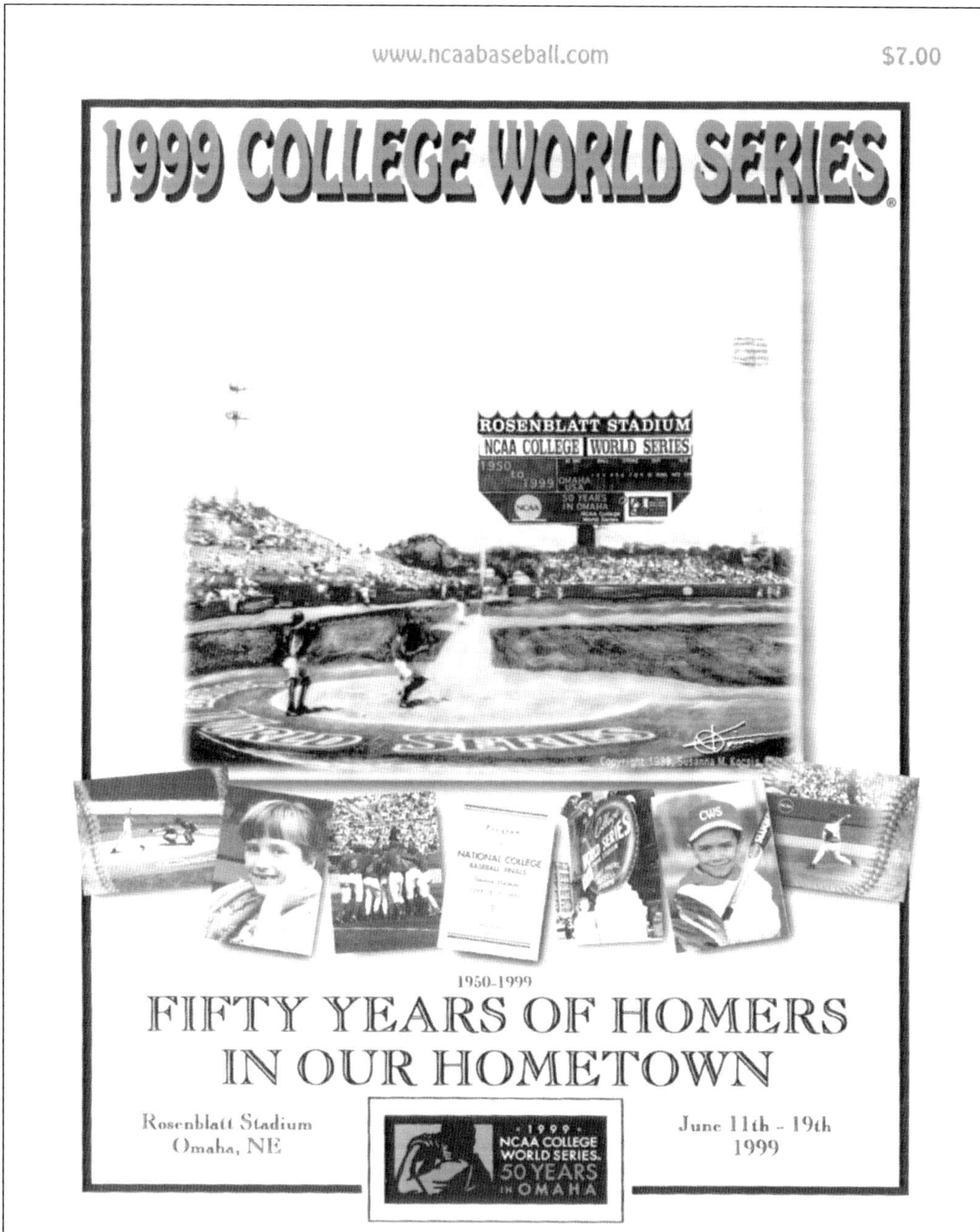

The 1999 CWS marked the 50th anniversary of the event at Rosenblatt Stadium in Omaha. The first CWS in 1950 pitted Washington State University against the University of Texas. In the 1999 CWS, the Miami Hurricanes took the championship with a win over Florida State. In addition to Miami and Florida State, the 1999 CWS brackets included Oklahoma State, Alabama, Rice, Texas A &M, Cal-State Fullerton, and Stanford. (Courtesy of Mark Johnson Photography.)

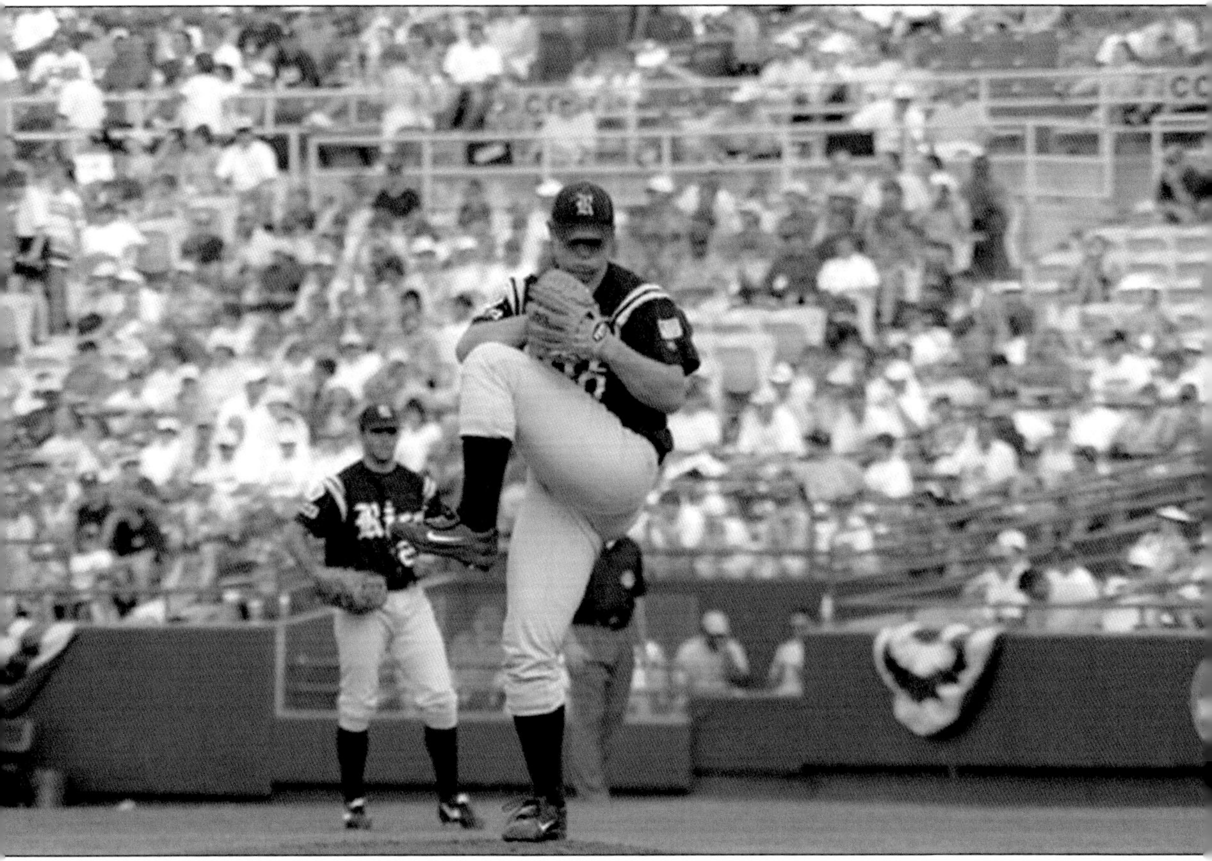

Rice University's Wade Townsend earned the win in a 12-2 win over Texas in Game 8 of the 2003 College World Series. Rice eventually won the 2003 CWS by defeating Stanford. (Courtesy of Mark Johnson Photography.)

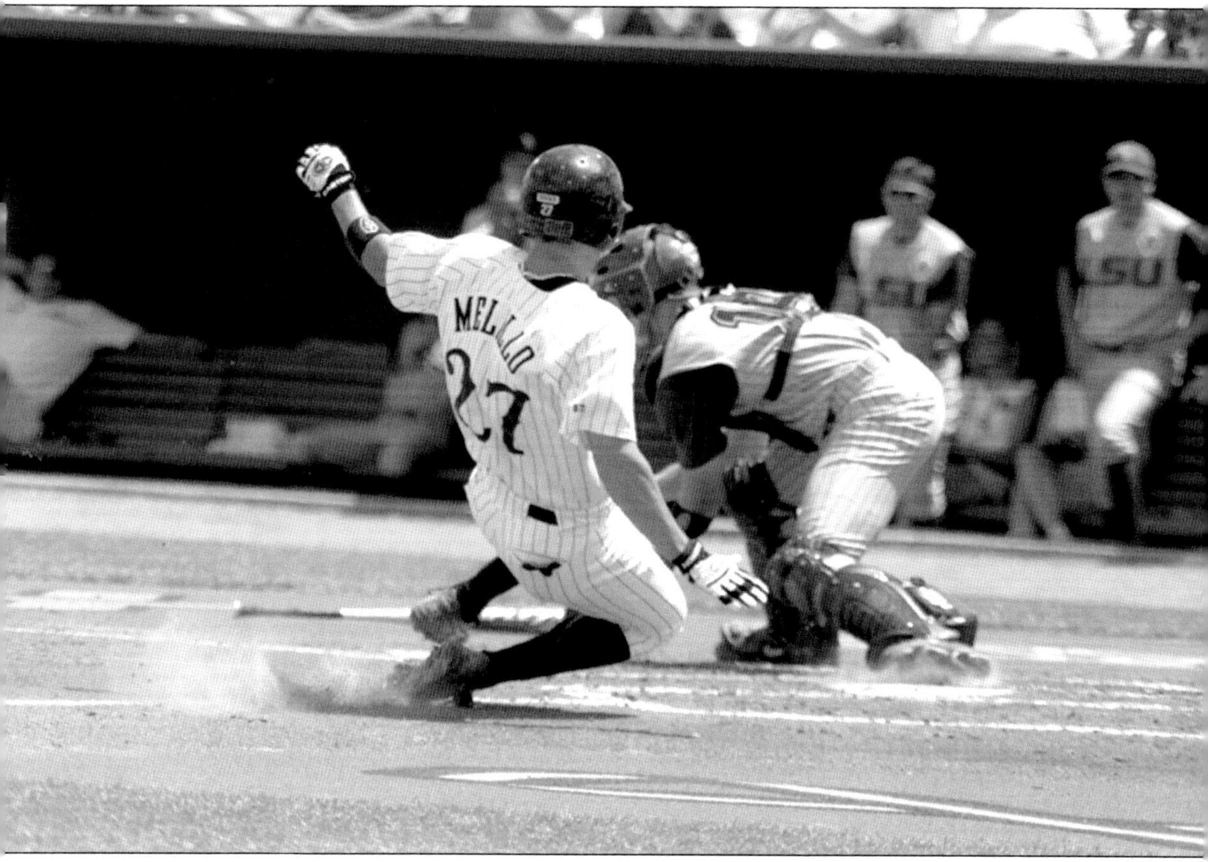

South Carolina Gamecock second baseman Kevin Melillo hit a solo homerun in the seventh inning to bring the Gamecocks an 11-10 win over LSU in the 2003 CWS. The Gamecock victory eliminated LSU from the series. (Courtesy of Mark Johnson Photography.)

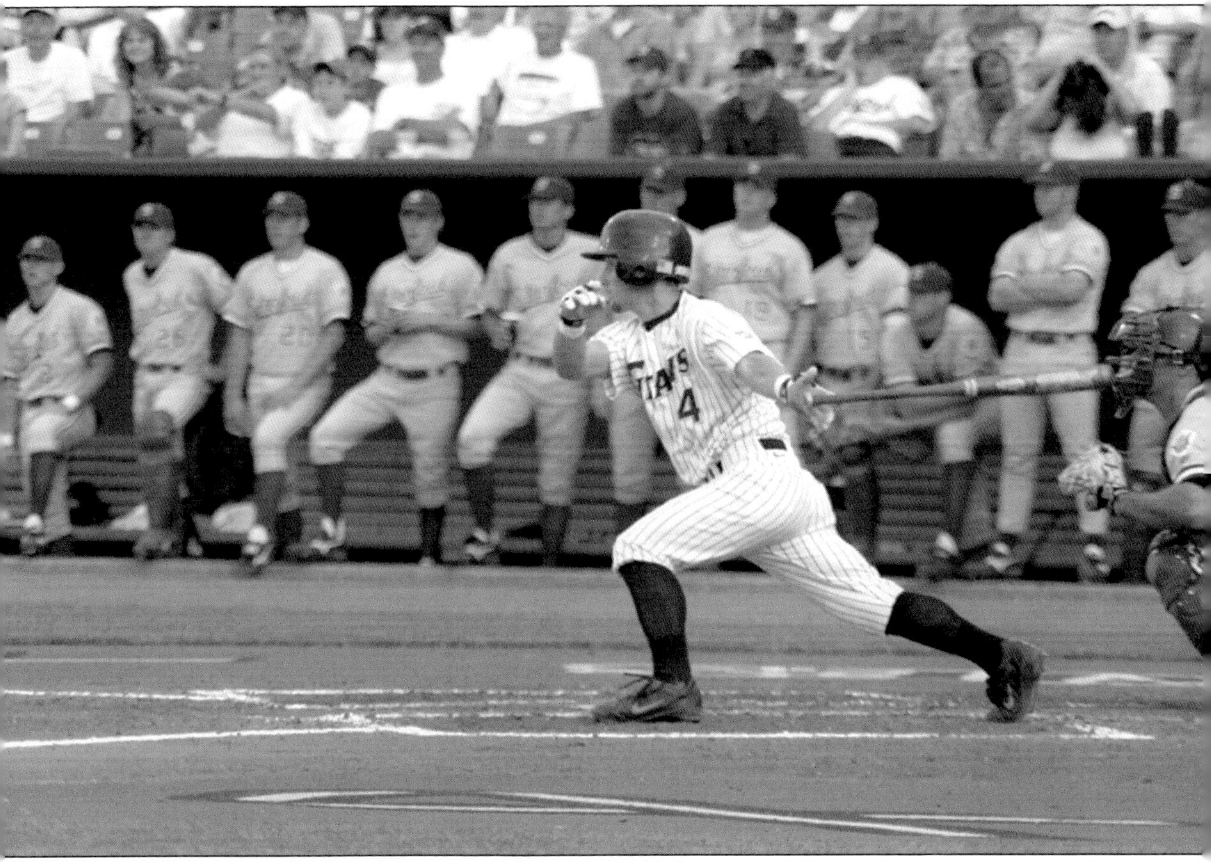

In the 2003 CWS match-up between rivals Cal-State Fullerton and Stanford, the Titans won 6-5 over the Stanford Cardinals, breaking Stanford's 10-game post-season win streak, which included 2 victories over the Titans in the 2001 CWS. (Courtesy Mark Johnson Photography.)

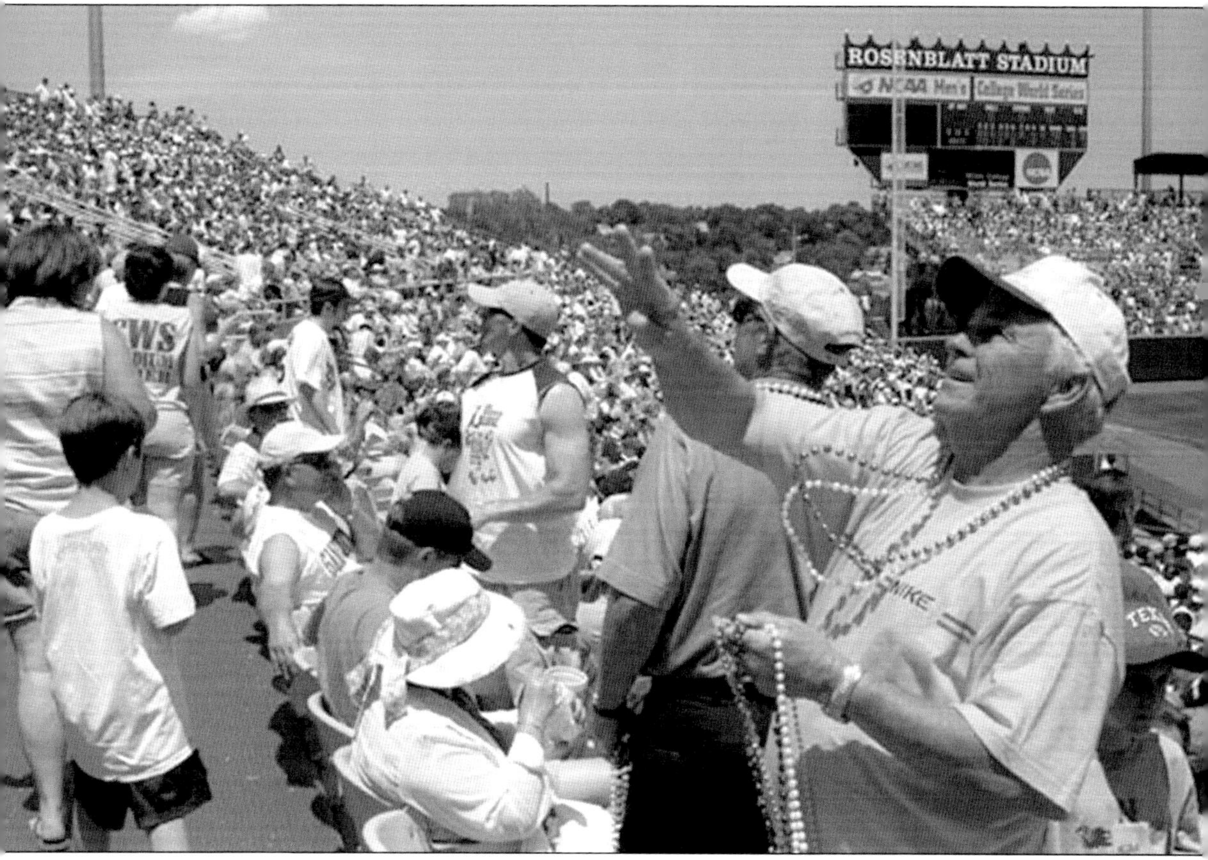

An essential part of CWS culture at Rosenblatt Stadium, the fans return season after season. (Courtesy of Mark Johnson Photography.)

FOUR

Omaha Builds a Ballpark

Rosenblatt and Community

Buried in the *Omaha World Herald* sports page for October 17, 1949, is a single column of text beneath the headline *Stadium Gets A Test Today: Ceremonies Start at 2, Game at 2:40.* The opening of the fought-for and much anticipated Omaha Municipal Stadium at 13th and Deer Park coincided with the 44-13 University of Nebraska Cornhusker loss to Notre Dame at Lincoln's Memorial Stadium. Given second-billing on that fateful day, the inaugural festivities for the structure with "grandstand and bleacher seats for 20 thousand…infield sod ready… outfield grass (that has) started to grow," featured an exhibition game between a team of major leaguers including Richie Ashburn of Tilden, NE, Johnny Hopp of Hastings, NE, and Mel Harder, playing against the Johnny Monaghan Storz crew. "Senator Wherry, Governor Peterson, Mayor Glenn Cunningham, the Original Stadium Committee, and the current Stadium Committee" were expected to attend.

Typographical error or not in the October 17 *OWH*, Original Stadium Committee was a capital letter-worthy effort. Breaking ground for the Omaha Municipal Stadium, raising it up from wood, steel, concrete, politics, bonds, and charters, was all no easy feat in 1940s Omaha. The city had the promise of the Class A Western League Cardinals for 1947, but home games would have to be played across the river in Council Bluffs. Sandlot, Legion, and CYO ball games were played at Brown Park, Burdette, Fontenelle, Riverview, and Miller Park across the city, a city still a few years from being traversed via I-480, a city that did not yet have the Civic Auditorium, or anything much past 72nd Street, other than cornfields and a very distant Boystown.

A young, local Roberts Dairy sales director, Johnny Rosenblatt, along with Eddie Jelen, pulled together the grassroots Original Stadium Committee with the vision of a stadium that would house the Class A Western League Cardinals and eventually bring Triple A ball to Omaha while serving as a community center. Jelen died in the war, but Rosenblatt continued the work that was merely an extension of his involvement in Omaha as a sandlot star in his own right.

Rosenblatt won two letters for his baseball efforts at Technical High before graduating in 1926. As a sandlot fixture, Rosenblatt switched uniforms, sometimes in the same day, for local All-Star teams, Northwestern Bell Telephone Company, the Clay Commission team, the Carter Lake Ball Club, Omaha Prints for Clint Miller, the Murphy-Did-Its for Clink Clair, and the Omaha Crickets of the Western League under manager Pug Griffin.

For decades, Rosenblatt was Omaha baseball. Rosenblatt was on the Omaha Print team that welcomed Ruth and Gehrig in 1927. Facing Satchel Paige in a Negro League exhibition game in Omaha, Rosenblatt ran the count full before striking out. The starting job with Roberts Dairy allegedly came about as a means of getting Rosenblatt on the company baseball team. The young Rosenblatt's battles for the stadium began with the issue of whether or not to use Fontenelle Park for games. Western League officials and Bill Walsingham of the Class A Cardinals were willing to build a fence around Fontenelle Park and install lights, but the people of the neighborhood opposed the likely noise, traffic, and distractions of night stadium lights. Omaha Parks and Recreation found parking to be a potential problem.

After much debate and after putting issues to votes, Rosenblatt and the committee oversaw the fruition of the physical part of the dream, breaking ground at the current site at 13th and Deer Park. Carlson Construction Company cleared the site of brush. Leo A. Daly Co. submitted plans, revisions, and more plans, including several changes in the number of seats accommodated. Peter Kiewit held the building contract. One of the most pressing challenges was the acquisition of steel during a 1947 coal strike; trips were made to Gary, Indiana, to expedite steel shipments to Omaha. By April 1947, steel was trickling in, with a major portion of the Stadium completed by January 1, 1948. By April of that year, John Rosenblatt was on the ballot for City Commissioner.

Omaha Municipal Stadium was finally ready to welcome the Western League Omaha Cardinals back to Omaha (from Council Bluffs) on April 25, 1949. Rosenblatt lauded the lighting system of the new park, a system patterned after the lighting in New York's Yankee Stadium. Specifically, Municipal Stadium featured nine light towers, with the two towers atop the grandstand roof boasting 28 reflectors each. Two towers along the baselines contained 40 reflectors, and the five outfield towers had 50 reflectors each. Each reflector ran on a 1500-watt bulb. Outfield dimensions were patterned after Chicago's Wrigley Field, with distances running 343 feet down the foul lines, 370 feet to right and left field, and 420 feet to dead center. A 20 by 30-foot scoreboard in left center field would serve both baseball and football game scoring. As City Commissioner, John Rosenblatt wrote a memo to Bert Murphy, member of the Omaha Stadium Advisory Committee and president of Andrew Murphy and Sons:

Marking the years of paper pushing, negotiating, postponements, and even the natural elements, Bert Murphy presented John Rosenblatt with a gold watch for his effort in bringing a

> *Dear Mr. Murphy:*
> *Will you please make arrangements regarding plaque for the Stadium Dedication Day. Our present plans call for dedicating the stadium October 17, 1948, so it will be necessary to give this immediate attention in order to have theplaque completed by that time.*
>
> *Very truly yours,*
> *John Rosenblatt*
> *Commissioner*
> *Department of Public Property*

new stadium to Omaha. The plaque lists the names of 30 individuals; 12 Omaha City Council members and 18 members of the original and 1948 Stadium Advisory Committee. Stars in front of two names, John Rosenblatt and Edward Jelen, designate founders of the stadium.

In the days before Opening Night, a healthy Nebraska gust toppled one of the light towers, with the damaged tower covered by insurance.

Also in 1949, the Junior World Series came to Omaha Municipal Stadium. The Junior World Series continues to be American Legion ball's equivalent of the NCAA College World Series. Having the JWS scheduled in Omaha for 1949 was a boon for Omaha and Rosenblatt, with the event returning again in 1950, marking the first time any city has played host to the event two straight years. Attendance in 1949 leveled out at 45,727 paid, breaking all previous JWS records.

The College World Series came to Municipal Stadium in 1950, a decade which also saw the dwindling years of the Negro League games. The Kansas City Monarchs played many exhibition games at 1930s League Park, continuing the tradition at Municipal Stadium. Cool Papa Bell, Buck O'Neil, Goose Tatum...they played in Omaha, including a game between the Kansas City Monarchs and the House of David team. Tickets for the Negro League games often sold at Johnson's and the Lone Star in North Omaha.

On April 21, 1955, Mayor John Rosenblatt threw out the opening pitch for the first game between the AAA Omaha Cardinals and the Louisville Colonels, a game Johnny Keane's Cardinals lost 7-1, but, at last, Omaha had Triple A ball and a spot in the American Association.

Over the years and under the watch of Charlie Mancuso, Frank Mancuso, and long-term public address announcer Jack Payne, the Stadium housed not only Cardinals, Dodgers, and

Royals baseball, but exhibitions of major league teams, benefit games between the All-American Girls including Delores Lee, Maxine Kline, and Dolly Vanderlip pitching for the local Mel Harder League teen-agers against their mates.

Dizzy Dean and Joe DiMaggio sat in the dugouts, with a young Steve Rosenblatt meeting DiMaggio. From 1963 through 1968, when no club resided at Rosenblatt, Charlie Mancuso booked Central High football games, with Gale Sayers playing in those years for the Eagles; the semi-pro Omaha Mustangs also played at Rosenblatt.

Sandlot teams booked games for summer mornings, with Ryan High and Creighton Prep playing home ball games there.

Kid Gavilan fought a match at Rosenblatt and the Ringling Brothers Circus and the Beach Boys performed there.

Anything done at Municipal Stadium was at the risk of Omaha weather. Before a July 18, 1969 ballgame with the new Omaha Royals, the public address announcer issued a special thanks to Frank Mancuso and the grounds crew for making the field playable. Rosenblatt Stadium had received over 2.5 inches of rain between 4:30 and 7:30AM; the area around home plate had to be scooped away and resurfaced. Jesse Cuevas remembers gathering a group of kids, at the summons of Frank Mancuso, to take shovels to the basepaths, clearing an April snow before an exhibition ballgame.

Omaha Municipal Stadium was renamed Rosenblatt Stadium in 1964. Somewhere in the middle of the tournaments, concerts, wrestling matches, and football games the stadium had become the center of community envisioned by John Rosenblatt and the Original Stadium Committee.

Today Rosenblatt Stadium stands, renovated, greeting ball fans with an entryway of interlocking, cantilevered steel beams, girders, and approximately five-story tall columns. John Rosenblatt himself might not recognize much of the original structure, with only the concrete skeleton and those storied steel towers remaining of the 1949 structure, but the park itself is a symbol of Omaha and in the spirit of Frank Mancuso, Jesse Cuevas is a keeper of the grass and stories, the kind that begin, "As it was told to me . . ."

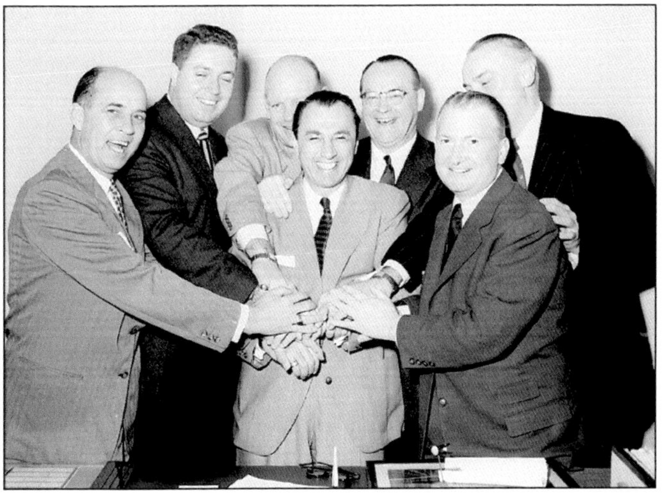

Then-sales director for Roberts Dairy Company, Steve Rosenblatt and Eddie Jelen set about the task of organizing a committee to bring American Association baseball to Omaha, to be played in Omaha at a new baseball stadium. In the mid-to late-1940s, the Omaha Cardinals played home games in Council Bluffs. Omaha Mayor Charles Leeman wanted Triple A baseball, while Western League commissioner Harry Trustin supported use of existing Fontenelle Park for games. The original stadium committee included Edward Hinton, Robert Hall, Bert Murphy, William Lane, Frank Ryan, Floyd Olds, Tom Dailey, Edward Lawler, Charles Winston, Rudy Tesar, Dick McCann, and Chip Bowley. Hinton supported the new stadium, offering that the park would be used for Legion and sandlot games, college and pro football, boxing and wrestling, political meetings and conventions, music festivals, and ice-skating. (Courtesy of the Durham Western Heritage Museum.)

ALL STARS

		1	2	3	4	5	6	7	8	9	10	R	H	E
CF	Ashburn													
SS	Marion													
1B	Hopp													
LF	Hazen													
RF	Basso													
3B	Henningsen													
2B	Babe													
C	Wilber													
P	R. Barney													

IF Ray Henningsen—Denver
IF Marty Marion—St. Louis
IF Johnny Hopp—Pittsburg
IF Loren Babe—Beaumont
OF Westy Basso—Shreveport
OF Rich Ashburn—Philadelphia
OF Vaughan Hazen—Allentown
C Del Wilber—St. Louis
P Mel Harder—Cleveland
P Rex Barney—Brooklyn

Manager—Duce Belford

The major league team included Beemer and Nebraska born Mel Harder—a football, baseball, and basketball stand-out at Omaha Tech High School, who pitched his entire 20 season major league baseball career with the Cleveland Indians. In those 20 seasons, Harder pitched five 20-game seasons. In All-Star game competition, Harder pitched 13 innings without allowing a run. At the time of the 1948 exhibition game, Harder was pitching coach for the Cleveland Indians. Also in the line-up for the exhibition team, J.V. Duce Belford was a coach for a number of Omaha's top amateur and semi-pro teams including the Murphy Did-Its. In addition to scouting for the Dodgers (and credited with recruiting Omaha's Rex Barney for the Brooklyn club), Belford served as Creighton University's Athletic Director from 1943 to 1946, reappointed to the post in 1952 and serving up until his death in 1961. Never far from baseball, Bedford also coached Creighton's freshman baseball teams for 14 seasons, beginning in 1929. (Courtesy of Gary Kastrick, Project Omaha.)

Opposite page, top: In his seasons with the Brooklyn Dodgers, Rex Barney was known more for his inability to find the strike zone with his screaming fastball. Barney was 18 in 1943 when he accepted an invitation to join the Dodgers. In five seasons with the Brooklyn Dodgers, Barney compiled 410 walks and 336 strikeouts, with 1948 being the highlight of this career. Pitching for the Dodgers at Ebbets Field against the New York Giants, Barney threw a no-hitter with 75 out of 116 pitches tossed that day being strikes. The Dodgers won 2-0. Barney started the 1948 exhibition game for the All-Stars, planning to last five innings. In 1948, Hastings, Nebraska native Johnny Hopp played for the Pittsburgh Pirates, having started his major league tour in 1939 with the St. Louis Cardinals. Hopp began his tenure with the Cardinals substituting for an injured Johnny Mize at first base, but finished his seasons in St. Louis in the outfield. Philadelphia Phillies' Richie Ashburn of Tilden, Nebraska, went 3 for 4 as the All-Star lead-off man, generating excitement for freezing fans by "running wild on the bases," including a steal of third in the first inning. (Courtesy of Gary Kastrick, Project Omaha.)

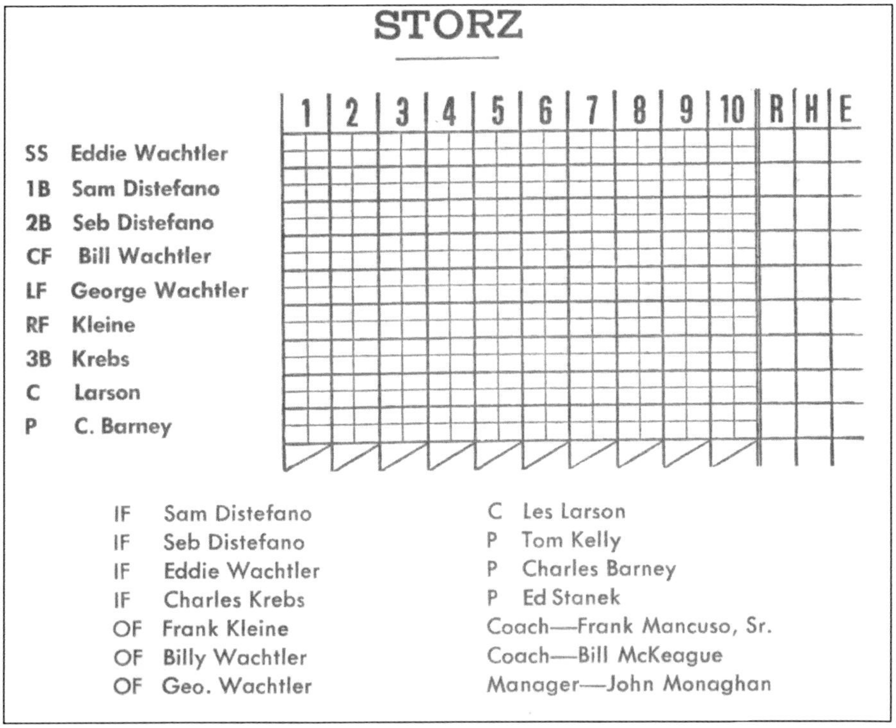

STORZ

		1	2	3	4	5	6	7	8	9	10	R	H	E
SS	Eddie Wachtler													
1B	Sam Distefano													
2B	Seb Distefano													
CF	Bill Wachtler													
LF	George Wachtler													
RF	Kleine													
3B	Krebs													
C	Larson													
P	C. Barney													

IF Sam Distefano
IF Seb Distefano
IF Eddie Wachtler
IF Charles Krebs
OF Frank Kleine
OF Billy Wachtler
OF Geo. Wachtler

C Les Larson
P Tom Kelly
P Charles Barney
P Ed Stanek
Coach—Frank Mancuso, Sr.
Coach—Bill McKeague
Manager—John Monaghan

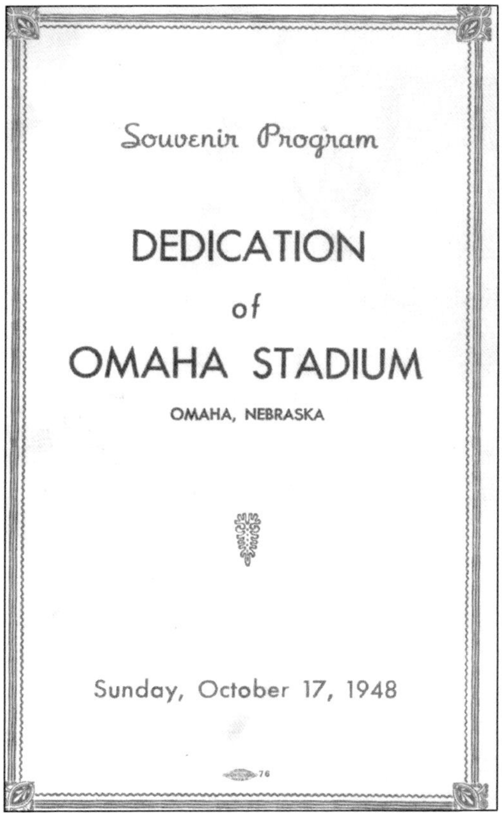

Souvenir Program

DEDICATION
of
OMAHA STADIUM
OMAHA, NEBRASKA

Sunday, October 17, 1948

On a chilly, football weather Sunday, October 17, 1948, the new stadium, Omaha Municipal Stadium, was dedicated with an exhibition ballgame played between a major league traveling exhibition team composed primarily of players with Omaha and greater Nebraska ties, and the Johnny Monaghan Storz semi-pro team. Mayor Glenn Cunningham tossed the ceremonial opening pitch for a game eventually won by the All-Stars, 11-3. (Courtesy of Gary Kastrick, Project Omaha.)

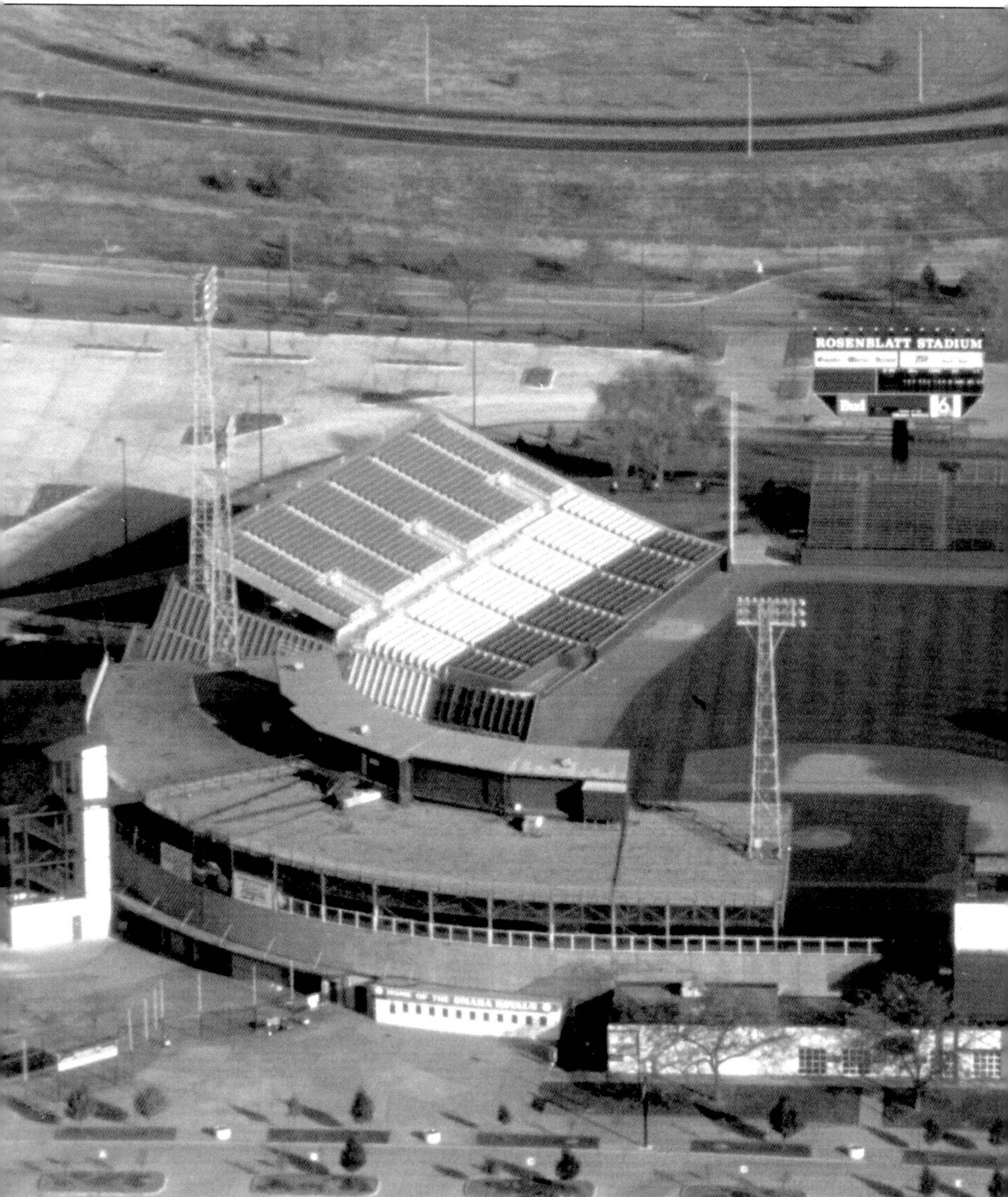

Here is a glimpse of Rosenblatt Stadium before many of the renovations stipulated by the National Collegiate Athletic Association. Overlooking the site of old Riverview Park (now the Henry Doory Zoo), Rosenblatt Stadium is still very much the field on a hill, overlooking

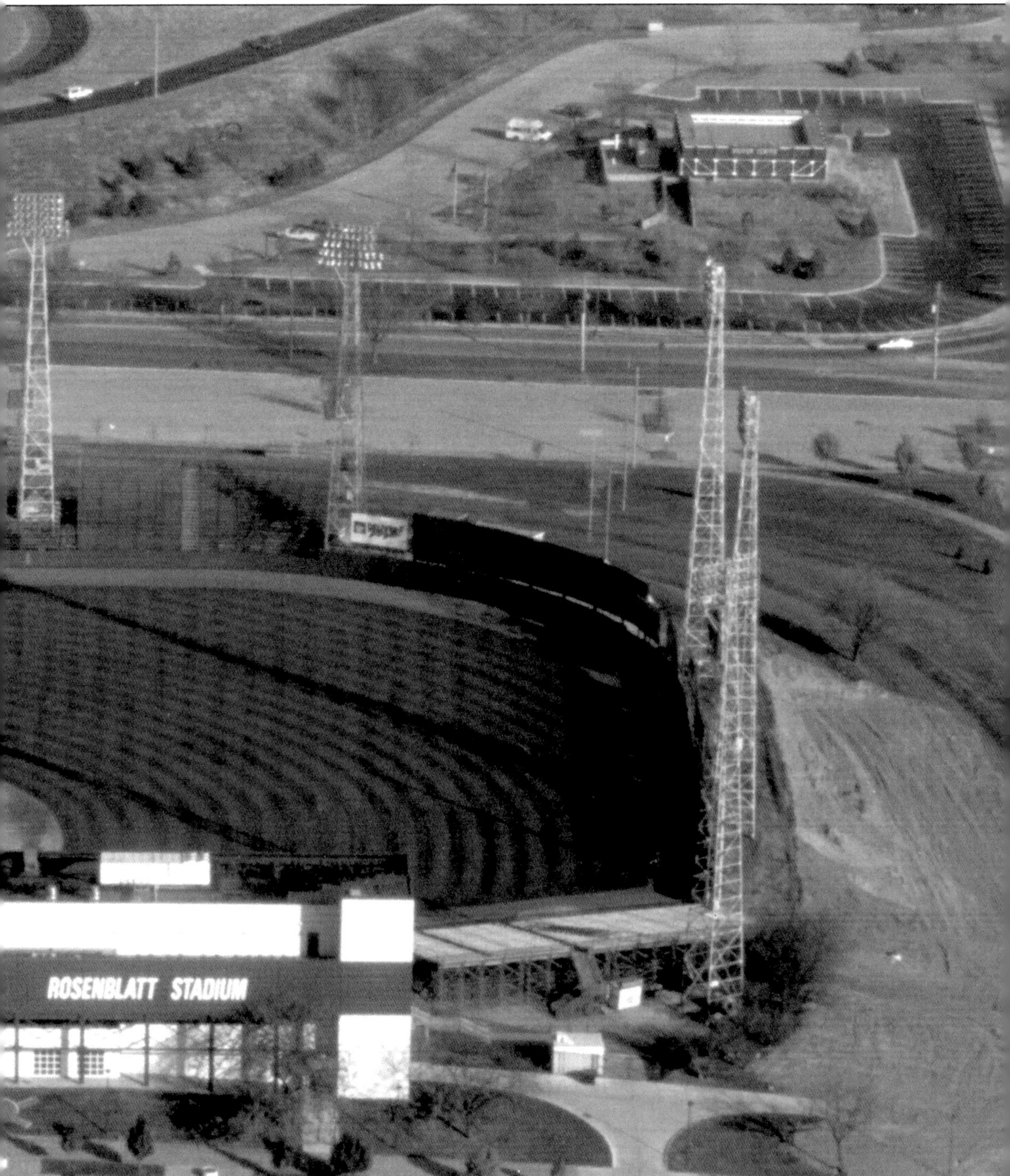

the Missouri River and recalling the days when neighborhoods gathered to watch ballgames and children woke early on weekday mornings to play ball until sunset. (Photo courtesy of the Omaha Royals.)

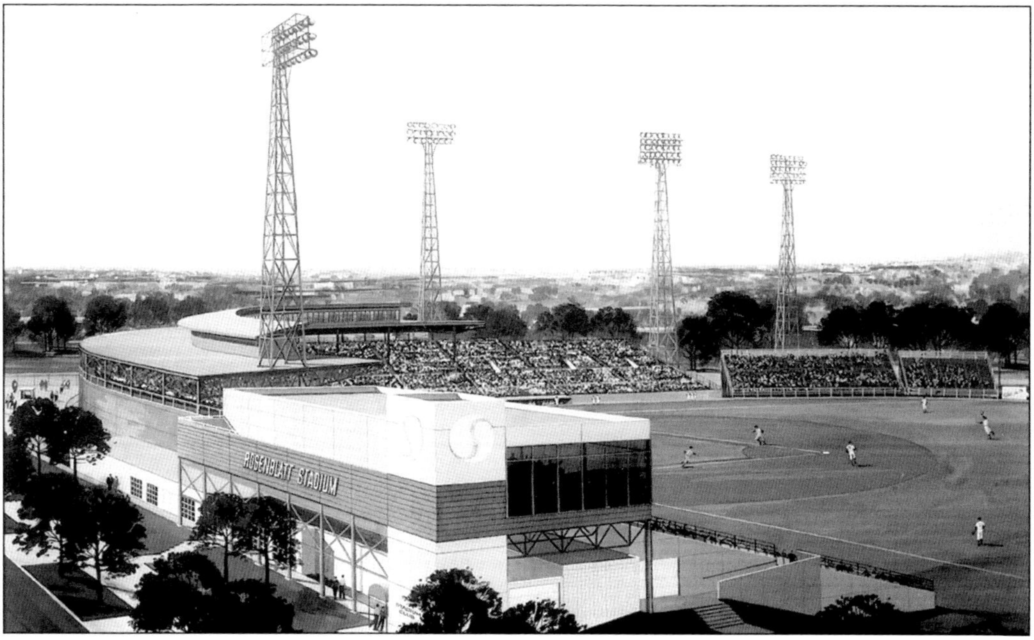

1992 marked the 47th anniversary of the ballpark on Deer Park Boulevard and also perhaps the year of the most visible changes to the park at which John Rosenblatt tossed many opening pitches. In 1992, the ballpark was only in the second year of a five year, $9.5 million dollar renovation, including a 13,500 square foot, three-tiered Stadium View Club, 700 field box seats, media tower and camera supports, and a new playing field with a new sand-based drainage system that included finely crushed brick on the warning track and along foul lines. The field and drainage system, laid following the 1991 season were the first of their kind in a minor league park. The pressbox, rated one of the best in the country, still houses the traditional ballpark organ, in addition to 200-capacity television, print, and radio media members. (Courtesy of the Omaha Royals.)

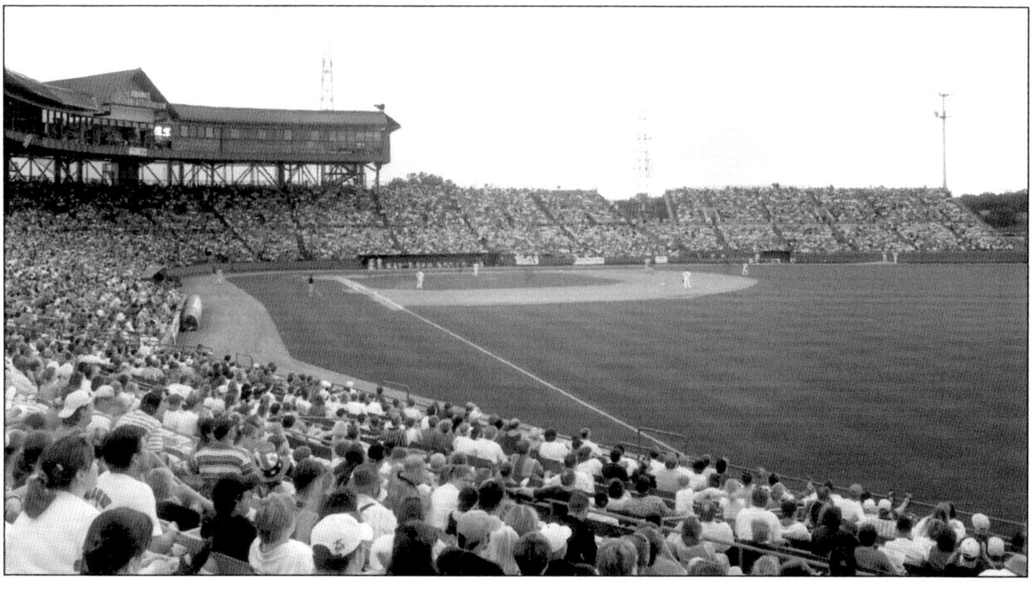

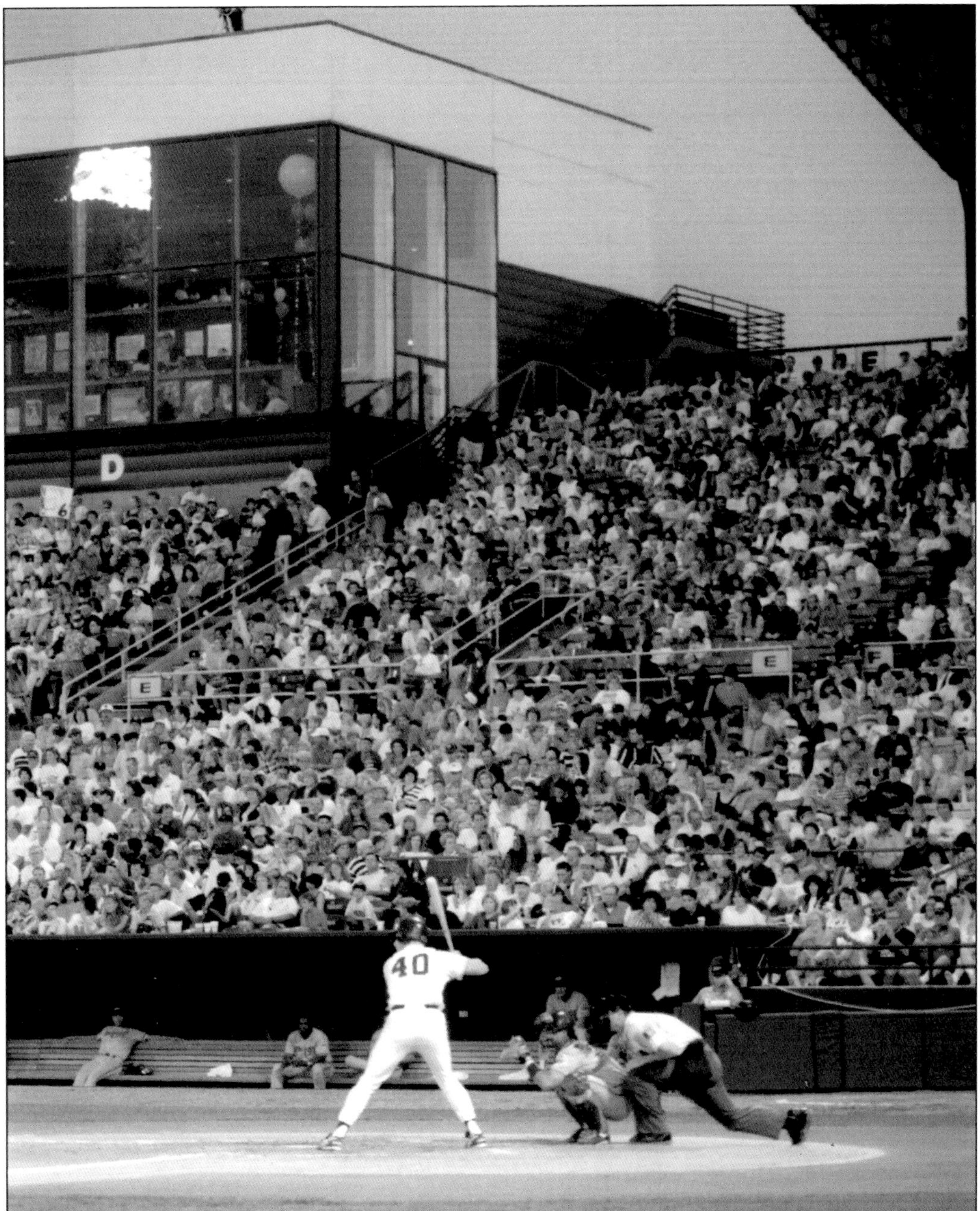

A new, three-tiered Stadium View Club houses photos from the early Omaha Royals clubs and also includes a restaurant, dining area, and concessions. The Stadium View Club was part of the five-year Rosenblatt Stadium Expansions and Renovations package as identified by the National Collegiate Athletic Association's (NCAA) suggested improvements to keep the College World Series in Omaha through the 2000 season. Improvements were carried out by the architectural firm of Bahr Vermeer Haecker (BVH). In additional to fulfilling an NCAA requirement, the Stadium View Club also provided a facility envisioned for use by the Omaha community. (Courtesy of the Omaha Royals).

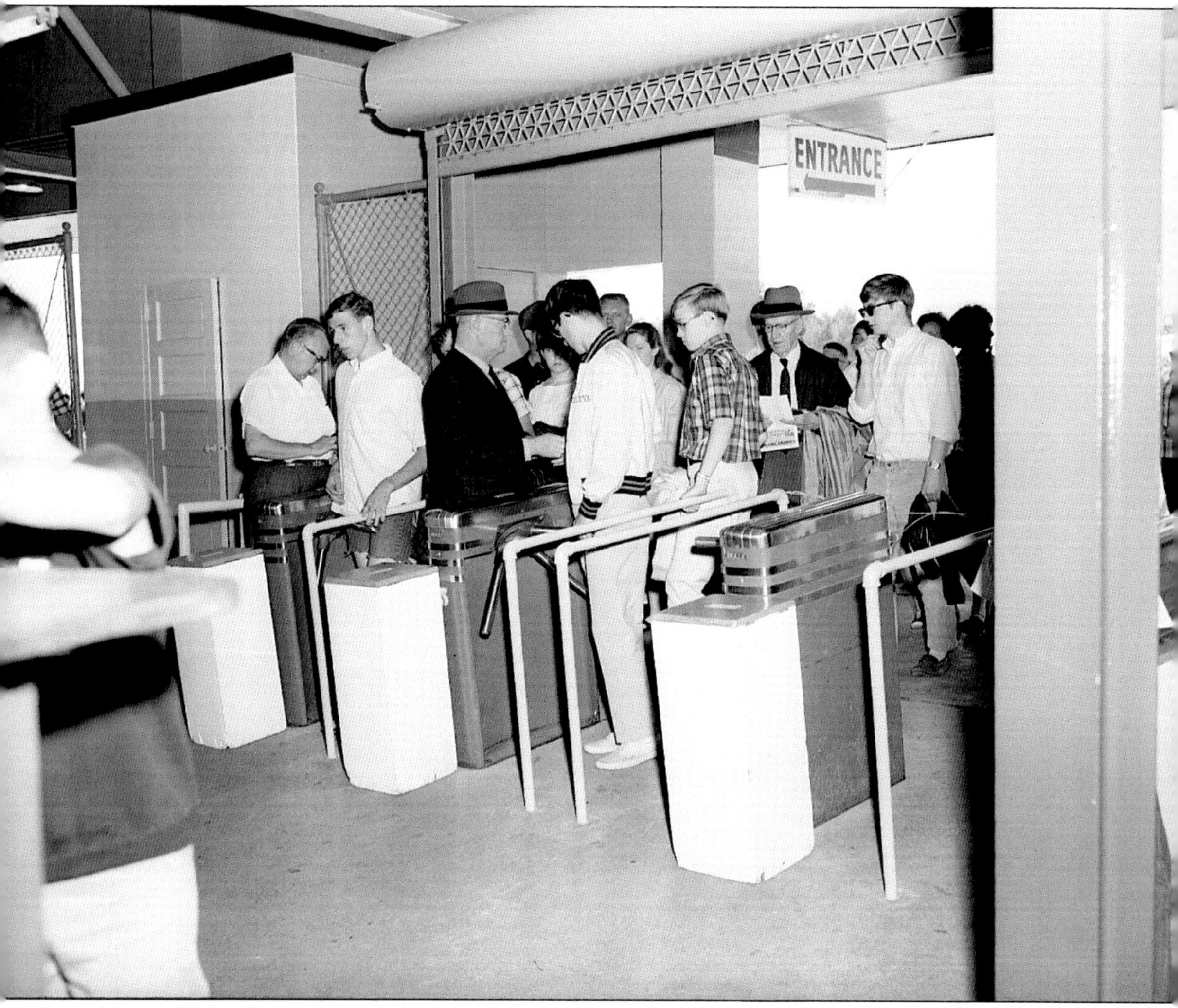

By 1967, Omaha's Municipal Stadium had been renamed Johnny Rosenblatt Stadium. Though Omaha was still two seasons away from hosting the AAA farm club for the Kansas City Royals, Rosenblatt Stadium remained an active hub for local baseball action including American Legion, CYO, and semi-pro baseball and football games. Archbishop Ryan High School and Creighton Prep played home baseball games at Rosenblatt Stadium and CYO games were often played from 8:00 a.m. through noon during the summer. The semi-pro football Mustangs held games in the Stadium, and Walter Payton played for Jackson State in a 17-10 victory over the University of Nebraska at Omaha. (Courtesy of the Durham Western Heritage Museum.)

Pictured is the Omaha Stadium dedication. Today the plaque hangs to the right of the main concourse as one enters Rosenblatt Stadium. Four years, seven months, and 20 days passed from John Rosenblatt and his committee securing approval for the stadium to the day of dedication. The Leo A. Daly firm submitted original plans for an "L" shaped stadium with 8,000 seats under a "horseshoe covering" behind home plate. 27,500 seats would fit around the playing field proper, with parking for 1000. Revisions over time included a reduction in stairways, fewer permanent seats, and adjustments to the grandstand roof. Peter Kiewit, Co. spent the summer of 1947 searching for steel and ways to bring it to Omaha despite coal strikes on the East coast. (Courtesy of Devon Niebling.)

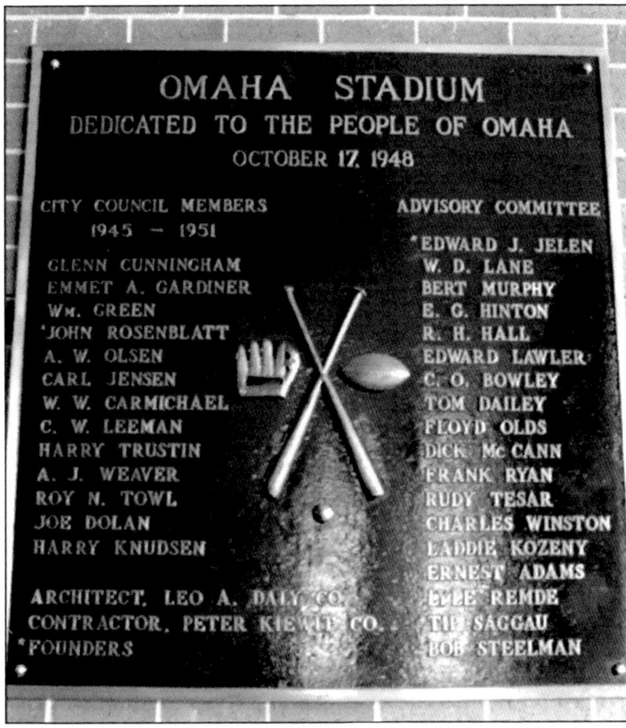

This is the best game. And this is the best atmosphere. I love watching these guys play. They always work hard. And we always root for the underdog.

–Baseball fan quoted in *2000 Omaha World-Herald*

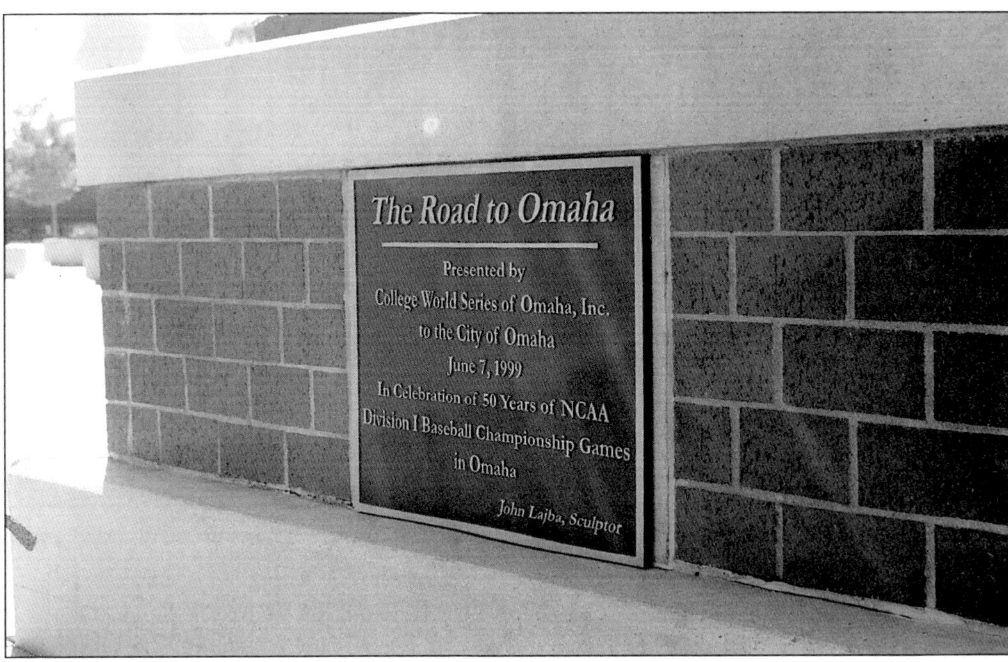

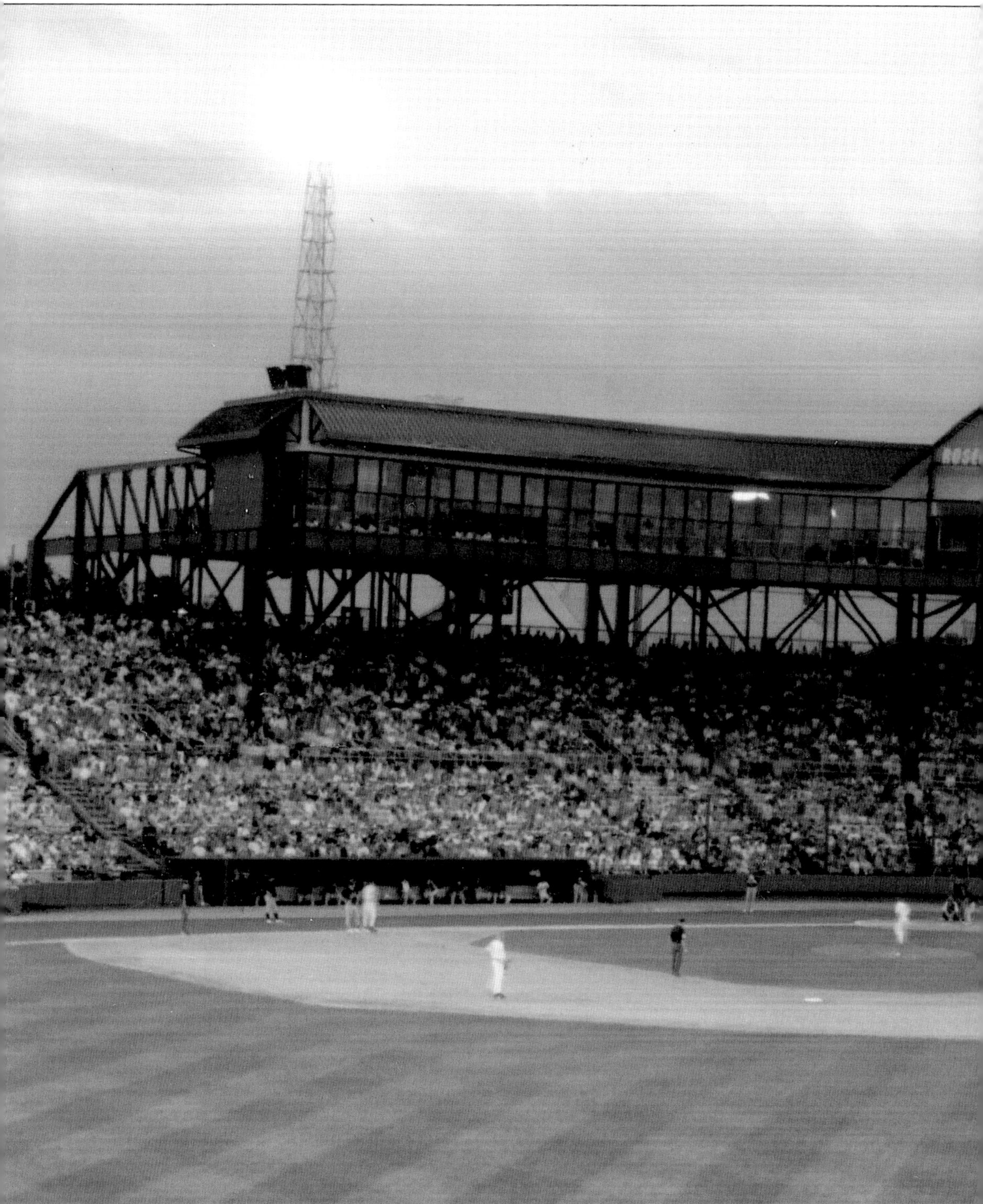

Rosenblatt is seen here under lights. One of the larger ballparks in the Pacific Coast League, Rosenblatt Stadium packs in a crowd early in the season. Pressbox windows above the backstop

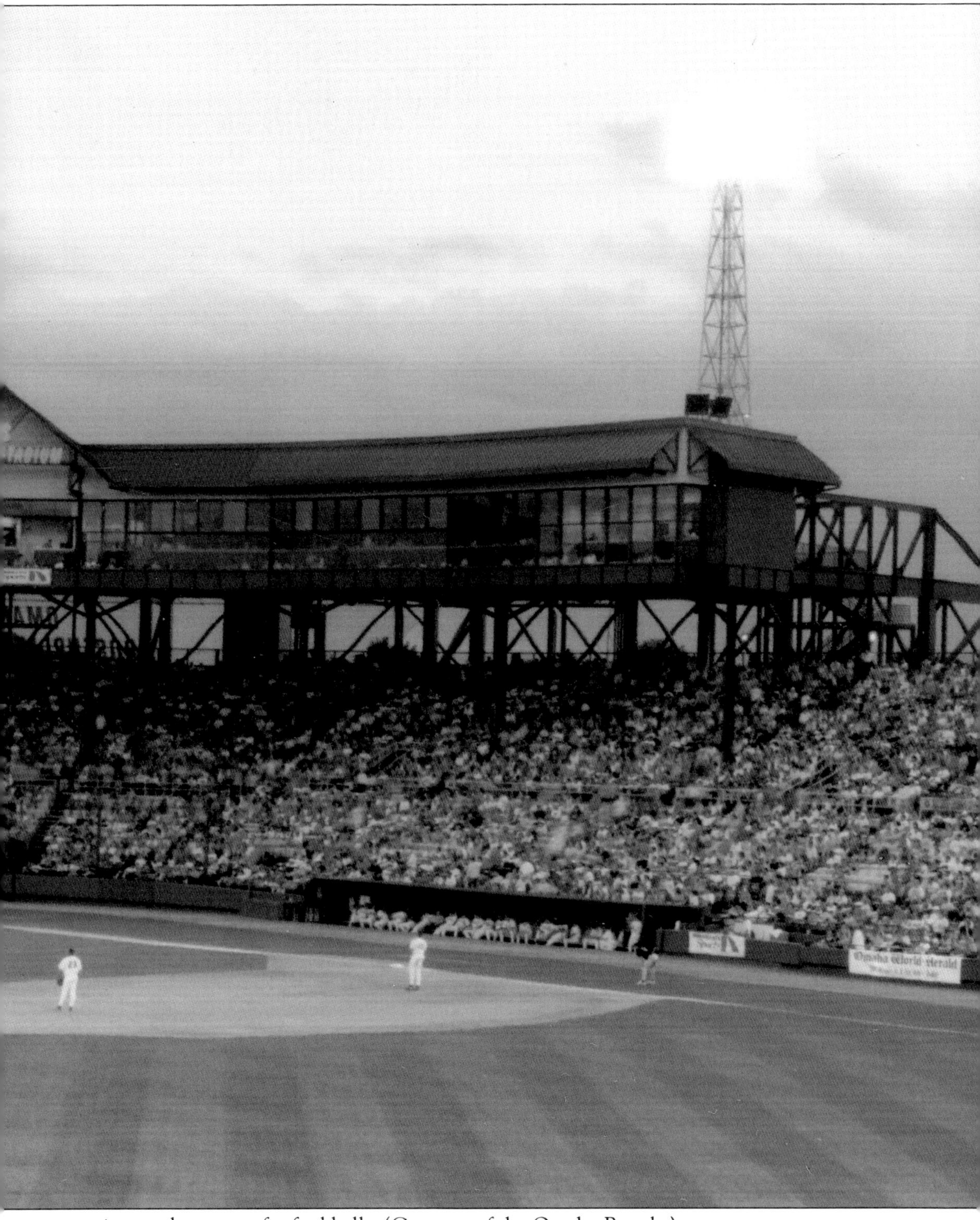

remain popular targets for foul balls. (Courtesy of the Omaha Royals.)

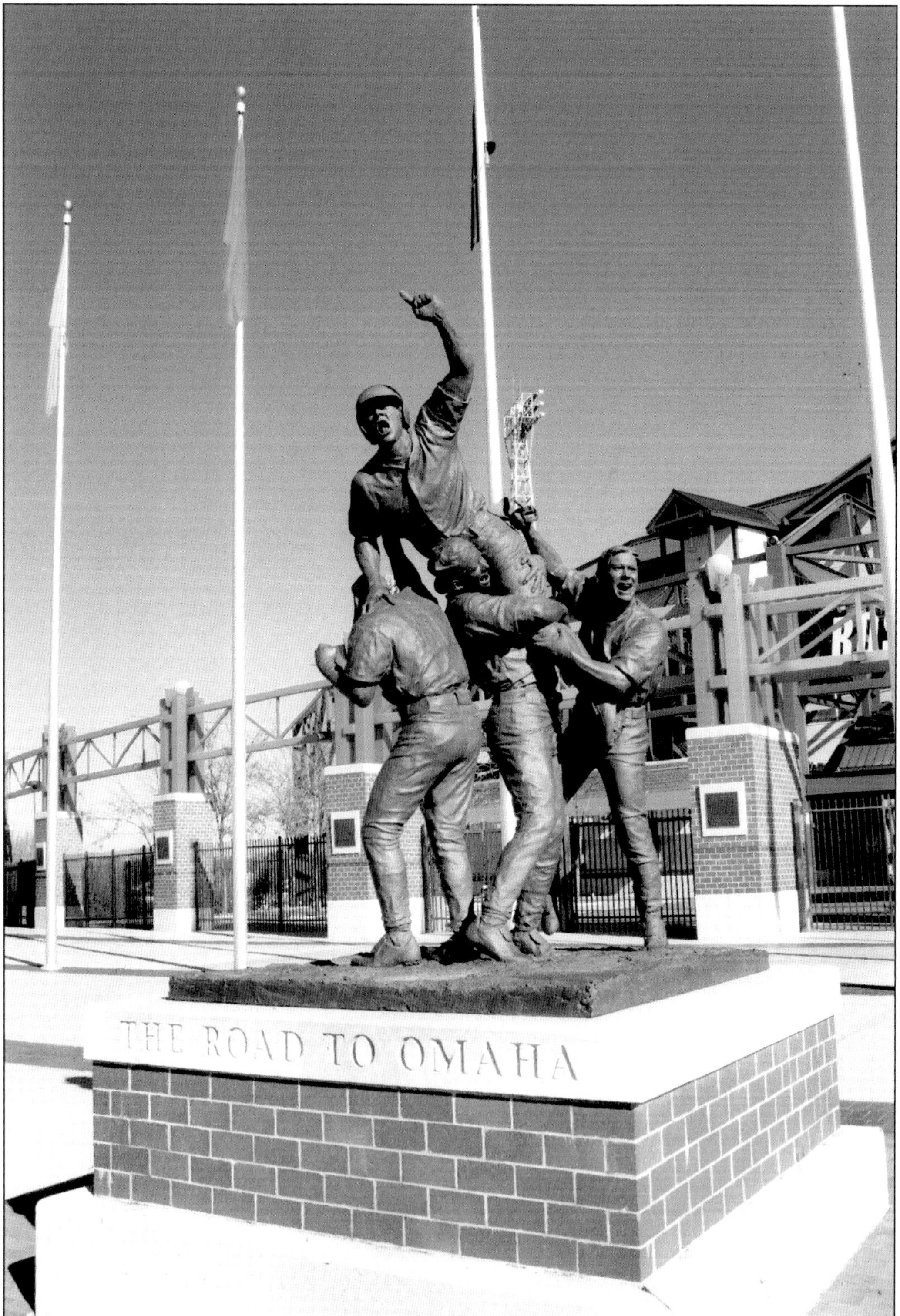
THE ROAD TO OMAHA

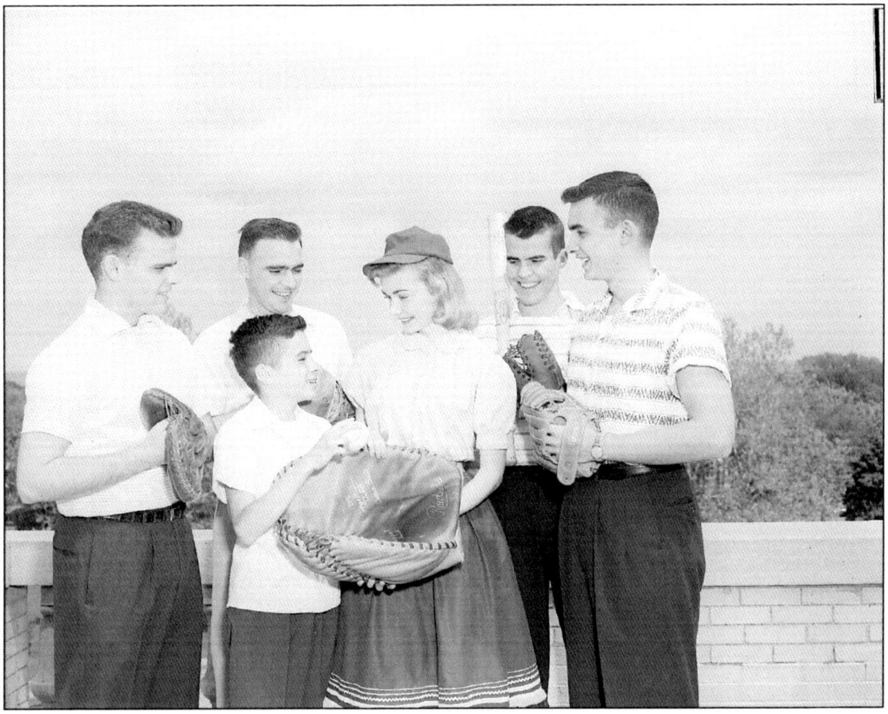

Before its inception as the College World Series Ambassador Program in 1992, the local program aimed at college students, and coupled with the NCAA College World Series, was known as the Sweetheart Program. A connection between the CWS and host-city Omaha, the Sweetheart Program involved the selecting of one female representative from each of the nine local colleges, universities, and nursing schools. Eligible representatives had to be single, full-time college students, and between the ages of 17 and 22. From the nine sweethearts, local sportscasters and sportswriters elected one to serve as the College World Series Queen. The Queen made public appearances, while the remaining eight representatives were assigned to a team participating in the CWS. The eight members of the court appeared at events with area service clubs for each team, in effect functioning as liaisons at the local level for the CWS. (Courtesy of the Durham Western Heritage Museum.)

Opposite page: Reaching to the sky in victory, the players of *The Road to Omaha* celebrate not only the tradition of the NCAA College World Series in Omaha, but the relationship of the series with Rosenblatt Stadium. Sculpted and dedicated in 1999 by Omaha artist John Lajba, *The Road to Omaha* stands to welcome visitors to the main gates of the ball park where over 5 million fans have passed in the over 50 years of CWS action in Omaha. For a large percentage of those 5 million fans, the CWS is an annual trip. The Omaha World Herald's Todd Cooper wrote of such a tradition in a 2000 feature story about Council Bluffs' couple Lauren and Lila Leaders. The 2000 CWS marked the 48th year of attendance for the Leaders, the 52nd of their marriage. Youth, camaraderie, and the joy of competition glow in the faces of Lajba's players when struck by the sun. The statue has become a testimonial to the game and tradition, recalling perhaps for Omaha baseball fans a sign that once stood outside the ballpark, a doff of the cap to Mayor John Rosenblatt, celebrating the June 12, 1964 renaming of Omaha Municipal Stadium as Johnny Rosenblatt Stadium and establishing "The Fourth Sunday of Every June as Johnny Rosenblatt Baseball Day." (Courtesy Devon M. Niebling.)

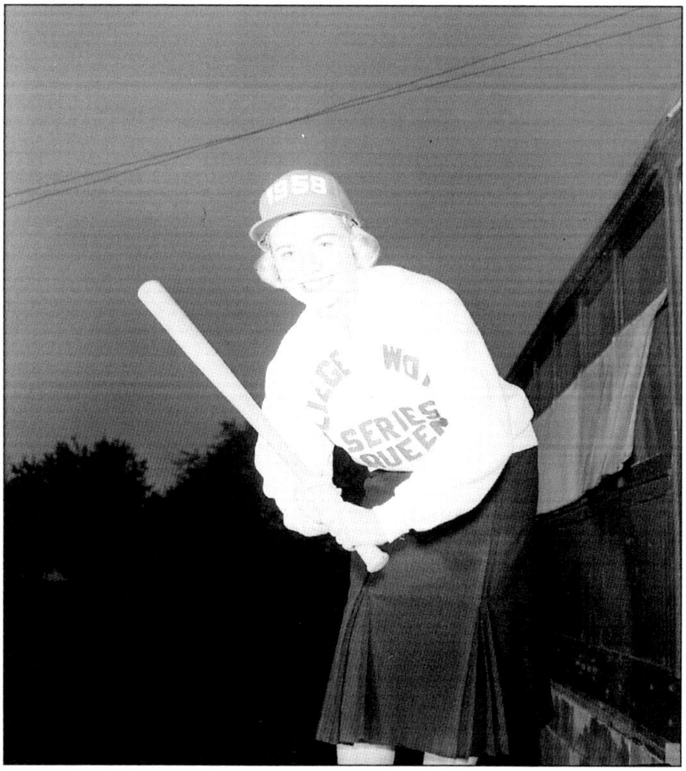

In 1991, the Sweetheart Program became part of a reorganization effort led by Meeting & Event Design (MED) and the NCAA. Recognizing the importance of sustaining local ties, the committee retained the original premise of the Sweetheart Program, but widened the scope beneath a new name, College World Series Ambassador Program. Opening the program to any full-time college student, the committee also brought the selection process of representatives under the umbrella of the College World Series of Omaha, Inc. Prospective Ambassadors were required to submit an application and participate in interviews from which eight Ambassadors were selected to assist in the NCAA office and Box Office at Rosenblatt Stadium, prepare player welcome packages, work in the CWS of Omaha offices, participate in promotional media interviews, and sell general admission ticket books. (Courtesy of the Durham Western Heritage Museum.)

Opposite page, bottom: In preparation for a 1969 major league exhibition game between the Montreal Expos and Cleveland Indians, the Rosenblatt Stadium crew, led by Frank Mancuso, called in a helicopter. Over the years, baseball in Omaha has meant battling the elements including snow in April, thunderstorms in June, and early frost near the end of the baseball season. The 1969 exhibition game at Rosenblatt drew only 2,874 fans, the smallest in history for a major league exhibition game in Omaha. Heavy rain the morning of the game required extreme clean-up measures including the hiring of the helicopter at $65.00 an hour to help dry the field. Approximately 660 gallons of liquid were used to burn the infield surface dry, with the bill for the entire clean-up going to Mid-America Expositions, sponsor of the exhibition game which brought Maury Wills, then shortstop for the Expos, Russ Snyder, Nelson (a Nebraska native and Cleveland outfielder), and others to Omaha. Anyone sitting close to the pressbox during the game could have heard the Montreal radio announcer providing play-by-play in French for a Montreal network. (Courtesy of the Durham Western Heritage Museum.)

A fan favorite for the parent St. Louis Cardinals club, Stan Musial was also a favorite for the Omaha crowds at Municipal Stadium. In December 1954, the St. Louis Cardinals announced the movement of its AAA club from Columbus, Ohio, to Omaha, the American Association, and Omaha Municipal Stadium. Johnny Keane was named manager and Mayor John Rosenblatt invited the "St. Louis family" to Omaha for a January baseball dinner and promotion of the new relationship between the two cities. Musial made additional appearances at Municipal Stadium, including a 1958 exhibition game between the Chicago White Sox and St. Louis Cardinals. The Chisox-Cardinal contest had first billing the weekend of August 6, followed by a Sunday afternoon game between the San Francisco Giants and Cleveland Indians. Sunday afternoon brought 14,070 fans to Municipal Stadium where Cleveland and Rocky Colavito won 8-5 over the Willie Mays and the Giants. (Courtesy of the Durham Western Heritage Museum.)

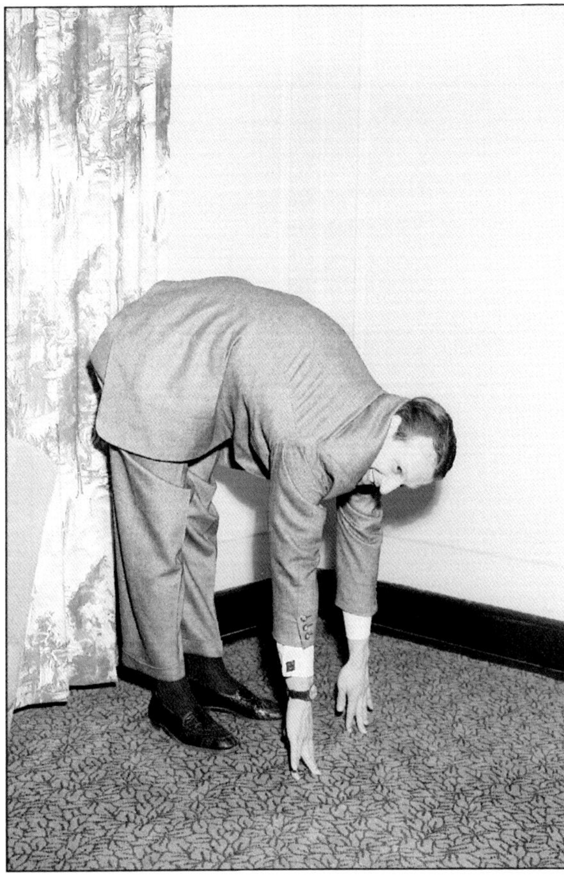

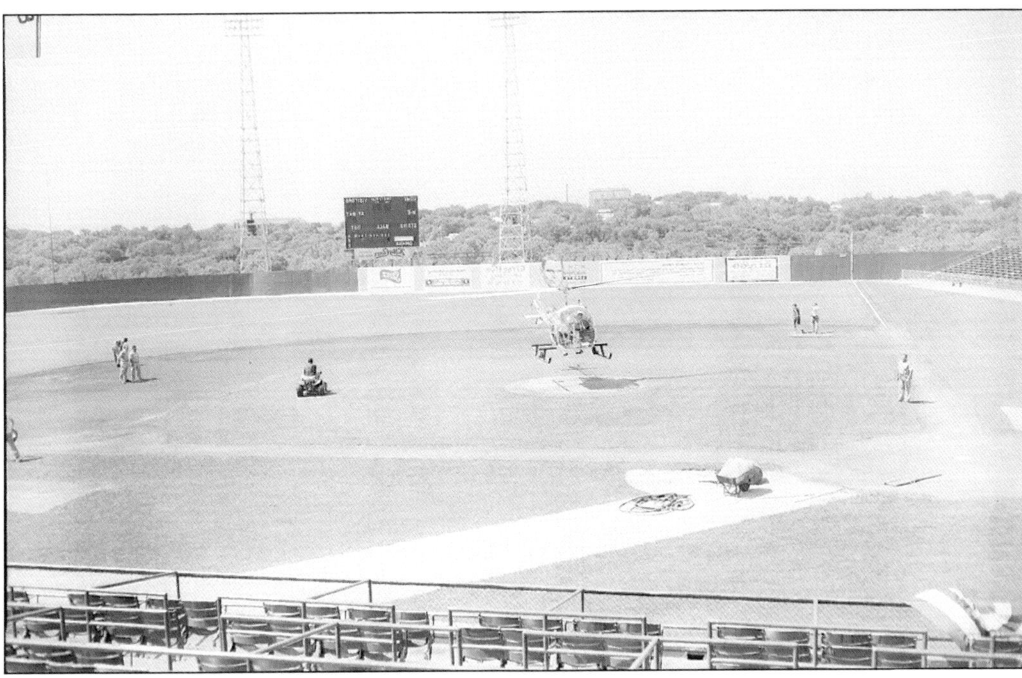

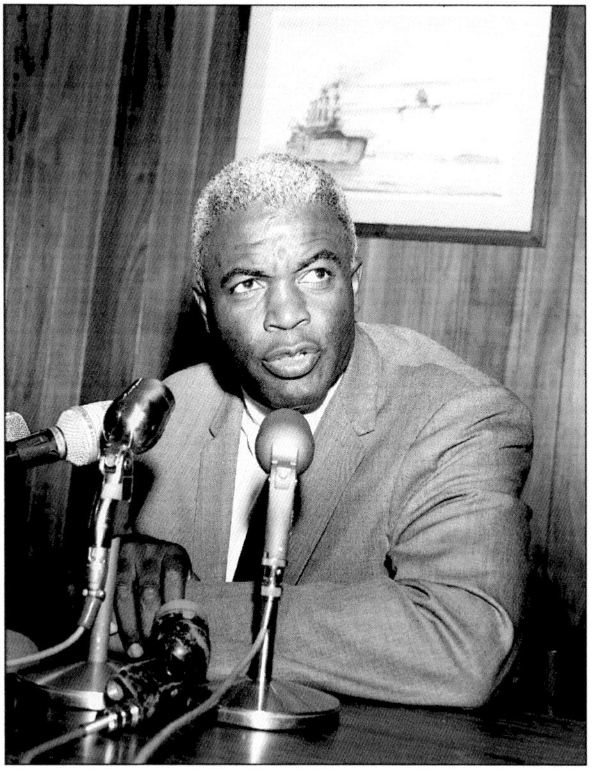

Jackie Robinson came to Omaha in the late '60s, post-playing days, to visit Sacred Heart School and Parish. (Courtesy of the Durham Western Heritage Museum.)

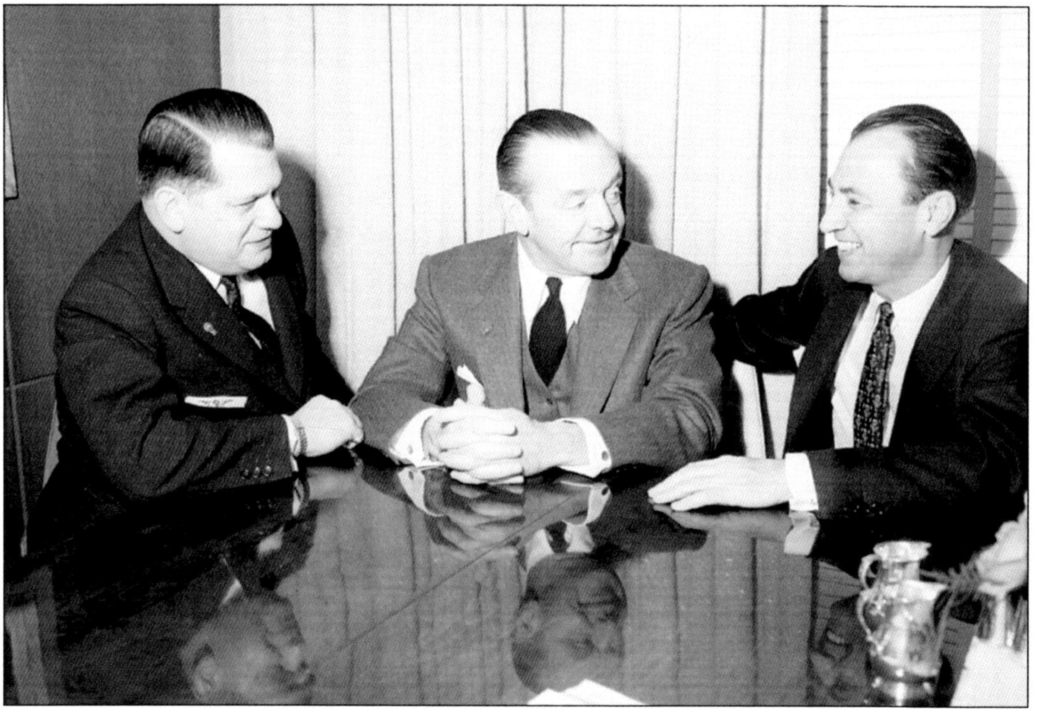

Mayor Rosenblatt with unidentified gentlemen reputed to be Dodger ownership.(Courtesy of the Durham Western Heritage Museum.)

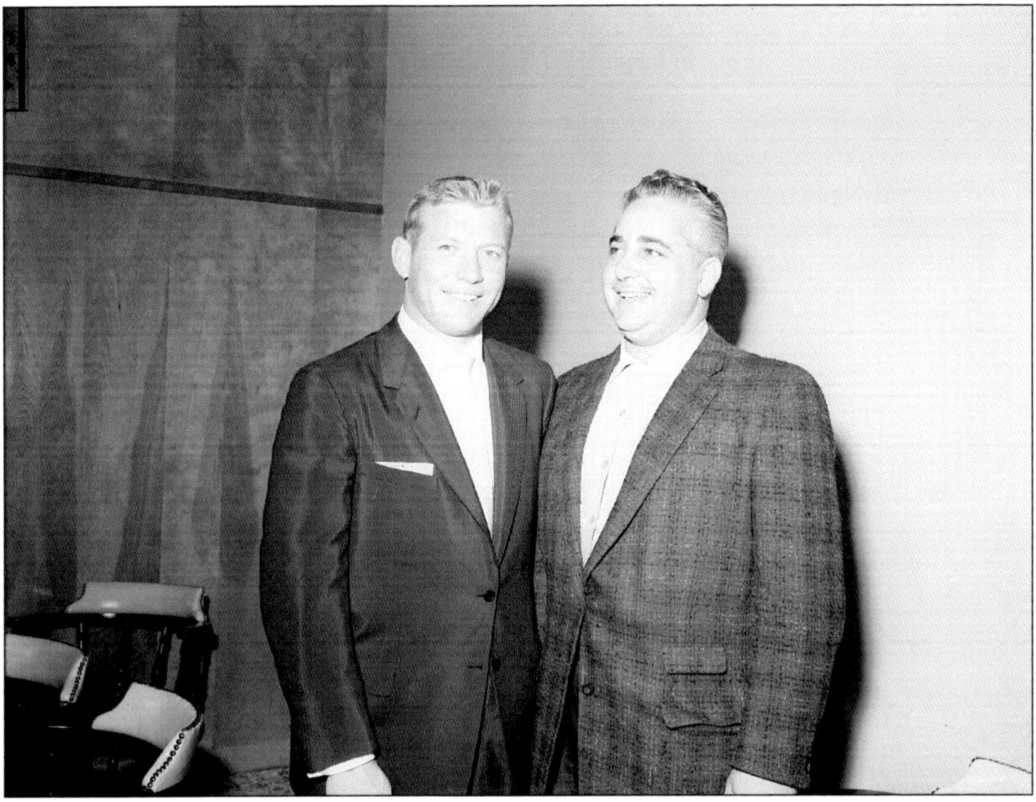

In Omaha for a February 1959 appearance at the second annual Omaha Sportscasters' Association Banquet, the New York Yankees' Mickey Mantle dined at Ross' Steakhouse, meeting owner Ross Lorello. The dinner/benefit was for the vocational workshop of the Omaha Opportunity Center. Ross' Steakhouse, an Omaha restaurant landmark at 72nd and Pacific Street, hosted many visiting sports legends. Mantle's appearance at the off-season baseball banquet, his only for the 1958–1959 winter season, put him on the dinner docket with new Omaha Cardinal manager Joe Schultz, American Association president Ed Doherty, and St. Louis Cardinal business manager Art Routzong. Future Hall of Fame broadcaster Jack Buck was the master of ceremonies. Joe Schultz, succeeding Johnny Keane, made his first appearance before Cardinal boosters and local fans, arriving from Winter League play-offs in the Dominican League where his Licey-sponsored team won a best-of-nine series over Escogido for the championship. Schultz's stop in Omaha marked a six-day midwinter vacation, the new manager's first following the Class A Eastern League Season with the York White Roses and the winter season in the Dominican Republic. Following his Omaha vacation, Schultz reported early to the parent club St. Louis Cardinal training camp in St. Petersburg, Florida. While in Omaha, Mantle participated in a Tuesday afternoon press conference at Omaha's Ranch Bowl. He answered questions about his Yankee contract negotiations, and promoted Omaha's penchant for bowling and the rise to national prominence on the women's professional bowling tour of Pauline Bickel. Mantle bowled an exhibition against Bickel, racking up several strikes on his way to a 192-point game. Bickel scored 220 to take the game from Mantle. (Courtesy of the Durham Western Heritage Museum.)

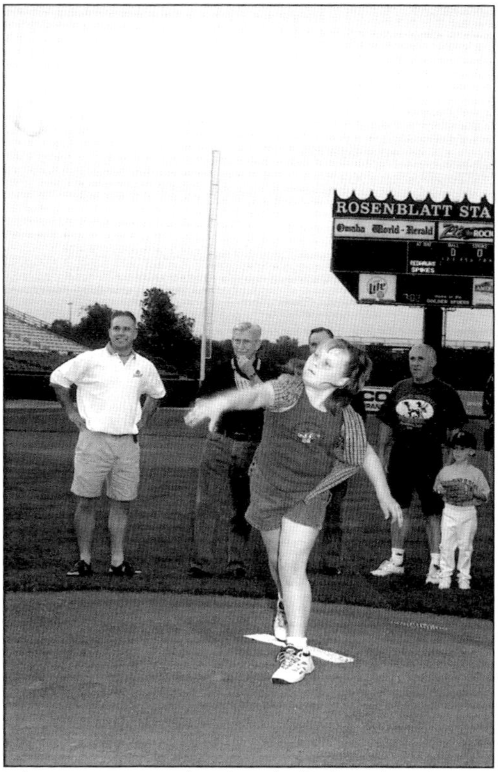

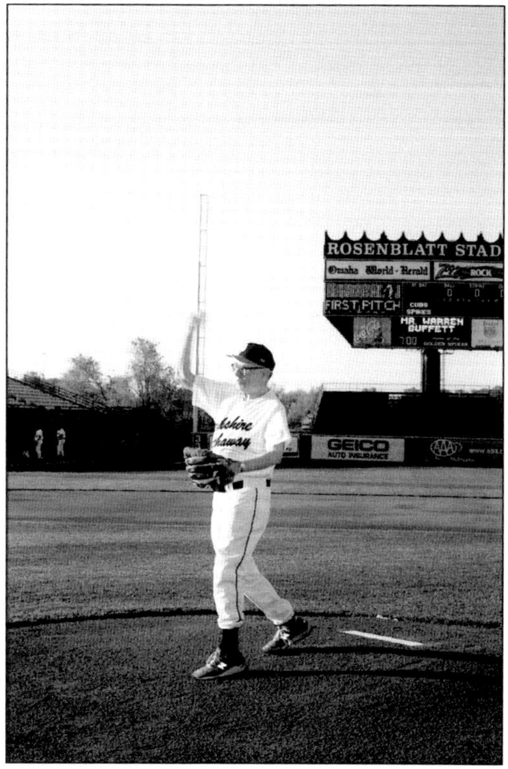

The opening pitch is baseball's bond with the community, with fans, and with history. Presidents beginning with William Howard Taft have fired the ball 90 feet to open major league seasons in parks across the country. Season opening and regular season game opening pitches at Rosenblatt have found their mark courtesy of Buck O'Neal, Ernie Banks, Warren Buffet, local dignitaries, school teachers, transplant survivors, and even children from the community. (Courtesy of the Omaha Royals.)

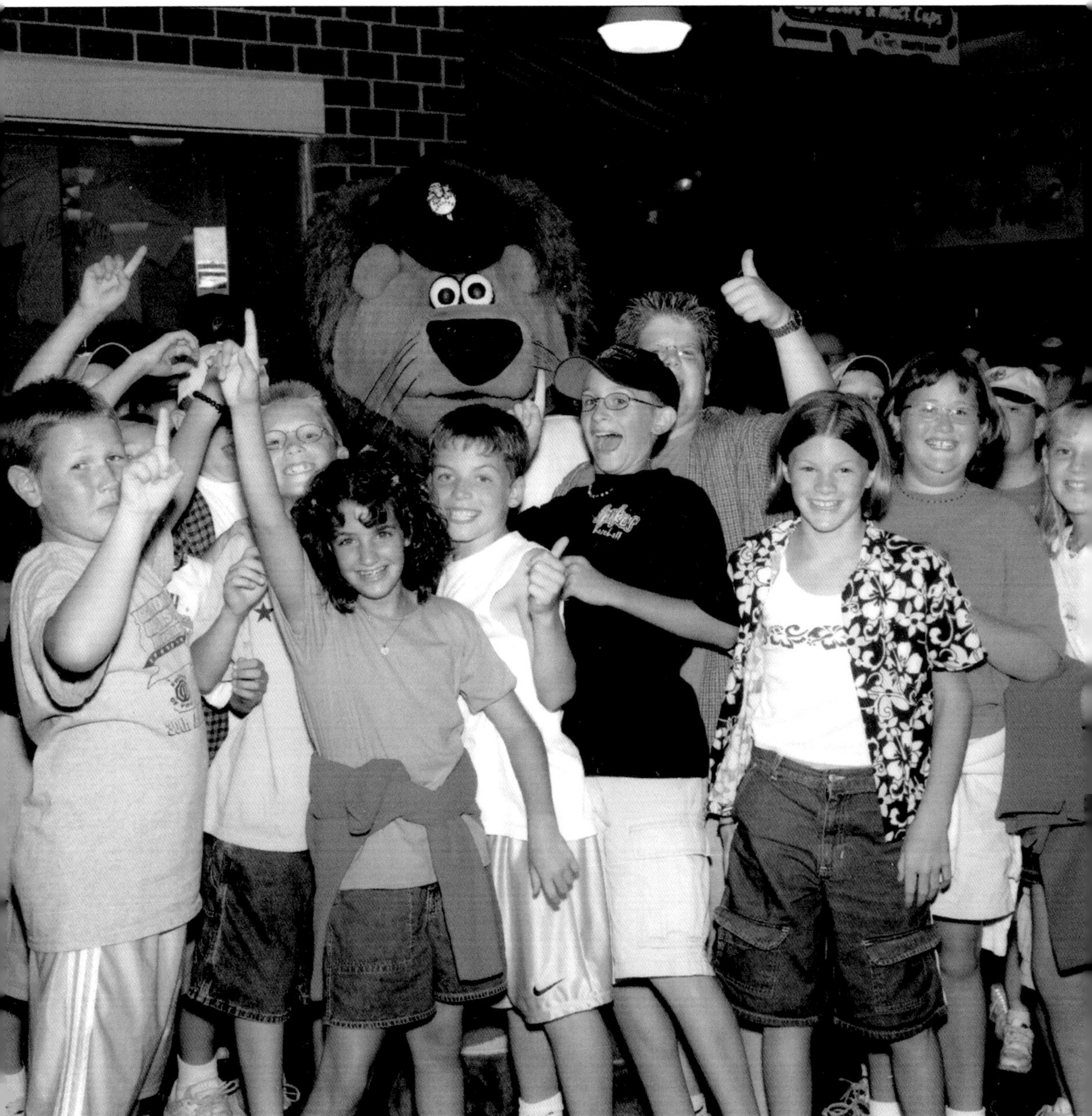

Along with bat races, balloon races, and the occasional water-in-the-teaspoon race down the first base line, mascots have provided grassroots entertainment not only at Rosenblatt Stadium, but minor league venues across the country. Casey with Omaha's children is a familiar sight at Royals' games, complimenting the ever-popular giveaway nights and promotions including the Casey Bobble Head Giveaway, Halloween in June, Grab Bag Night, and Kids Mini-Camp. (Courtesy of the Omaha Royals.)

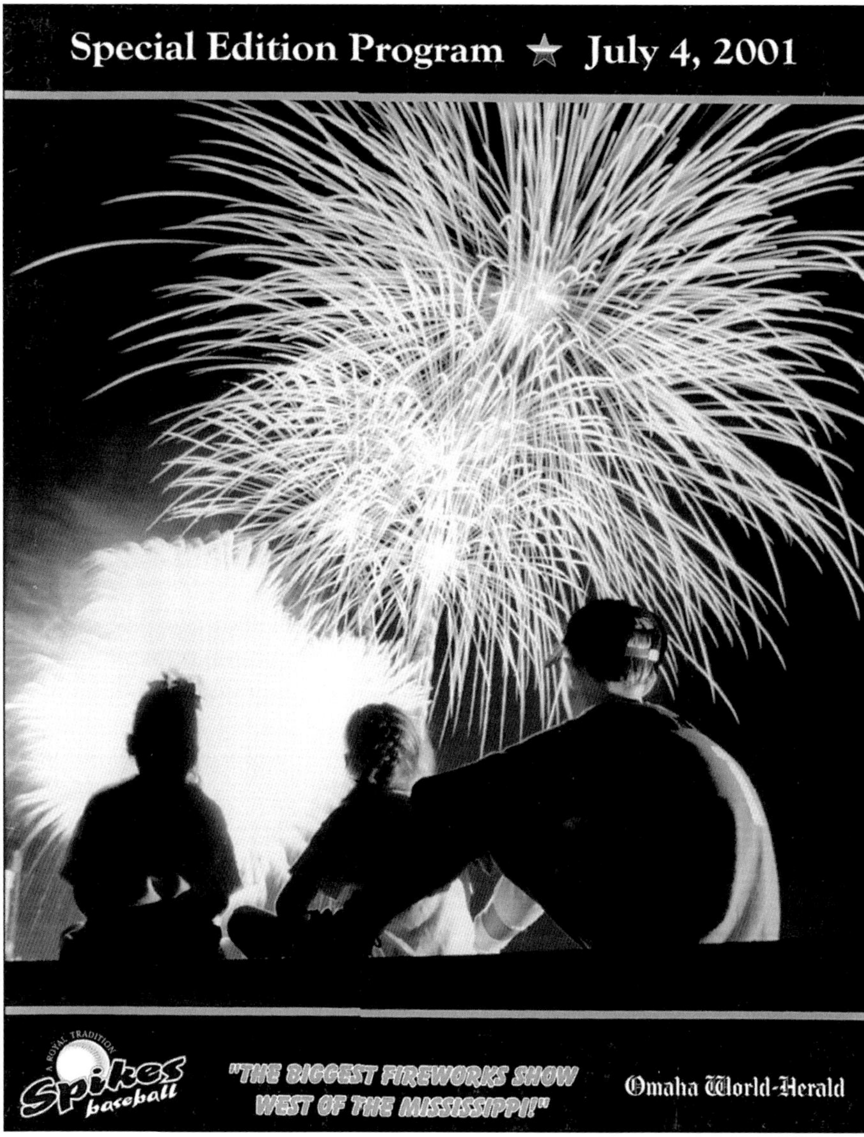

Since 1985, Rosenblatt and Fireworks by Grucci have headlined Fourth of July celebrations in Omaha. The almost two-decade-old tradition has meant capacity crowds for the Royals game, followed by the traditional clearing of stands along the right-and left-field base lines. Once a season, fans file down onto the first base side of the infield where they find a space of grass or packed infield dirt to settle in for the spectacle of lights. Residents of surrounding neighborhoods gather to watch from porches, parking lots, and rooftops as Grucci specialists launch works crafted in Australia, Canada, China, France, Great Britain, Taiwan, Japan, and the United States. The show, sponsored each year by the *Omaha World-Herald*, garnered recognition in 1999 by the *Wall Street Journal* as the fifth largest Independence Day fireworks display in the United States.

On average, Fireworks by Grucci requires five days of preparation for a fireworks display the size of the Fourth of July celebration at Rosenblatt. In addition to the shells themselves, materials used include 50 tons of sand to fill the firing batteries and 33 miles of wire to circuit the batteries. (Courtesy of the Omaha Royals.)

Five

And the Band Played...
Cardinals, Dodgers, and Polka

Omaha welcomed Johnny Keane and his 1958 Omaha Cardinal club home for their first homestand of the season with a parade, an open-car caravan through downtown Omaha, and band music. The *Omaha World Herald*'s Robert Phipps sketched the welcome itinerary in his April 22 article for the sports page:

> *Col. William Campbell, base commander at Offutt Air Force Base, will make the first pitch. Surrounding that action will be considerable pageantry involving more than three hundred persons. The show includes the complete Shrine band, the Chanters, Corvette Corps, Marching and Horse Patrols from Omaha Tangier Temple, Vincent Emanuel and his Oom-Pah Band; the Marine Corps Color Guard; Managers and players on both squads.*

The 15-game homestand began with a series against Wichita; Cardinal officials expected upwards of 5000 in attendance for the mid-week games.

Though the 1958 Cardinals finished in the lower tier of their American Association division, the team drew the support of Omaha with personalities such as the "little Texan" Johnny Keane, Curt Flood, Jim Frey, Lee Tate, and Bob Gibson, all of whom garnered headlines in the *World-Herald* sports page. Tate, a Texas League discovery of Johnny Keane, set the American Association record of 55 consecutive errorless games in 1958. Omaha Cardinal fans probably remember Tate just as much for the $4500.00 lilac-colored car parked in the stadium lot, accented with personalized gold plates. Flood was one of the "speed boys in the Cardinal chain." Gibson was already an acclaimed, local sports figure from his childhood years at Tech High, and later Creighton University, who played parts of the 1958 and 1959 season with the Omaha Cardinals.

The Omaha Cardinals of 1958 were part of a strong, steady Omaha baseball tradition and a sign of the solid relationship with parent club St. Louis that began in 1955 when St. Louis moved its Triple A franchise from Columbus, Ohio, to Omaha, fielding a team that included Tom Alston, Don Blasingame, Charlie "the Mule" Peete, and Dan Schell. Along with the Triple A franchise came a spot in the American Association. Previously, the Omaha Cardinals had been a Class A Western League organization (1949–1954). The move to the American Association guaranteed a higher caliber of player, but also meant that Omaha would see many roster changes as the St. Louis Cardinals called players up from Omaha, particularly towards season end. Raids on the farm club made top season finishes difficult, with the Cardinals finishing second in 1955, third in 1956, fifth in 1957 and 1958, and sixth in 1959.

On paper, the Cardinal seasons appeared mediocre. In the *Omaha World-Herald*, from the pen of Robert Phipps and thanks to good players, big local events that brought major league exhibition teams to Omaha Municipal Stadium, the Omaha Cardinals, from start to finish, had the attention of the hometown. Each day, Phipps told a story, flushing out the characters on the hometown team and setting the stage for the seasons.

Writing of a late season game between the 1955 Cardinals and Denver Bears, Phipps described Denver pitcher (and Omaha native) Jack Urban as "a cocky and loquacious towhead of medium size."

The final home game of that season was a "last stand...from the way things have been happening to them, it may resemble Custer's last stand."

Don "The Blazer" Blasingame once "gave the home crowd something to cheer for in the early part of the game. He raced into the outfield and made a diving catch of Don Buddin's Texas leaguer."

Of Charlie Peete, 1956 batting champion with a .350 average, Phipps waxed poetic of the sprite in centerfield: "Charlie Peete had another one of his good days in centerfield. He roamed widely to make six putouts. Charlie, who covers ground with deceptive ease, ran into rightfield to take Frank Malzone's sacrifice fly away from Dan Schell."

Of Johnny Keane and the 1958 Cardinal club in a late season game, "Johnny Keane put a muscular lineup on the field against Phoenix here Friday and beat the Coast Leaguers to a pulp with homeruns. Yes—home runs which soared over the distant walls in a standard-size park. The Cards clobbered Max Surkont and his reliever for 19 hits in a 14-4 victory."

And finally, there was the night the Cardinals "stuck a thumb into a 14-inning pudding and pulled out a plum, a prized victory timed to help the team's morale." The Cardinals took that game, 8-7, against Rocky Colavito and Indianapolis.

The stories on the field have long required good storytellers in the town paper, honest storytellers with second nature, tongue-in-cheek turn of phrase. Phipps took the games apart, inning-by-inning, weaving them together again for a daily tale.

Omaha gave its Cardinal teams parades and booming band salutes through the downtown. At least twice, Omaha welcomed Bob Gibson home with Bob Gibson Days; the first was to celebrate Gibson winning the 1964 World Series MVP Award, the second following the 1967 season when Gibson was named honorary governor for the day by then-Governor Norbert Tiemann. Gibson won his second World Series MVP in 1967 and third consecutive Gold Glove.

The Omaha Cardinals impacted the Omaha community to the extent that plans for a Hall of Fame to include standout Cardinal players were initiated and supported. Photo murals of each Hall of Fame member were to be displayed in the ballpark concourse near the Charlie Peete Memorial Plaque; Peete played parts of the 1955 and 1956 season with the Omaha club. At the end of the 1956 season, following 23 games with the St. Louis Cardinals, Peete decided to work through a thumb injury and find his timing at the plate by playing Winter League ball in Venezuela. On November 27, 1956, Peete, his wife Nettie, and their three children died in a plane crash outside Caracas. Peete was 27 years old.

To qualify for the Hall of Fame, a player had to receive three-fourths of votes cast by television, press, and radio representatives. Early leading candidates were Don Blasingame, Dick Schofield, Tom Alston, Mo Mozzali, Lee Tate, Charlie Peete, Bobby Gene Smith, Stu Miller, Willard Schmidt, Tom Cheney, Bob Mabe, and Frank Barnes, who threw a no-hitter for the Cardinals in 1958 against Louisville, the first in Cardinal American Association history.

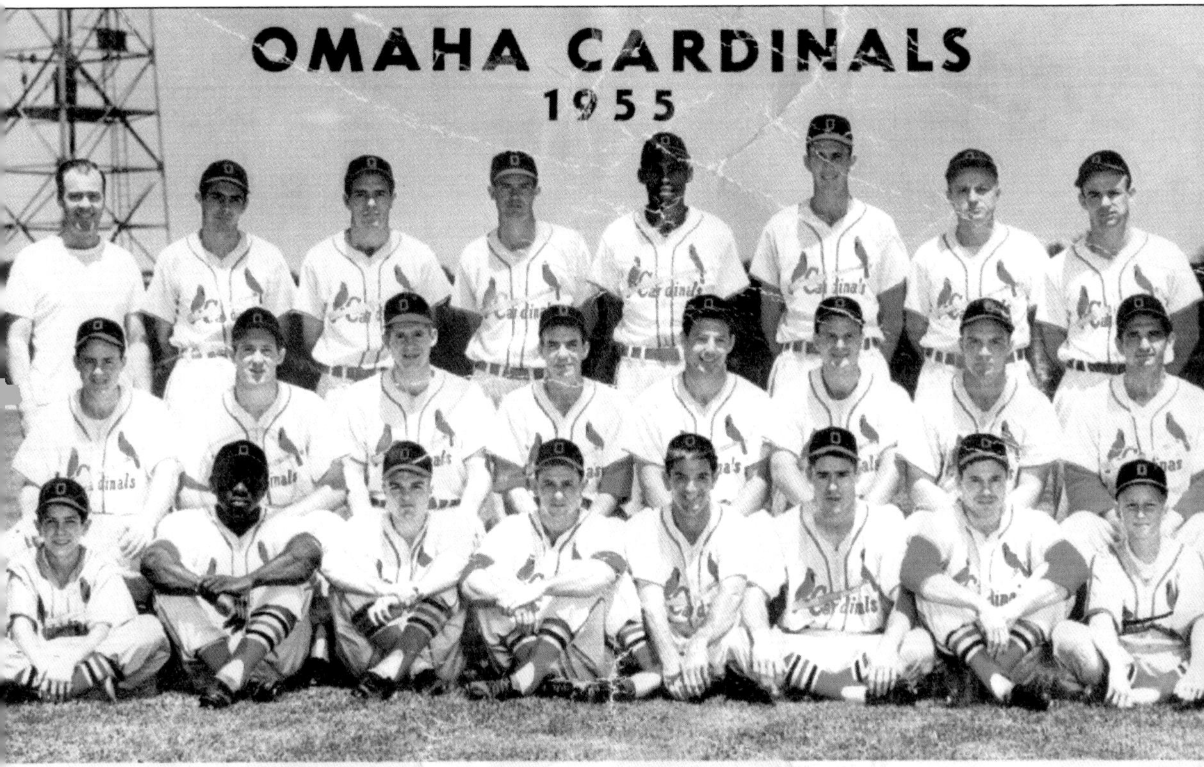

Left to right, rear row: **Paul Kippels, Trainer; Dick Rand, Catcher; Bobby Tiefenauer, Pitcher; Jim Willis, Pitcher; Tom Alston, Infielder; Jim Pearce, Pitcher; Frank Carswell, Outfielder; Willard Schmidt, Pitcher.**

Left to right, 2nd row: **Wally Lammers, Infielder; Gerry Thomas, Infielder; Danny Schell, Outfielder; Johnny Keane, Manager; Pete Riggan, Catcher; Eddie Phillips, Outfielder; George Spencer, Pitcher; Bob Clear, Pitcher.**

Left to right, front row: **Eddie Vlacek, Batboy; Charlie Peete, Outfielder; Dick Schofield, Infielder; Joe Presko, Pitcher; Mo Mozzali Infielder; Don Blasingame, Infielder; Stu Miller, Pitcher; Steve Petruconis, Batboy.**

The 1955 Cardinals, led by Manager Johnny Keane, marked the arrival of AAA baseball in Omaha. The club finished second in the standings behind Minneapolis and ranked third in the league in attendance with 316, 012 paying fans. Keane looked to Willard Schmidt, Stu Miller, and Jim Pearce for pitching strength, while offensive leadership came from Frank Carswell, Charlie Peete, Dan Schell, and Don Blasingame. Johnny Keane guided the Omaha Cardinals from 1955 through the 1958 seasons, after which Joe Schultz took over for the Cardinals' last season in Omaha. Keane saw several of his Omaha Redbirds again, including Bob Gibson and Curt Flood, on the 1964 St. Louis Cardinal squad that took the World Series from Mickey Mantle and the New York Yankees. (Courtesy of Gary Anderson.)

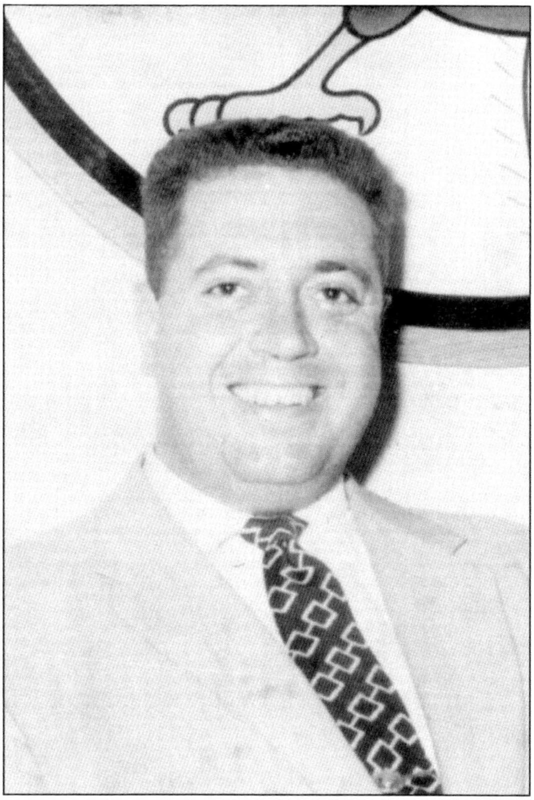

General Manager of the Cardinals through the transition from Western League class A status to American Association AAA status, Bill Bergsch was instrumental in negotiating the deal that brought the St. Louis top farm club to Omaha. In a meeting held in the office of Mayor John Rosenblatt, Bergsch announced, "Negotiations for the purchase of the Omaha territory from the Western League were completed at nine o'clock this morning. The Cardinals have authorized me to announce that the way now has been cleared to move their AAA operation from Columbus to Omaha." Bergsch worked hard to promote the AAA Cardinals in Omaha, including bringing exhibition games to Rosenblatt; season ticket holders could see the exhibition games free of charge. Bergsch also gave fans a vote on the starting times for the games, with 7:30 starting times winning by a landslide over 8:00pm starting times. Despite Bergsch's best efforts, attendance by 1958 at Cardinal games was poor. Fans were unhappy with the raiding of the minor league team by the parent club, while Bergsch himself attributed low attendance to a long, rainy weather season in Omaha. Even Mayor Rosenblatt's presence at the games dropped off with the 1958 season. 1959 marked the final season for the Cardinals in Omaha. (Courtesy of Gary Kastrick, Project Omaha.)

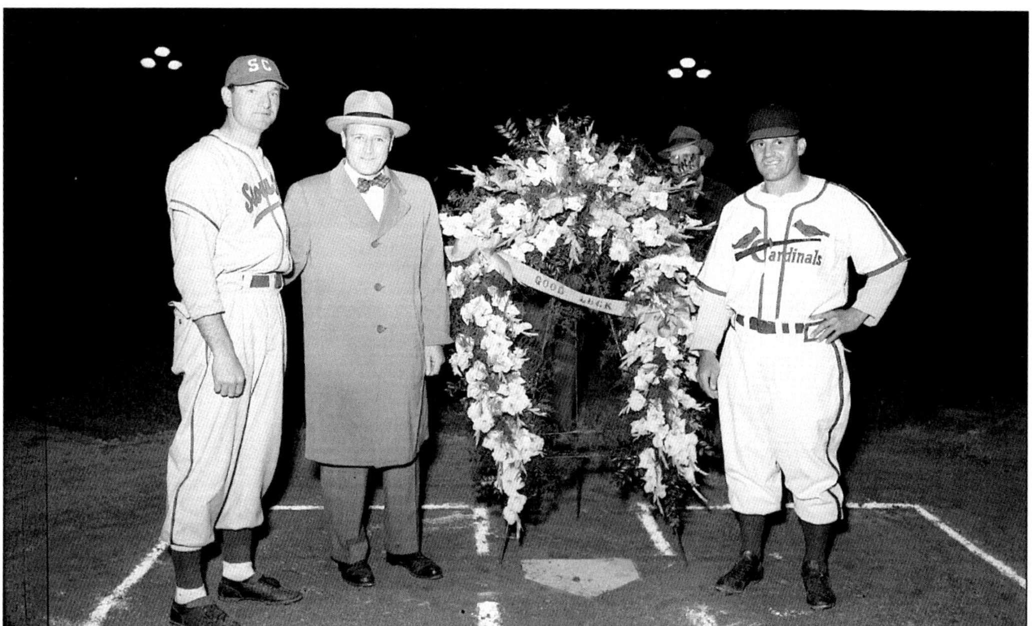

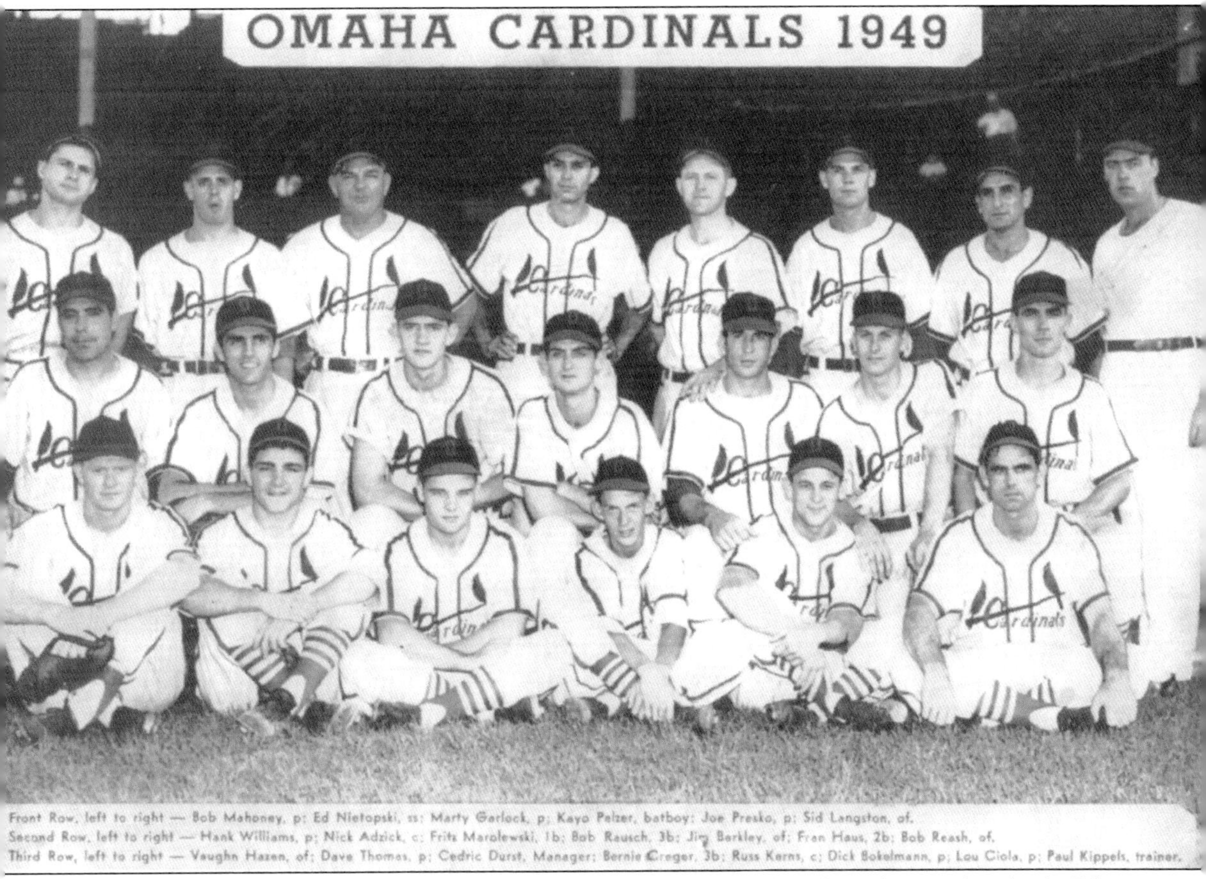

The 1949 Omaha Cardinals, from left to right, are (front row) Bob Mahoney (pitcher), Ed Nielopski (shortstop), Marty Garlock (pitcher) Kayo Pelzer (batboy), Joe Presko (pitcher), and Sid Langston (outfield); (middle row) Hank Williams (pitcher), Nick Adzick (catcher), Fritz Marolewski (first base) Bob Rausch (third base), Jim Barkley (outfield) Fran Haus (second base), and Bob Reash (outfield); (back row) Vaughn Hazen (outfield), Dave Thomas (pitcher) Cedric Durst (manager), Bernie Creger (third base), Russ Kerns (catcher), Dick Bokelmann (pitcher), Lou Ciola (pitcher), and Paul Kippels (trainer). (Courtesy of Gary Kastrick, Project Omaha.)

Opposite page, bottom: Opening Day at Omaha Municipal Stadium on April 25, 1949 was "the first dress inauguration of the new million-dollar Muny Stadium at Thirteenth and Deer Park Boulevard," according to the *Omaha World Herald's* Robert Phipps. Though the stadium had been dedicated the previous October, events had been limited to exhibition contests; necessities such as concession stands, outfield fences, lights, and a scoreboard were not added until late spring of 1949. The Western League Omaha Cardinals played home games at Legion Park in Council Bluffs, Iowa. The Opening Day game pit the Omaha Cardinals against the Des Moines Bruins with 9,416 fans in the stands to witness a 9-8 Cardinal win in 12 innings. The game finally ended at 11:45 p.m., with manager Ced Durst down to his last rabbit. As reported by Robert Phipps, Durst had "pulled rabbits out of a hat" all night after the Cardinals lost a 4-0 lead to a seven-run tear by the Bruins in the sixth and seventh innings. At final tally, Durst sent five pitchers to the mound and four pinch hitters to the plate. "Little" Joe Presko started the game for the Cardinals. (Courtesy of Gary Kastrick, Project Omaha.)

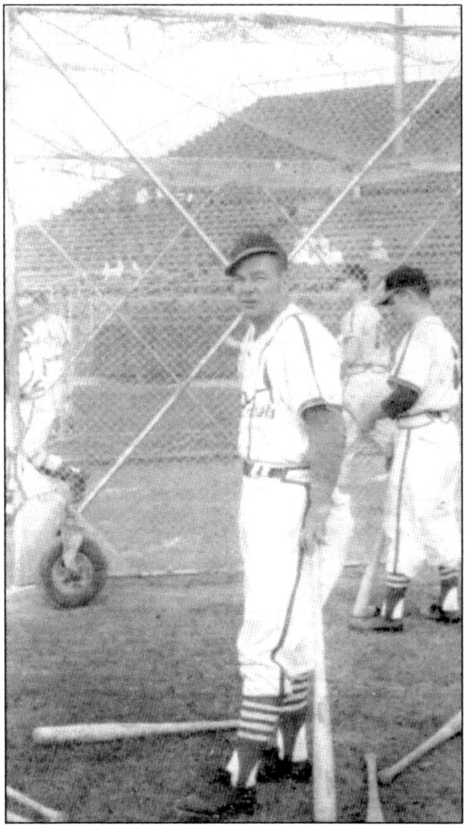

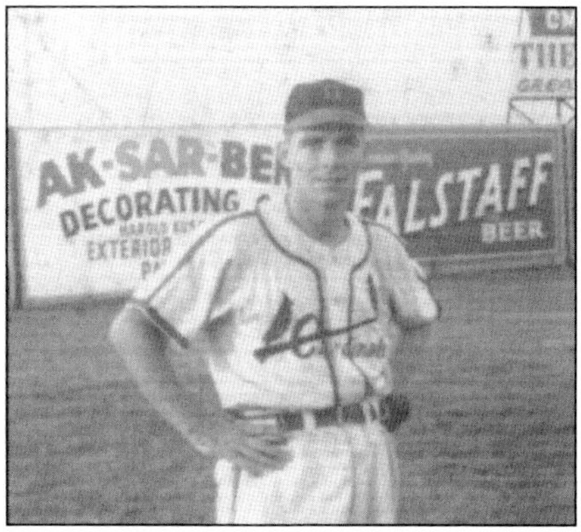

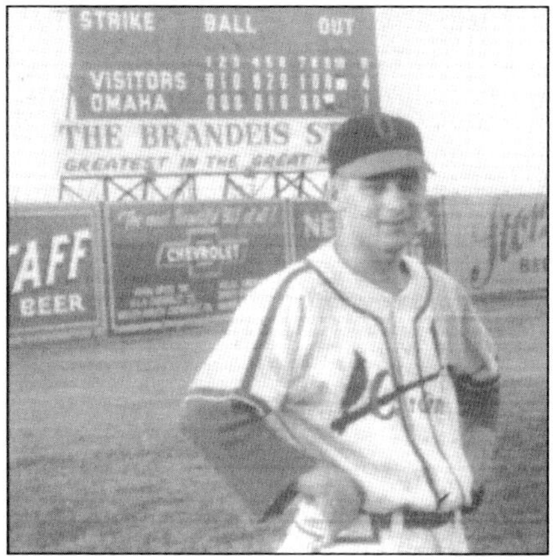

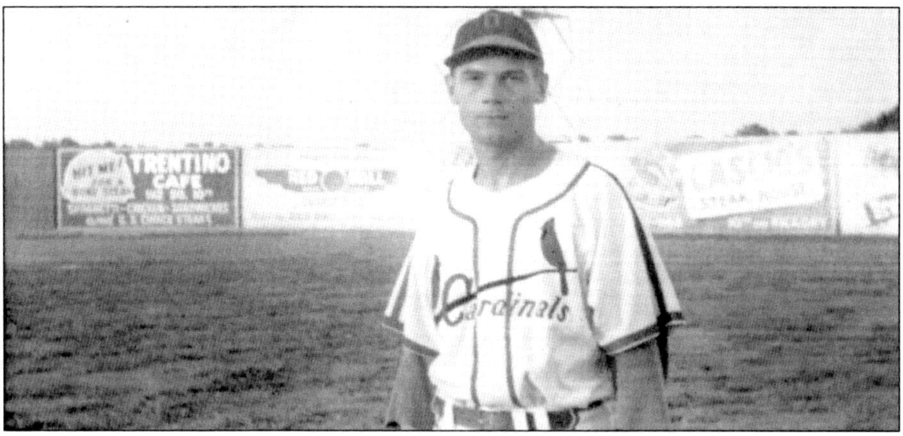

Top left: Cedric Durst was the manager of the '49 Cardinals. *Top right:* Bob Reash played outfield for the '49 Cardinals. *Center:* On the way to six seasons in the major leagues with St. Louis and Detroit, Joe Presko led the 1949 Cardinal pitching staff with a 14-9 record. The Omaha Cardinals finished second to last in their Western League division, ahead only of the Sioux City Soos. *Bottom:* Dick Bokelmann was a pitcher with the '49 Cardinals. (Courtesy of Gary Kastrick, Project Omaha.)

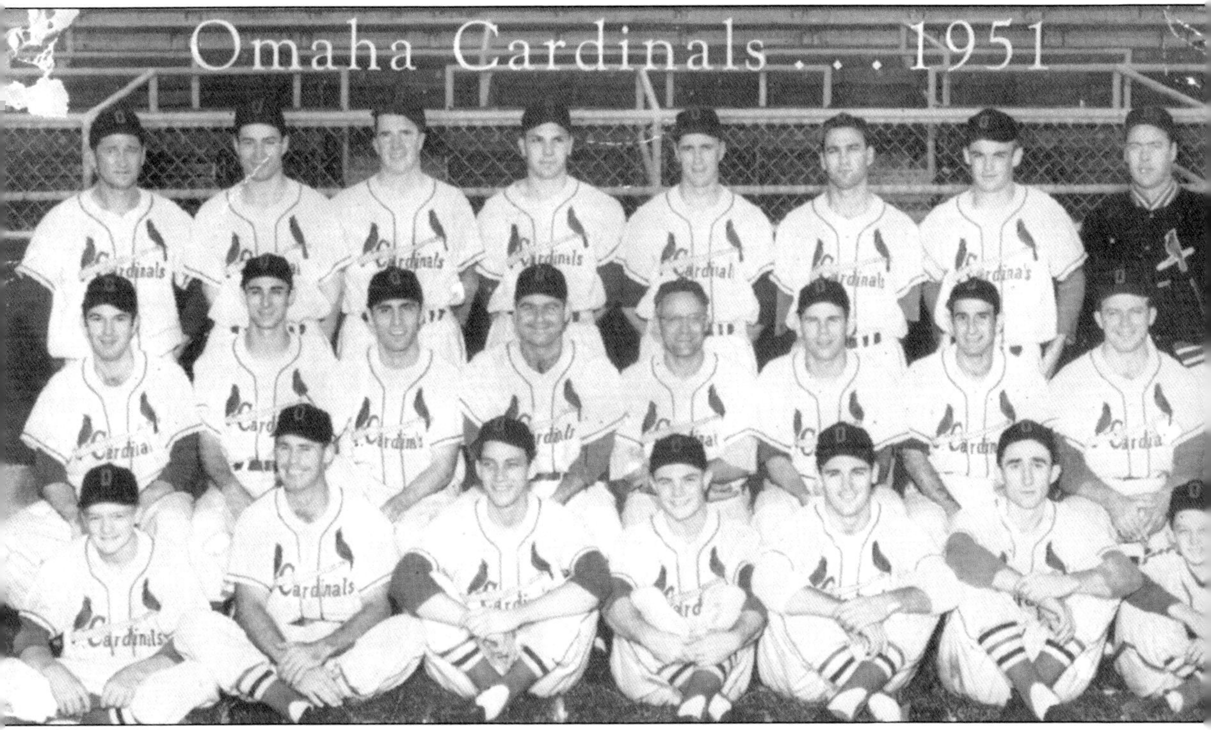

The 1951 Omaha Cardinals, from left to right, are (front row) Billy Saint (batboy), Roy Huff (outfield), Hal Coffman (pitcher), Earl Weaver (second base), Jack Shirley (pitcher), Bob Stephenson (shortstop), and Billy Richardson (batboy); (middle row) Harvey Zernia, (first base), Jim Neufeldt (outfield), Nick Adzick (catcher), Buddy Phillips (catcher) George Kissel (manager), Russell Rac (outfield), Lou Ciola (pitcher), and George Eyrich (pitcher); (back row) John Grodzicki (pitcher), Jim Hercinger (outfield),Tom Keating (pitcher), Ken Boyer (third base), Roy Pounds (pitcher), Joe Chuka (pitcher), Willard Schmidt (pitcher), and Paul Kippels (trainer). (Courtesy of Gary Kastrick, Project Omaha.)

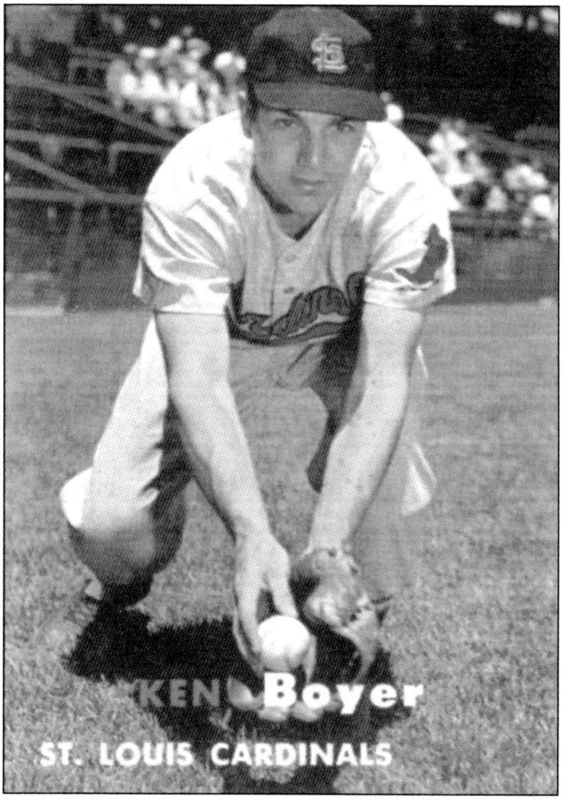

TOPPS 122

KENTON L. BOYER 3rd base ST. LOUIS CARDINALS

Ht: 6'1½" Wt: 190 Bats: Right Throws: Right

Born: May 20, 1931; Liberty, Missouri

Ken had a great sophomore year in '56 placing just behind Stan Musial in Cards' R.B.I.'s, Homers and Hits. He also led the N.L. 3rd Sackers in Assists and Double Plays last year. Appearing in his first All Star Game, Ken was the batting and fielding star for the N.L. getting 3 hits and making 3 great plays at third.

WHO HURLED THE LONGEST SHUTOUT IN THE NL?

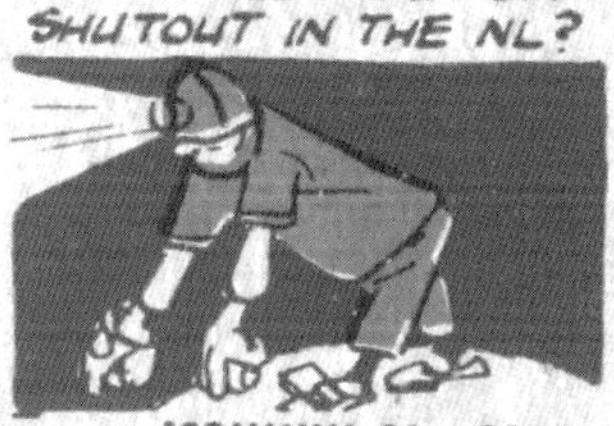

ANS: HUBBELL—GIANTS 1933—18 INNINGS.

COMPLETE MAJOR & MINOR LEAGUE BATTING RECORD

YEAR	CLUB	LEA.	G	AB	R	H	2B	3B	HR	RBI	AVG.
1949	Lebanon	No. Atl.	16	33	10	15	1	1	3	9	.455
1950	Hamilton	Pony	80	240	41	82	17	6	9	61	.342
1951	Omaha	West.	151	565	87	173	28	7	14	90	.306
'52-3	Houston	T. L.			(In Military Service)						
1954	Houston	T. L.	159	634	116	202	42	7	21	116	.319
1955	St. Louis	N. L.	147	530	78	140	27	2	18	62	.264
1956	St. Louis	N. L.	150	595	91	182	30	2	26	98	.306
Major League Totals		2 Yrs.	297	1125	169	322	57	4	44	160	.286

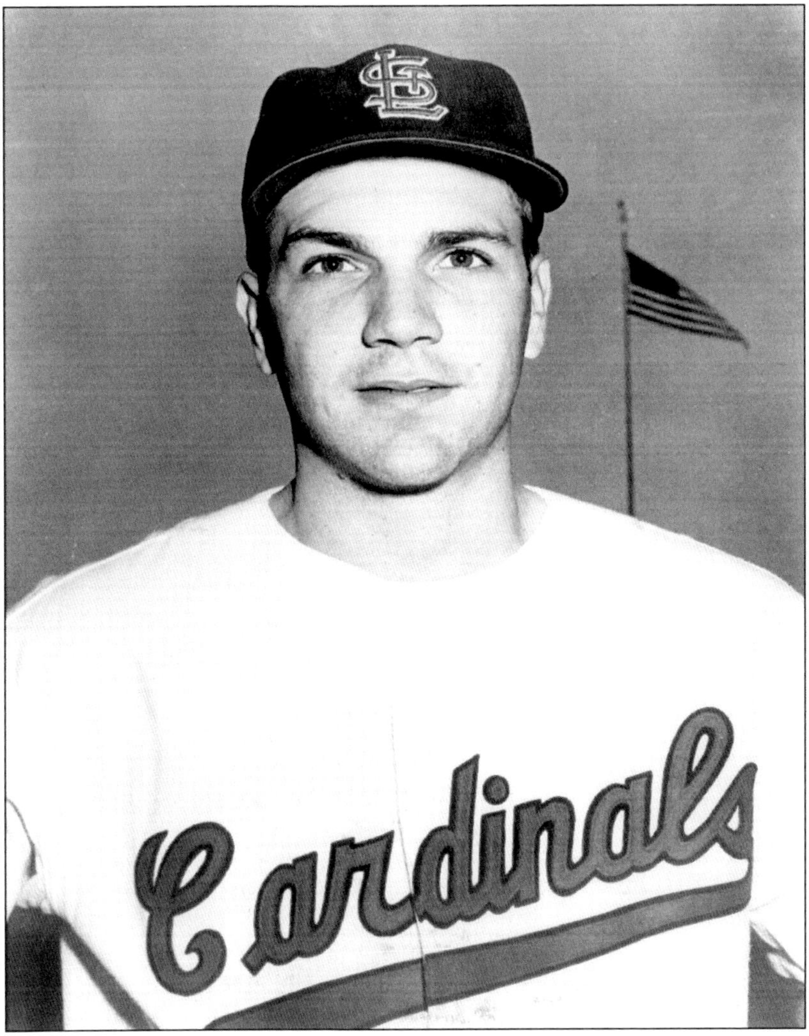

Ken Boyer, one of seven baseball playing brothers from Alba, Missouri, played one season for the Western League Omaha Cardinals, batting a respectable .306 for the season. In his 1951 season with the Cardinals, Boyer shared the infield with Earl Weaver, playing third base and occasionally right field. Despite a first place finish in the Western League, the Cardinals lost the division playoffs to the Sioux City Soos. Boyer, following 1953–1954 seasons with Houston of the Texas League and military service in the Korean War, was brought to the major league Cardinals in 1955 for a $6,000 salary. During his tenure with St. Louis, Boyer earned five Gold Gloves at third and maintained a consistent bat for Cardinal teams that included Stan Musial, Curt Flood, and Wally Moon. In his 11 seasons with the Cardinals, Boyer experienced his best years in the early 60s, culminating in the 1964 season and MVP of the National League honors. Boyer also hit two clutch homeruns against the Yankees in the 1964 World Series; in Game Four, a grand slam gave the Cardinals a 4-3 win, and in Game Seven, a seventh-inning homerun led to a 7-5 victory and the World Championship. Traded from the Cardinals in 1965, Boyer played several more seasons with the New York Mets, Chicago White Sox, and Los Angeles Dodgers. Boyer returned to the Cardinals as manager from 1978 through the mid-1980 season. (Courtesy of the National Baseball Hall of Fame, Cooperstown, New York.)

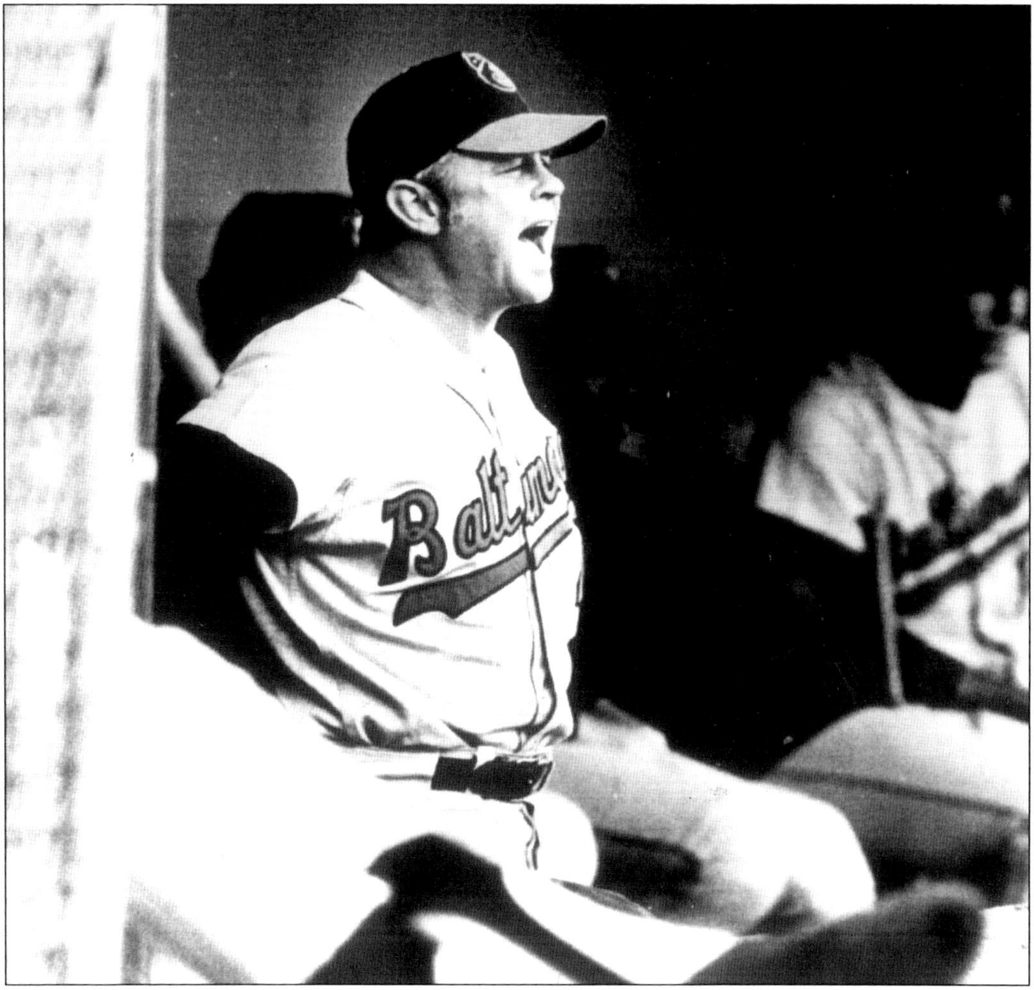

Before he was the "The Earl of Baltimore," Earl Weaver wore the "O" for the Western League Omaha Cardinals on his cap. *Omaha World-Herald* sportswriter Robert Phipps eulogized ground balls to Weaver at second as, "the sure recipe for extinction." Weaver played second base for the Western League Omaha Cardinals beginning in 1948, and ending by 1956 with the Denver Bears. In 1957, Weaver became a manager in the Baltimore system, where his teams never finished below fourth place. Weaver's minor league career playing highlights include being named to the Western League All-Star Team in 1952, with the Omaha club finishing third that year behind the Denver Bears and Colorado Springs Sky Sox. Named to the Western League All-Star team again in 1954, this time for the league leading Denver Bears, Weaver was also a league leader in runs scored with 124. In a 1951 game against the Pueblo Dodgers, Weaver's third walk of the game allowed him to score the winning run on doubles by Jim Neufeldt and Russ Rac. Playing second base for the Pueblo Dodgers was Omahan and former Mets All-American of 1947, Don Hunter. Hunter went 4 for 5 at the plate that day. That season, Hunter was among Western League batting leaders in doubles (33) and bases on balls (113). Pueblo pitcher Dick McCoy, also from Omaha, yielded 10 hits in eight innings against the Cardinals. The 1951 Cardinals finished first in the Western League behind the pitching of Louis Ciola, Willard Schmidt, and George Eyrich. Weaver shared the infield with Ken Boyer, who later became a steady presence for the St. Louis Cardinals. Weaver was elected to the Hall of Fame in 1996. (Courtesy of the National Baseball Hall of Fame, Cooperstown, New York.)

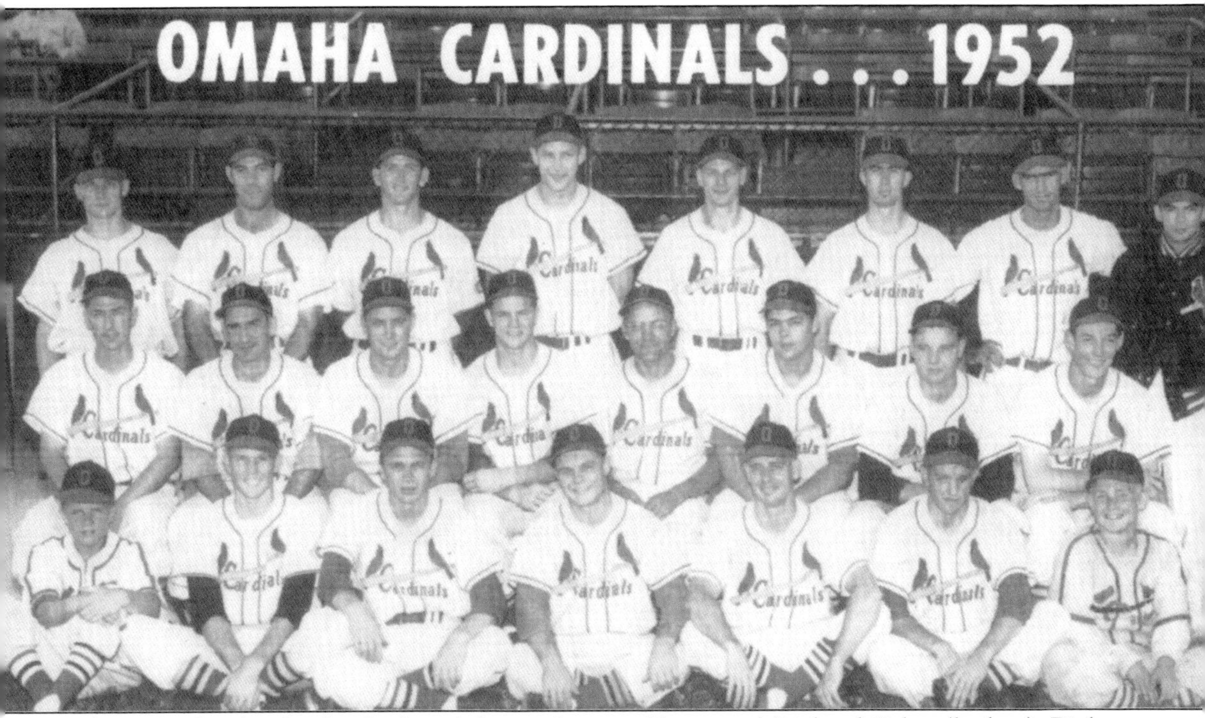

The 1952 Omaha Cardinals, from left to right, are: (front row) Richard Kubat (batboy), Dick Atkinson (pitcher), Willis McDonald (pitcher), Earl Weaver (second base), Dave Thomas (pitcher), Robert Slaybaugh, (pitcher), Kenneth Martin (batboy); (middle row) Bill Killinger, (infield), Lou Ciola, (pitcher), Gerry Mertz, (pitcher), Gary Blaylock, (pitcher), George Kissell, (manager), Walter Montgomery (pitcher), Marty Garlock (pitcher), Neal Hertweck (first base); (back row) Jay Drake (catcher), Joe Di Martino (catcher), Dave Johnson (outfield), Dick Cordell (outfield), Eddie Phillips (outfield), Sherwin Dixon (shortstop), Wally Moon (outfield), and Don Fauls (trainer). (Courtesy of Gary Kastrick, Project Omaha.)

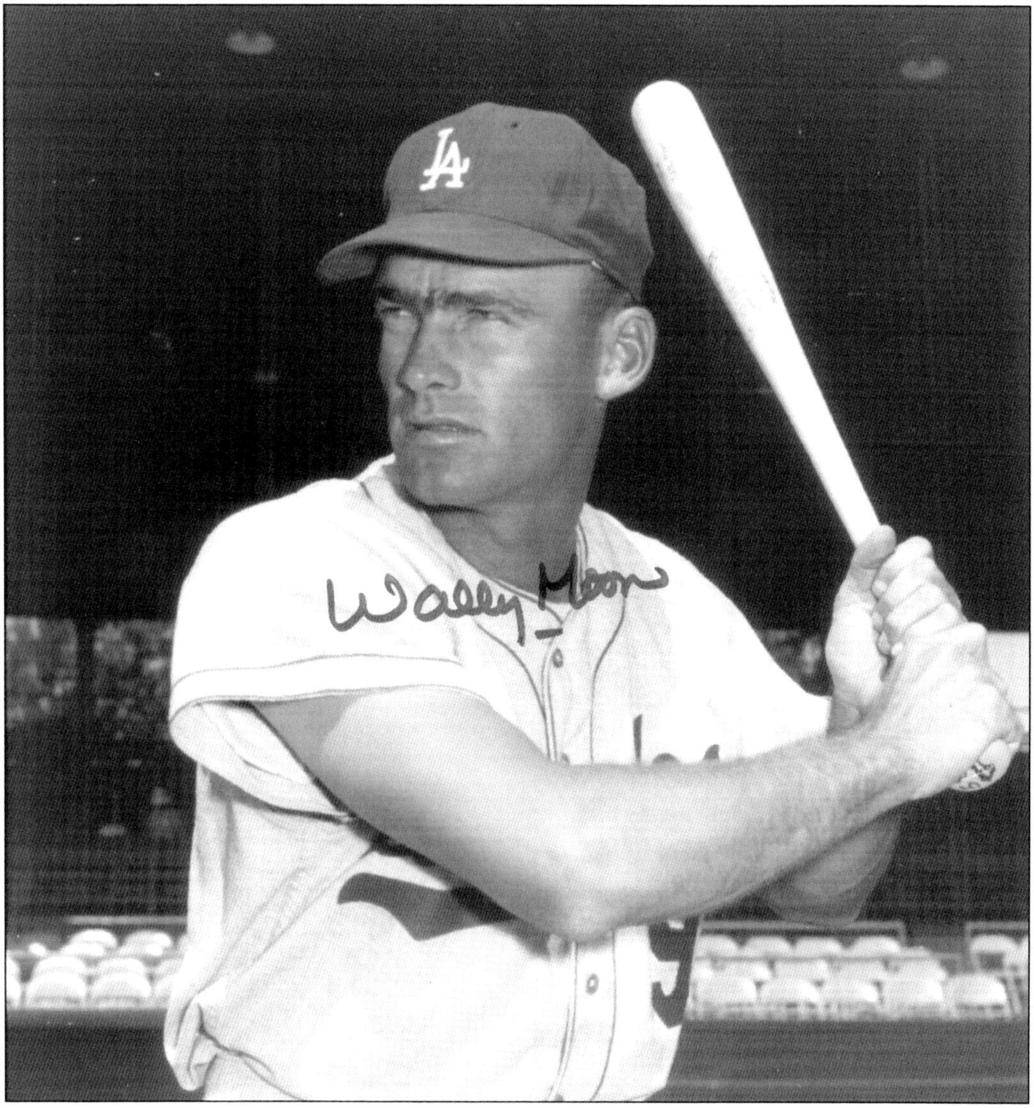

Wally Moon made a loud entrance in his 1954 Sportsman's Park debut replacing St. Louis Cardinal fan favorite Enos Slaughter in the outfield. Slaughter, a 16-season Cardinal veteran, had another six seasons ahead of him with the New York Yankees. Moon, meanwhile, in his first major league at-bat against the Chicago Cubs, drove a homerun over the right-field pavilion into the middle of Grand Boulevard. Moon went on to hit .304 for the season, winning National League Rookie of the Year honors. Altogether, Moon played five seasons for St. Louis and seven seasons for the newly relocated Los Angeles Dodgers, where his periodic homeruns over the L.A. Coliseum's 42-foot left field wall became known as "Moon shots." Two years before his debut with the St. Louis Cardinals, Moon made a dramatic rookie debut with the Western League Omaha Cardinals, driving a sixth-inning homerun over the right-centerfield fence to capture a 5-4 win for Omaha over the Sioux City Soos. The win maintained a three-game lead for Omaha in the Western League standings. Moon had opened Cardinal scoring in the third inning with a single. Despite the mid-season league lead, the Cardinals finished the 1952 season in third place. For his part, Moon was among the league batting leaders in triples, with 11. (Courtesy of Gary Kastrick, Project Omaha.)

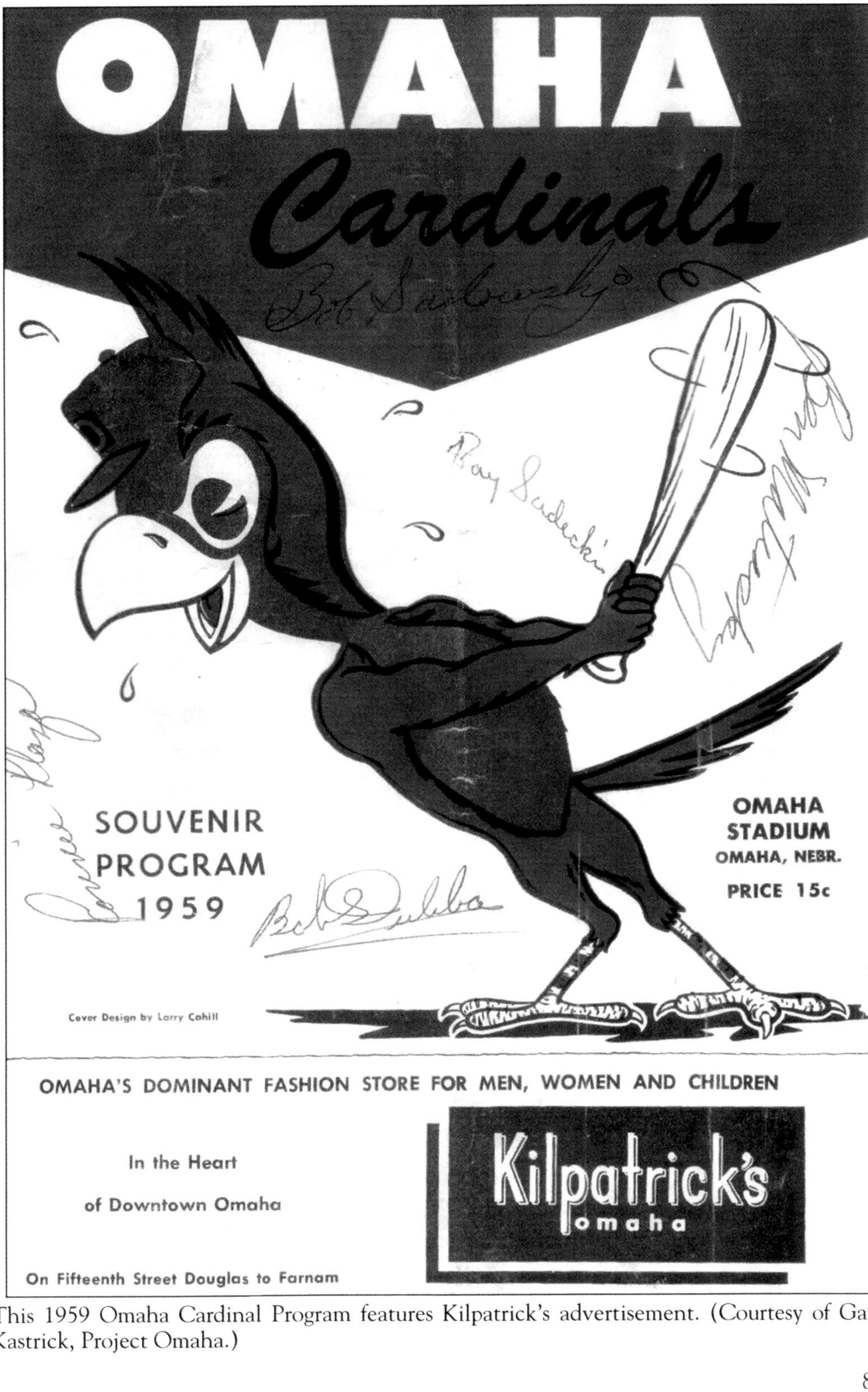

This 1959 Omaha Cardinal Program features Kilpatrick's advertisement. (Courtesy of Gary Kastrick, Project Omaha.)

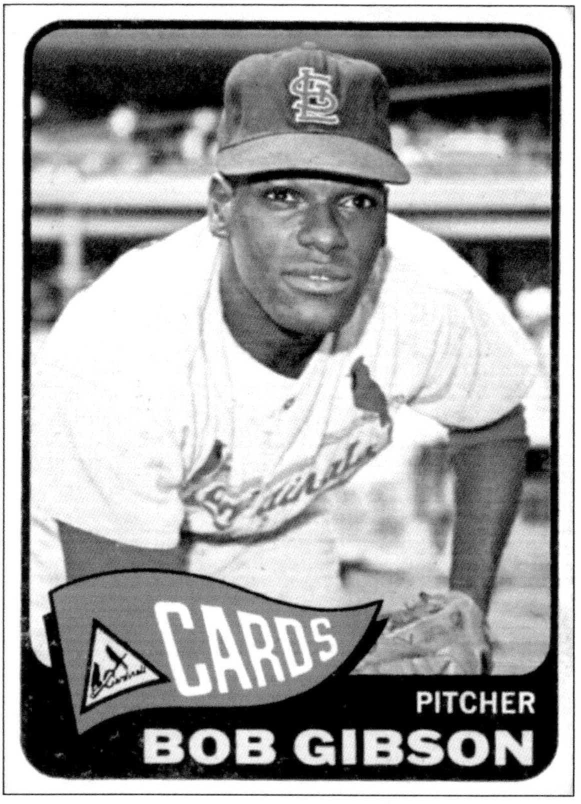

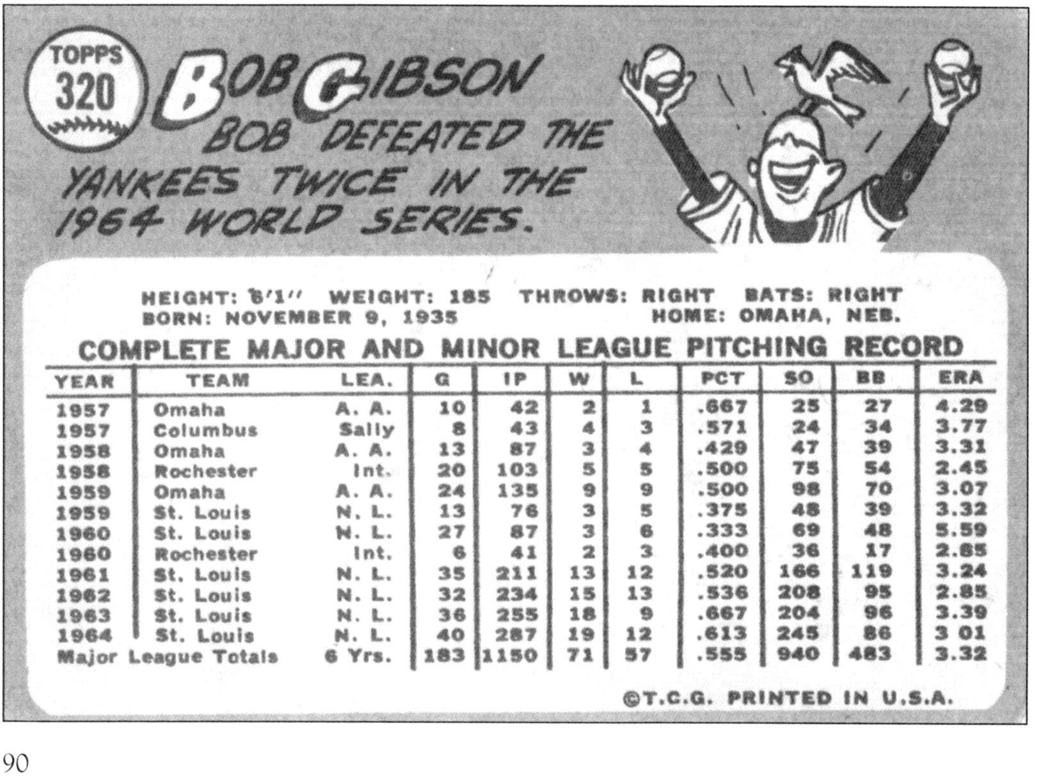

TOPPS 320

BOB GIBSON

BOB DEFEATED THE YANKEES TWICE IN THE 1964 WORLD SERIES.

HEIGHT: 6'1" WEIGHT: 185 THROWS: RIGHT BATS: RIGHT
BORN: NOVEMBER 9, 1935 HOME: OMAHA, NEB.

COMPLETE MAJOR AND MINOR LEAGUE PITCHING RECORD

YEAR	TEAM	LEA.	G	IP	W	L	PCT	SO	BB	ERA
1957	Omaha	A. A.	10	42	2	1	.667	25	27	4.29
1957	Columbus	Sally	8	43	4	3	.571	24	34	3.77
1958	Omaha	A. A.	13	87	3	4	.429	47	39	3.31
1958	Rochester	Int.	20	103	5	5	.500	75	54	2.45
1959	Omaha	A. A.	24	135	9	9	.500	98	70	3.07
1959	St. Louis	N. L.	13	76	3	5	.375	48	39	3.32
1960	St. Louis	N. L.	27	87	3	6	.333	69	48	5.59
1960	Rochester	Int.	6	41	2	3	.400	36	17	2.85
1961	St. Louis	N. L.	35	211	13	12	.520	166	119	3.24
1962	St. Louis	N. L.	32	234	15	13	.536	208	95	2.85
1963	St. Louis	N. L.	36	255	18	9	.667	204	96	3.39
1964	St. Louis	N. L.	40	287	19	12	.613	245	86	3 01
Major League Totals		6 Yrs.	183	1150	71	57	.555	940	483	3.32

©T.C.G. PRINTED IN U.S.A.

Omaha honored Bob Gibson on February 15, 1981 with a ceremony at the City Auditorium. The event marked Gibson's election to the National Baseball Hall of Fame in Cooperstown, New York. Gibson, retired from baseball since 1975, was planning to join the New York Mets that spring as an assistant pitching coach. Accepting the position put Gibson on a coaching staff with Joe Torre, a former Cardinal teammate. The Hall of Fame Day for Gibson was the culminating event in a series of Bob Gibson Days held in Omaha to honor the Cardinal pitcher. It followed the 1964 and 1967 World Series MVP honors, and a third consecutive Gold Glove in 1967. Before Gibson picked up a baseball for the St. Louis Cardinals, he attended Kellom Elementary in Omaha and played ball for his brother's North Side YMCA teams. In the late 1940s and 1950s, Josh Gibson was the North Side YMCA program director. His teams traveled in and around small towns in Nebraska, Missouri, and Iowa. A small notice in the July 5, 1950 *Omaha World Herald* records that Robert Gibson of the Y Monarchs pitched a no-hit game against the Mainelli's, with the Monarchs winning 22-0 in the Burdette Midget Baseball League game. In 1951, when Bob Gibson was 15 years old, the Y Monarchs became the first black team to win the Nebraska State Championship. Gibson also made the all-city team as an all-purpose player his senior year at Tech High. (Courtesy of Gary Kastrick, Project Omaha.)

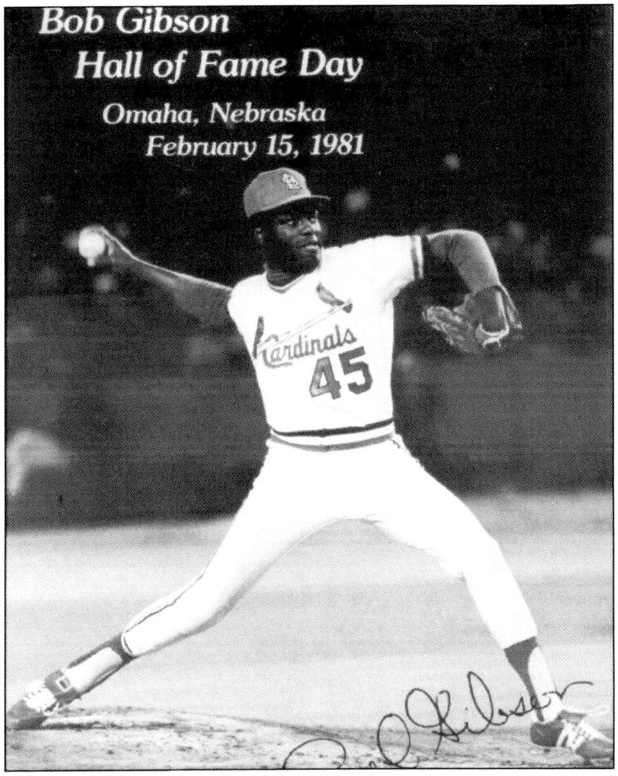

Bob Gibson Year-by-Year

Regular Season Record

Year—Club, League	G.	IP.	W.	L.	Pct.	H.	R.	ER.	SO.	BB.	ERA.
1957—Omaha, A.A.	10	42	2	1	.667	46	26	20	25	27	4.29
1957—Columbus, Sally	8	43	4	3	.571	36	26	18	24	34	3.77
1958—Omaha, A.A.	13	87	3	4	.429	79	45	32	47	39	3.31
1958—Rochester, Int.	20	103	5	5	.500	88	35	28	75	54	2.45
1959—Omaha, A.A.	24	135	9	9	.500	128	59	46	98	70	3.07
1959—St. Louis, Nat.	13	76	3	5	.375	77	35	28	48	39	3.32
1960—St. Louis, Nat.	27	87	3	6	.333	97	61	54	69	48	5.59
1960—Rochester, Int.	6	41	2	3	.400	33	15	13	36	17	2.85
1961—St. Louis, Nat.	35	211	13	12	.520	186	91	76	166	*119	3.24
1962—St. Louis, Nat.	32	234	15	13	.536	174	84	74	208	95	2.85
1963—St. Louis, Nat.	36	255	18	9	.667	224	110	96	204	96	3.39
1964—St. Louis, Nat.	40	287	19	12	.613	250	106	96	245	86	3.01
1965—St. Louis, Nat.	38	299	20	12	.625	243	110	102	270	103	3.07
1966—St. Louis, Nat.	35	280	21	12	.636	210	90	76	225	78	2.44
1967—St. Louis, Nat.	24	175	13	7	.650	151	62	58	147	40	2.98
1968—St. Louis, Nat.	34	305	22	9	.710	198	49	38	*268	62	*1.12
1969—St. Louis, Nat.	35	314	20	13	.606	251	84	76	269	95	2.18
1970—St. Louis, Nat.	34	294	x23	7	.767	262	111	102	274	88	3.12
1971—St. Louis, Nat.	31	246	16	13	.552	215	96	83	185	76	3.04
1972—St. Louis, Nat.	34	278	19	11	.633	226	83	76	208	88	2.46
1973—St. Louis, Nat.	25	195	12	10	.545	159	71	60	142	57	2.77
1974—St. Louis, Nat.	33	240	11	13	.458	236	111	102	129	104	3.83
1975—St. Louis, Nat.	22	109	3	10	.231	120	66	61	60	62	5.04
Major League Total	528	3885	251	174	.591	3279	1420	1258	3117	1336	2.91

*Led league. xTied for league lead.

Gibson established following major league records: lowest earned-run average, season, 300 or more innings (1.12), 1968; most seasons, 200 or more strikeouts (9), 1972; most consecutive games, starting pitcher, 303, August 31, 1965, through May 12, 1969 (seventh inning).

Gibson established National League record for most strikeouts, lifetime, right-handed pitcher (3,117), 1975.

World Series Record

Year—Club, League	G.	IP.	W.	L.	Pct.	H.	R.	ER.	SO.	BB.	ERA.
1964—St. Louis, Nat	3	27	2	1	.667	23	11	9	31	8	3.00
1967—St. Louis, Nat	3	27	3	0	1.000	14	3	3	26	5	1.00
1968—St. Louis, Nat	3	27	2	1	.667	18	5	5	35	4	1.67
World Series Totals	9	81	7	2	.778	55	19	17	92	17	1.89

Gibson established folowing World Series records: Most consecutive games won, total Series (7); most consecutive complete games won, total Series (7); most consecutive complete games, total Series (8); most strikeouts, game (17), October 2, 1968; most strikeouts, Series (35), 1968; most games, 10 or more strikeouts, total Series (5).

Gibson tied following World Series records: Most games won, seven-game Series (3), 1967; most games won, no losses, seven-game Series (3), 1967; most complete games, seven-game Series (3), 1967 and 1968.

All-Star Game Record

Year—League	IP.	W.	L.	Pct.	H.	R.	ER	SO.	BB.	ERA.
1962—National (2nd game)	2	0	0	.000	1	1	1	1	2	4.50
1965—National	2	0	0	.000	2	0	0	3	1	0.00
1967—National	2	0	0	.000	2	0	0	2	0	0.00
1969—National	1	0	0	.000	2	1	1	2	1	9.00
1970—National	2	0	0	.000	3	2	2	2	1	9.00
1972—National	2	0	0	.000	1	0	0	0	0	0.00
All-Star Game Totals	11	0	0	.000	11	4	4	10	5	3.27

Member of National League All-Star Team in 1962 (first game) and 1968; did not play. Named to National League All-Star Team for 1966 game; replaced due to injury.

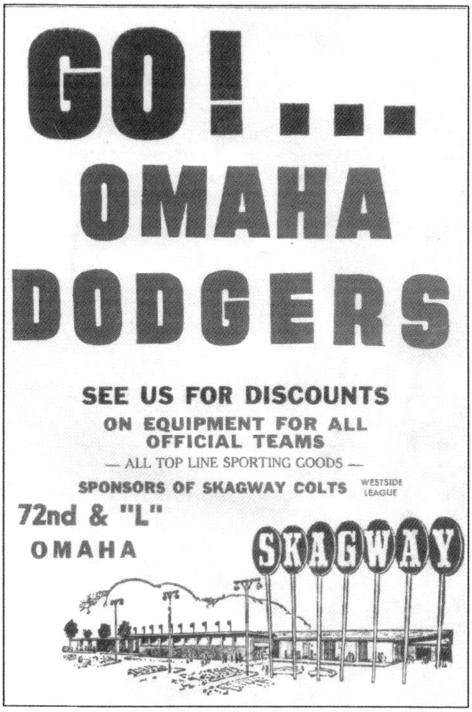

Omaha's baseball advocate, John Rosenblatt, refused to leave Omaha Municipal Stadium without an active professional baseball team. After the Omaha Cardinals left for Rochester following the 1959 season and the American Association reduced teams in the league from ten to eight, Rosenblatt searched for a franchise, commencing the search at a time when minor league baseball was in sharp decline. At post-war heights, the minor league family included 59 leagues with teams in 400 cities. By the mid-50s, leagues had been reduced to 43, dropping again to 27, and 21 by 1959. Against the odds, John Rosenblatt went looking for another ball club. An *Omaha World-Herald* survey indicated 84 percent of Omahans wanted another team and the American Association wanted Omaha back in the league following a year-long hiatus. The answer came when Minneapolis and St. Paul merged into the major league ranks, leaving two available franchises, one for the Los Angeles Dodgers, the other for the Boston Red Sox. On November 5, 1960, after terms had been discussed, E. J. Bavasi, executive vice-president of the Dodgers, came to town and helped Rosenblatt announce the return to Omaha of American Association baseball. (Courtesy of the Durham Western Heritage Museum.)

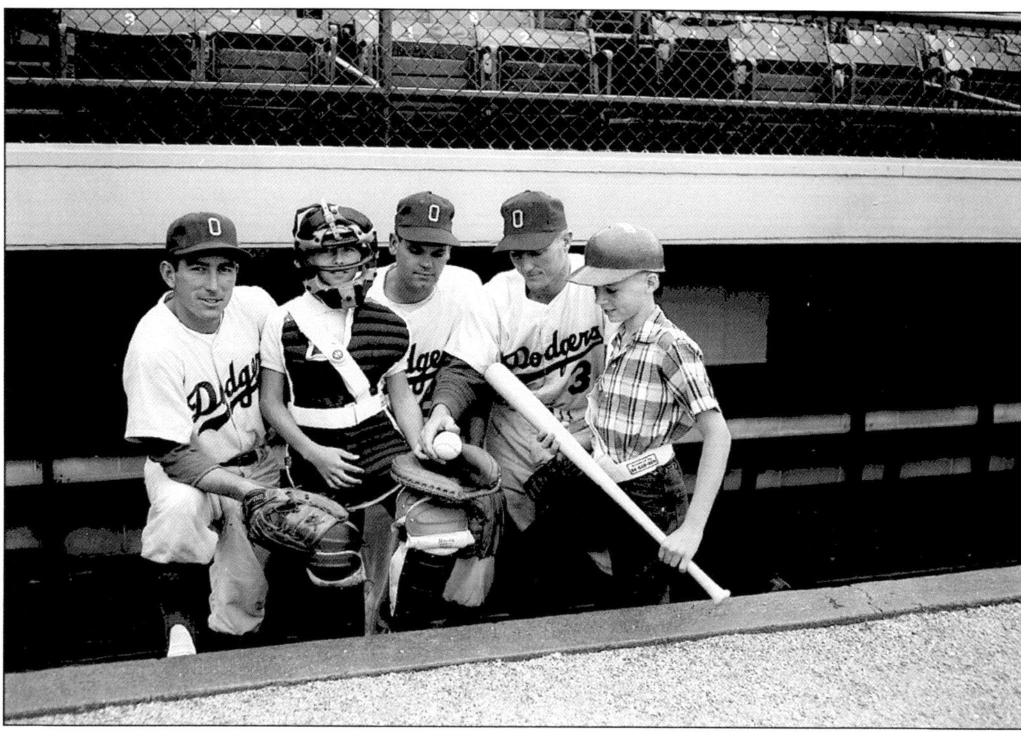

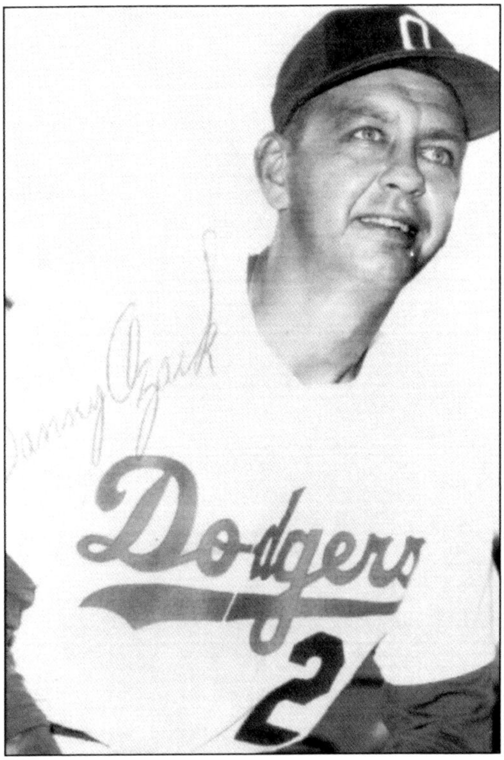

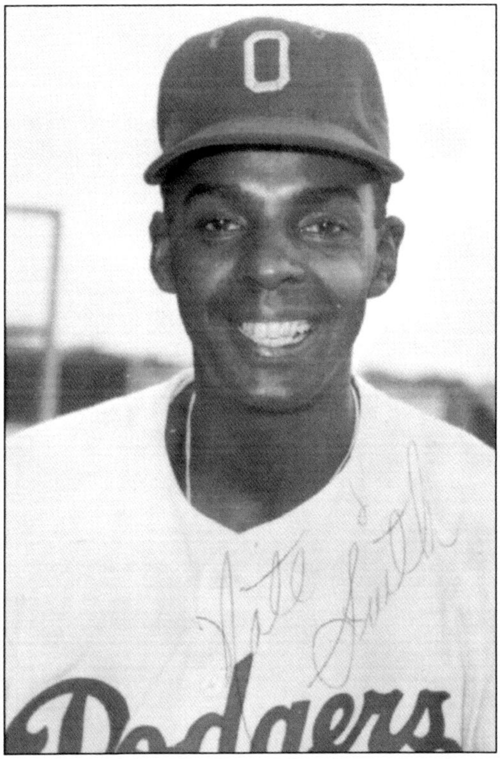

The year 1959 was the final one for the Cardinals in Rosenblatt Stadium. Omaha was without a minor league baseball team for the 1960 season, but welcomed the Dodger minor league farm club in 1961 and 1962. Manager Danny "the Wizard of Oze" Ozark (left) saw his Omaha Dodgers finish last in the American Association in 1961, but recover to finish second only behind Luke Appling's Indianapolis club in 1962. As a major league manager, Ozark saw his best seasons with the 1970s Philadelphia Phillies teams that included Mike Schmidt and Steve Carlton. The Phillies finished on top of their National League division three years in a row (1976–1979) in a stretch that also included Manager of the Year (1977) for Ozark. A low-key Yogi Berra, Ozark is known for two Ozarkisms that still make the baseball anecdote circuit. Said Ozark in response to a 10-game losing streak, "Even Napolean had his Watergate." And the popular advice, "Half of this game is ninety percent mental," is also attributed to the former Omaha manager. Nate Smith (right) caught for the 1962 Dodger team that fielded Joe Altobelli at first base and power hitters Jim Barbieri and Bart Shirley in the outfield. (Courtesy of Gary Kastrick, Project Omaha.)

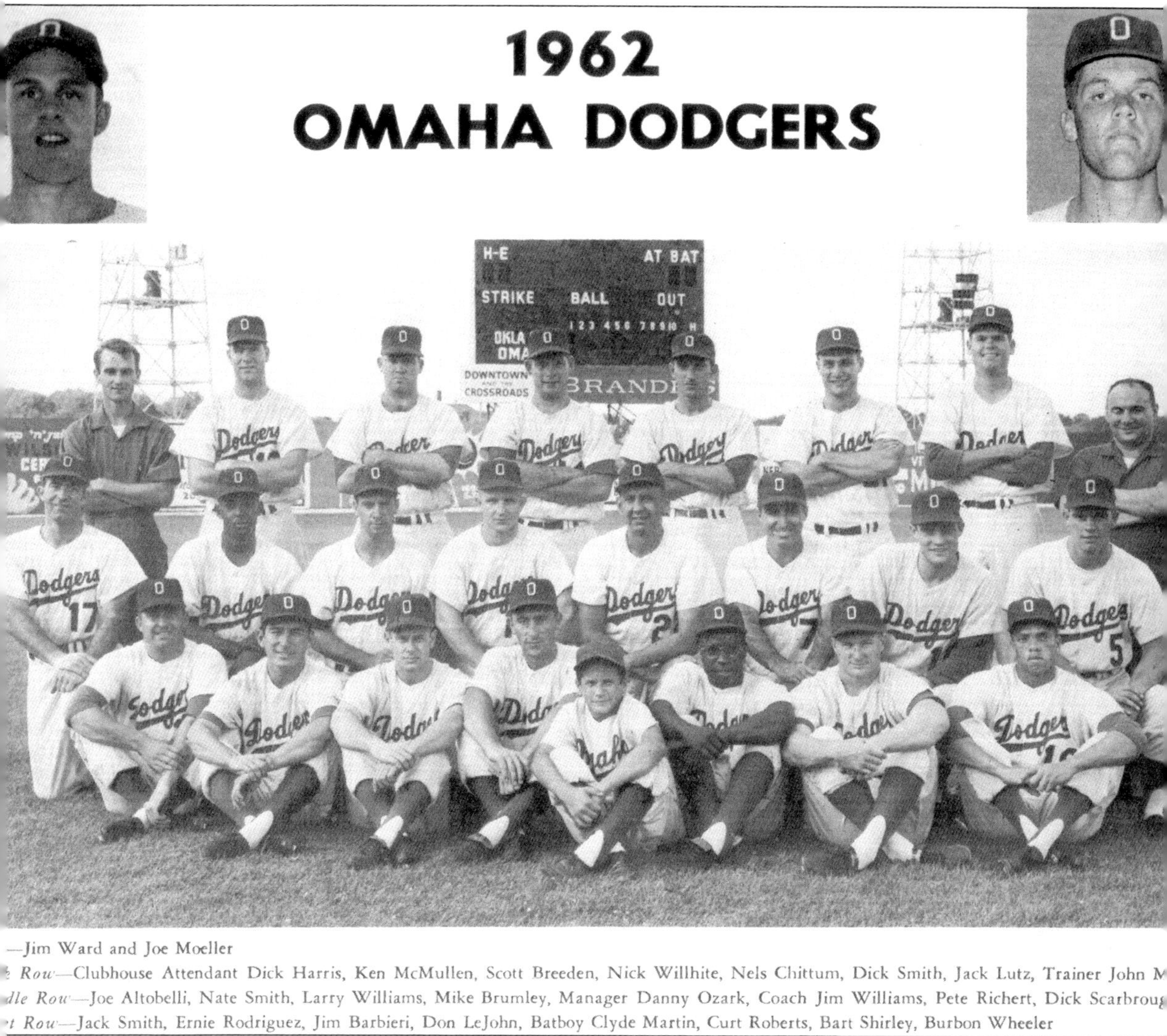

Pictured are the 1962 Omaha Dodgers. (Courtesy Gary Kastrick, Project Omaha.)

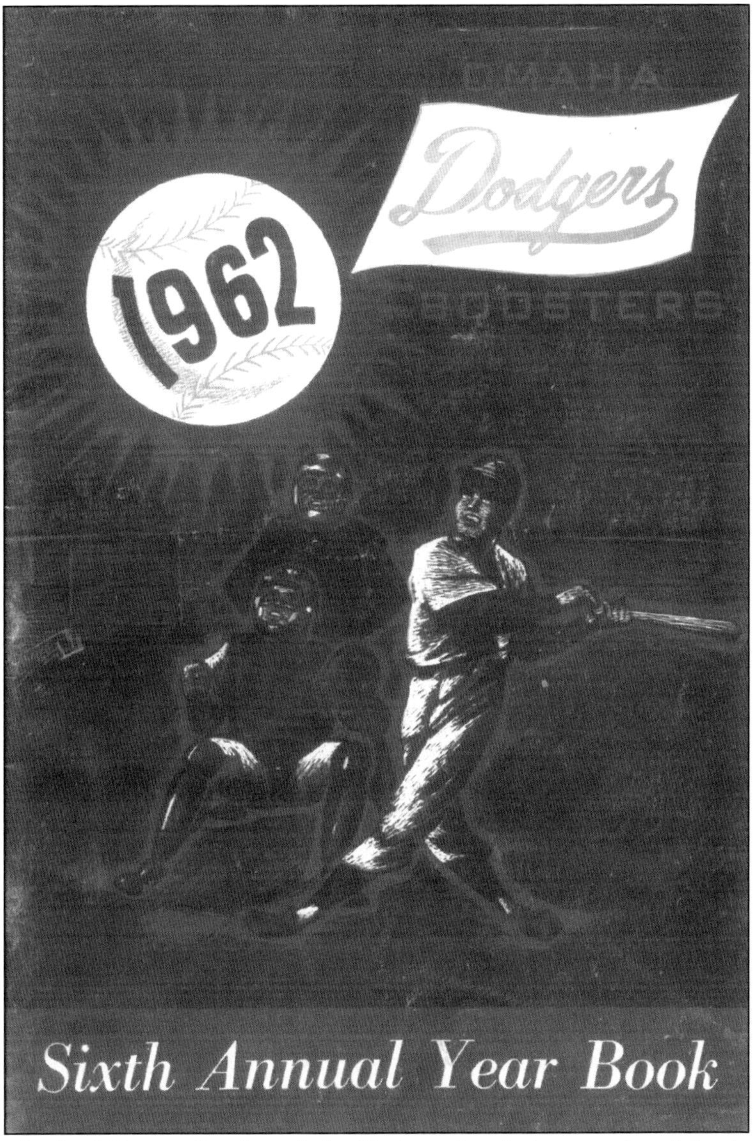

By 1962, Omaha had Danny Ozark and the Dodgers for their second and final season in the American Association. Housing the fourth largest railroad center in the country and the four-way junction for the then new interstate highway, the city itself had been labeled the Gateway to the West, the Crossroads of the Nation. Even in 1962, Omaha was on its way to a leading role in telecommunications with the manufacture of dial equipment for telephone systems. Food processing was still the largest industry with 19 meatpacking plants. Mutual of Omaha was already the largest insurance company with its home office in Omaha. As Omaha grew from the town of Edward Rosewater and his contemporaries, baseball was continuing a slow fade as a form of entertainment. Omaha was the bowling capital, supporting more lanes per capita than any other city of its size. The Omaha Knights of International League hockey pulled in fans. In the minor league baseball ranks, the Dodgers never generated the excitement of the Cardinals even as the major league club of Sandy Koufax and Johnny Podres battled the Giants for a World Series berth against the Yankees, a battle the Dodgers lost to Leo Durocher's team on four runs in the ninth inning. (Courtesy Gary Kastrick, Project Omaha.)

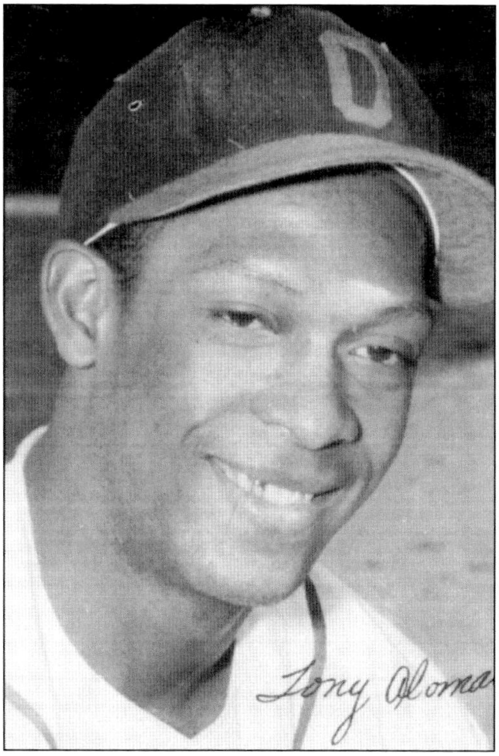

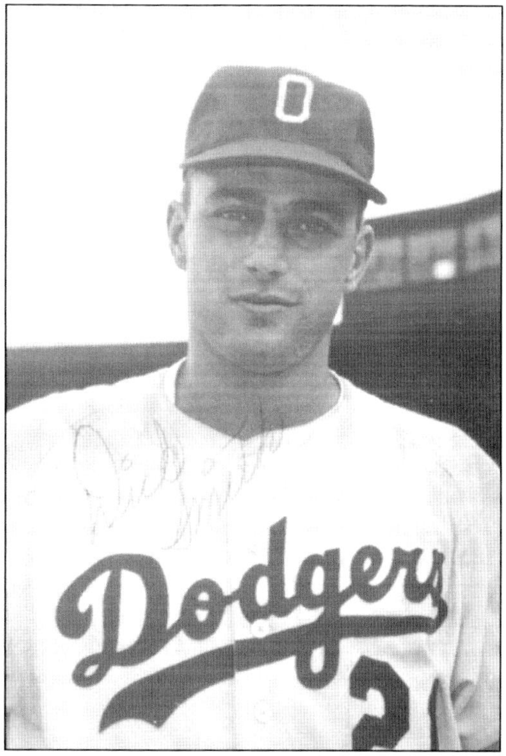

Tony Alomar (left) and Dick Smith (right) played for Danny Ozark's 1961 and 1962 Dodger teams. By the end of the 1962 season, the *Omaha World-Herald* indicated the departure of yet another minor league club from Omaha was imminent. In November, Municipal Stadium manager Charlie Mancuso told the *OWH* he thought a franchise through local ownership was a possibility, with a meeting at the Sheraton-Fontenelle Hotel planned to determine whether parties interested in raising the capital could be found. "This meeting, Mancuso said, "is Omaha's last chance to stay in organized baseball." The Los Angeles Dodgers had announced in previous weeks that they would return Omaha's franchise to the league and end two years of Dodger baseball in Omaha.Omaha's Mayor Dworak and predecessor John Rosenblatt attended the meeting, in addition to Jake Isaacson, general manager of Aksarban. The group decided to further explore the possibility of soliciting approximately $50,000 to $100,000 in capital deemed necessary to operate a franchise in 1963. Even if the money could be raised, nearly every major league club had its farm clubs in order for 1963. (Courtesy of Gary Kastrick, Project Omaha)

Six

Trader Jack Came to Omaha

The 2003 World Series pit the New York Yankees, baseball's giant in tradition and market-value, against the Florida Marlins, baseball's upstart, small-market expansion scrappers. The series was as much about managerial style, Joe Torre's calm, steady presence and Jack McKeon's fiery, vocal involvement, as storied Yankee Stadium and new-wave Pro Player Stadium; cool Mariano Rivera and lively Dontrelle Willis; an aging Roger Clemens and no-holds barred Josh Burkett; playing beneath the burden of expectations and flying on the wings of possibility, of fun.

He [McKeon] lulls you into a false sense of foolishness, and he wraps that around a level of intelligence that, from a baseball standpoint, is incredible.

–David Samson, Marlins President

Jesse Cuevas, Rosenblatt Stadium superintendent (and legend in his own right) recalls being a kid, hanging around the ballpark, doing odd jobs for then-field manager Frank Mancuso. In 1969, Jack McKeon was the first manager of Omaha's new Triple-A affiliate of the expansion Kansas City Royals. Coupled with the antics he wrapped around common sense was McKeon's pre-game ritual of wrapping three or four pieces of gum around a wad of BeechNut chew, a concoction that spewed and sputtered on the shirts of McKeon, umpires, and any player within talking distance over the course of a game. The then 10-year-old Cuevas hauled those shirts home for laundering (in the days before machines at the stadium) until Mrs. Cuevas discovered the source of the peculiar shirt-front stains.

Messy or not, meticulous wrapping of the Beechnut was indicative of McKeon style, of his view and participation in the game of baseball, of spitting and spewing bits of strategy and "keep your head in the game" advice. Before coming to Omaha, McKeon spread his blend of cigars, innovation, and common sense from Fayetteville, North Carolina, to Missoula, Montana; Vancouver, Washington to Minneapolis, Minnesota, where Lou Gorman, then-general manager of the new Kansas City Royals, hired McKeon away from a scouting job with the Twins, sending him to the Royals' Single-A club in High Point, North Carolina. That was 1968, with Gorman promoting McKeon to the new Triple-A Royals in Omaha for the 1969 season.

Before coming to Omaha and before he was Trader Jack, McKeon had a minor league playing career of his own that began in 1949 with the Pittsburgh Pirates organization. It was in Pittsburgh that McKeon began smoking cigars, even while jogging. In 1955, McKeon signed as a player-manager with Fayettesville in North Carolina, followed quickly by another assignment to play and coach with the new Missoula Timberjacks of the Class C Pioneer League and a farm club for the Washington Senators. Local play-by-play announcer Bob Bedard dubbed McKeon the "Little Bulldog" for his defensive skills behind the plate and his tenacity in the handling of the pitching staff, both as a catcher and a coach. In that first season, the Timberjacks finished seventh in an eight-team league with an average of 900 fans in attendance each night for 66 home games. By 1958, the Timberjacks had improved to a 70-59 record, drawing almost 64,000 fans. McKeon earned the first of many Manager of the Year honors in 1958.

The early-to-mid 1960s found McKeon managing the Pacific Coast League's Vancouver Mounties. While in Vancouver, McKeon experimented with radio receivers and hand-held transmitters to provide instant advice to new pitchers. McKeon was aided in his attempt at innovation by then-*Vancouver Sun* baseball reporter Jack Lee, who helped McKeon secure approval for the device from commissioner Ford Frick and baseball's rules committee. It was not long before the Mounties became known as the "Electronic Mounties" and the "Kids From Outer Space," with other teams attempting to intercept McKeon's signals to his pitchers. McKeon thwarted many attempts at interception by playing rock and roll music or pretending to be a taxi dispatcher (from Bob Macklin, *Vancouver Courier*).

By the time he arrived in Omaha for the 1969 season, McKeon had 11 seasons of managerial experience in his head and a team that included pitchers Jerry Cram, Don O'Riley, Alan Fitzmorris, Chris Zachary, and Paul Splittorff; Steve Boros at third base, Dennis Paepke at first base, and George Spriggs in the outfield. McKeon also had to accommodate raids on his bench from the parent club Kansas City Royals.

I had Paul Splittoff in Omaha when he was about 20 years old. They (KC) took him to the big leagues and started him, and he wasn't ready. He went up and got bombed. Come spring training, he didn't have a chance. The impression was he couldn't pitch out there. He was the first guy out.

–Jack McKeon

Splittorff went back to Omaha, but McKeon recommended him again, when Splittorff was ready. Splittorff made it to the majors on a one-hitter and twelve strikeouts over the Chicago White Sox and thus launched a 15-year career.

As the manager of the Omaha club, McKeon guided the Royals to American Association championships in 1969 and 1970, finishing ahead of Warren Spahn and his Tulsa Oilers in 1969, a year in which there were no postseason playoffs. Attendance figures registered 177,619 and 196,069 respectively and McKeon won the AA Casey Stengel Award for Manager of the Year both years. His record for wins, 298 in all four years (1969-1972) with the Royals still stands.

Given to antics in the clubhouse, McKeon was also a taskmaster, used to the small budgets of minor league organizations. In and around his second year with the Omaha Royals, McKeon summoned the young Cuevas to his office, assigning him the task to solve the problem of disappearing baseballs. Too many balls were being lost in batting practice; at two dollars a piece, with 15-20 balls being lost on an almost daily basis, the club could not afford the leak. Chuckling over the recollection, Jesse Cuevas described gathering a small group of neighborhood kids to investigate the fate of balls hit to the outfield and beyond the fence. He remembers staking out a spot to watch and being shocked the first time he saw the elaborate bamboo pole-wire basket contraption of a "professional scooper" coming through a hole in the bottom of the outfield fence. With Cuevas leading the charge, the boys startled the "adult" manipulating the pole from the hillside hideaway and Cuevas returned, triumphant, to lay the pole on McKeon's desk. Of course the victory was temporary, as scoopers continued to plague the grounds crew until outfield fences were reinforced.

After leaving Omaha in 1972, McKeon went to Kansas City where he managed the early careers of George Brett and Frank White, among others who first spent time in Omaha. After Kansas City, McKeon went to Oakland, San Diego (where he earned the moniker Trader Jack for trading Ozzie Smith, Terry Kennedy, and Kevin McReynolds), Cincinnati, and Florida. McKeon is currently baseball's third oldest manager behind Connie Mack and Casey Stengel. Overall, the cigar-chomping, daily walk-jogging, Mass-going McKeon has logged 52 seasons in professional baseball, his work with the young 2003 Florida Marlins merely reflecting a formula developed along the way.

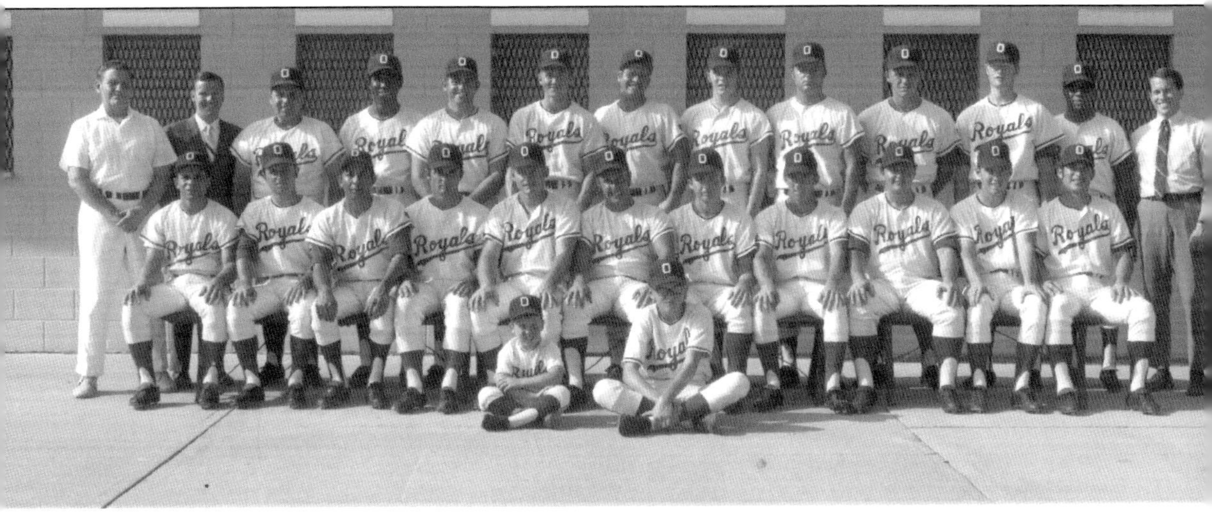

1969 AMERICAN ASSOCIATION AAA CHAMPIO

Front Row: Kelly McKeon and Jim Scriven (Bat Boys).

Second Row: Luis Alcaraz (2b), Paul Epperson (P), Orlando Pena (P), Gerald Cram (P), Steve Boros (INF), Bill Faul (P), Steve Jones (P), Northey (OF), Jim Campanis (C), Rich Severson (SS), Fred Rico (3b-OF).

Third Row: Jim Dudley (Trainer), Bob Quinn (Gen. Mgr.), Jack McKeon (Manager), Lee Green (OF), Dennis Paepke (1b), Joe Keough (OF Osborne (1b), Al Fitzmorris (P), Chris Zachary (P), Dave Nicholson (OF), Paul Splittorff (P), George Spriggs (OF), Bill Beck (Bus. Mgr.), Healy (C), Jon Warden (P), Absent when picture was taken due to military obligations.

In their first season in Omaha, the AAA Royals brought home the American Association championship, repeating the feat in 1970. The Kansas City affiliate joined a six-team league with no playoff structure in place. Between 1963 and the 1969 arrival of the AAA Royals to Rosenblatt Stadium and Omaha, the primary baseball focus was the NCAA College World Series. (Courtesy of Gary Kastrick, Project Omaha.)

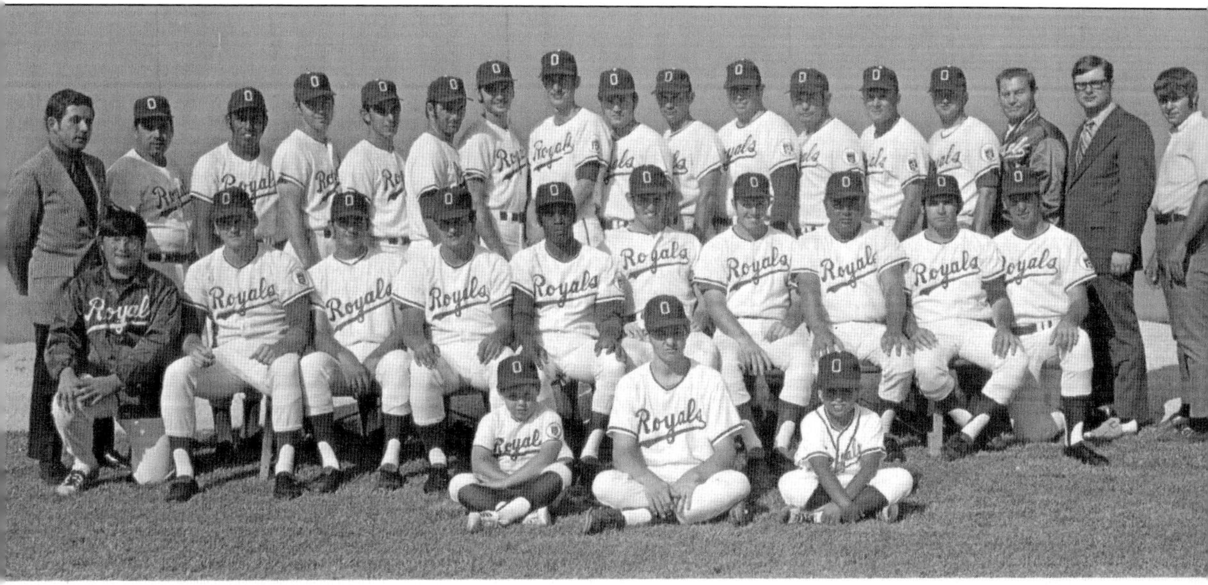

971 AMERICAN ASSOCIATION CLASS AA

Front Row: Kelly McKeon (Bat Boy), Paul Schmidt (Bat Boy), Mark Payne (Ball Boy).

Second Row: Jim Bayly (Clubhouse Boy), Lance Clemons (LHP), Chuck Murray (RHP), Wally Bunker (RHP), Mike Jackson (LHP), C Taylor (OF), Steve McMillan (INF), Ken Huebner (OF), Monty Monteagudo (RHP), Lloyd Gladden (RHP).

Third Row: Bill Gorman (Gen. Mgr.), Jack McKeon (Manager), John Matias (OF), Rich Severson (INF), Buck Martinez (C), Jerry Cra (RHP), Charlie Day (OF), Dennis Musgraves (RHP), Bill Sorrell (OF), Jay Ward (INF), Ken Wright (RHP), John Sullivan (C), T Hilgendorf (LHP), Ted Parks (INF), Jim Dudley (Trainer), Mark Holtz (Bus. Mgr.), Bill Quinlan (Adm. Asst.). Dan Haynes (INF) abs

Pictured are the 1971 Omaha Royals. (Courtesy of Gary Kastrick, Project Omaha.)

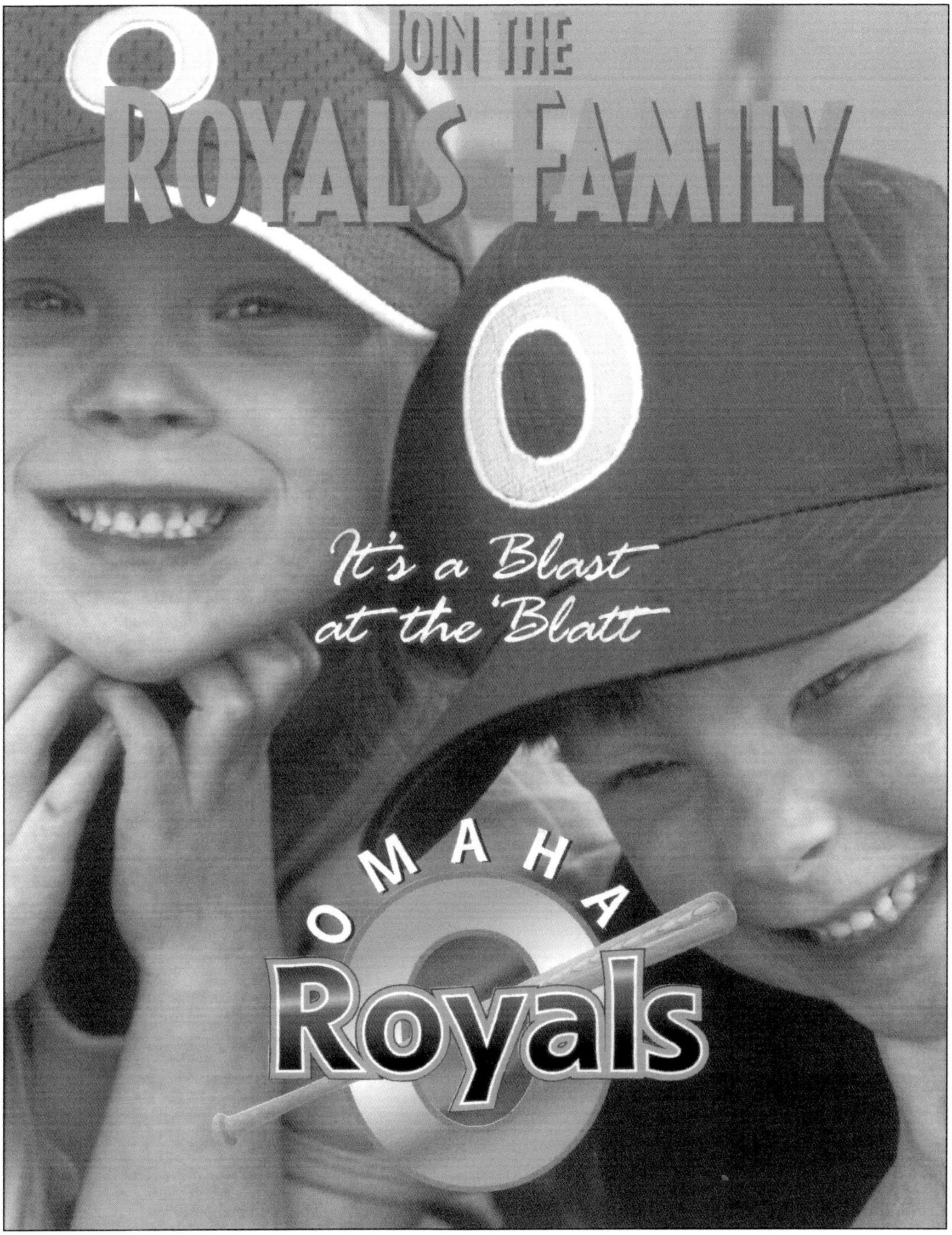

Minor league baseball in Omaha was a blast at the Blatt in 2003 with increased fan fare that included more promotional nights and activities for children. As part of the Pacific Coast League, Omaha shares league play with teams in Albuquerque, Colorado Springs, Des Moines, Memphis, Nashville, New Orleans, Oklahoma City, Fresno, Las Vegas, Sacramento, Tucson, Edmonton, Portland, Salt Lake City, and Tacoma. This strong network of mid-sized cities supports a wave of minor league baseball popularity coinciding with increased minor league attendance across the country. (Photo courtesy of the Omaha Royals).

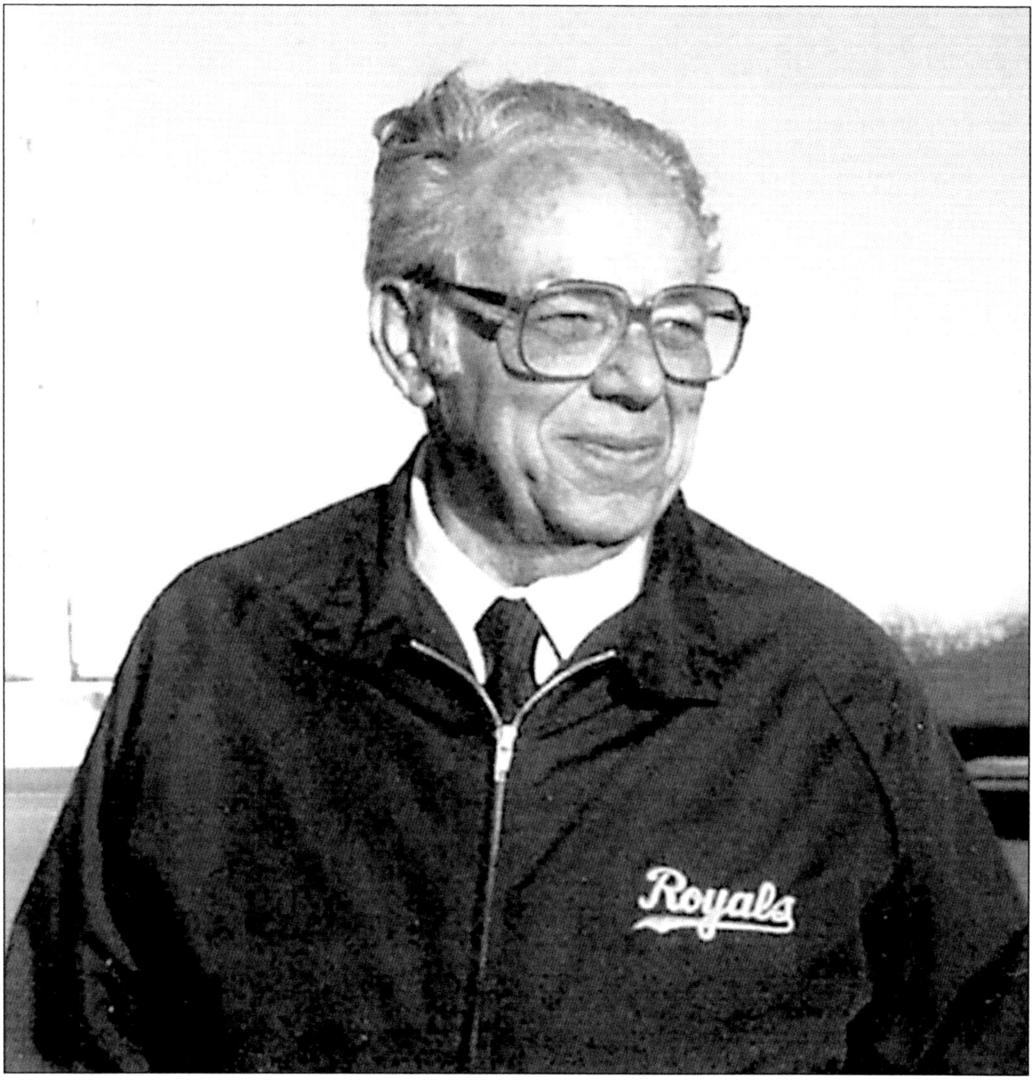

Irving "Gus" Cherry owned the Omaha Royals AAA club from 1985 to 1991, when he put the club up for sale, a sale that found buyers in Union Pacific Railroad, Warren Buffett, and Walter Scott, Jr. Buying the team when he did, Cherry broke into minor league franchise ownership at a time when, nationally, minor league baseball was surging in popularity. Franchise owners brought fans to the parks with promotions such as prizes for the dirtiest car in the parking lot. During Cherry's tenure, the Royals topped the 300,000 attendance mark in 1988, followed by increases in 1989 and 1990 when the Royals reached the AAA championship series. Poor health and difficulty of managing from out-of-town from his Evanston, Illinois office prompted Cherry to find a new owner for the Omaha Royals. Committed to keeping the team in Omaha, Cherry waited, waited, and waited until the ownership group of Union Pacific, Buffet, and Scott, Jr. came together. In an interview following announcement of the sale, Cherry attributed his patience to the fans, saying, "It's hard for me to put into words why I remained so firm in finding someone to keep the club there (Omaha). There were many factors, but one of the biggest was the loyal fans that supported this team. We've put a lot of hard work into this, and I think we've had some degree of success. I just found it difficult to turn my back and walk away from that." (Courtesy of the Omaha Royals.)

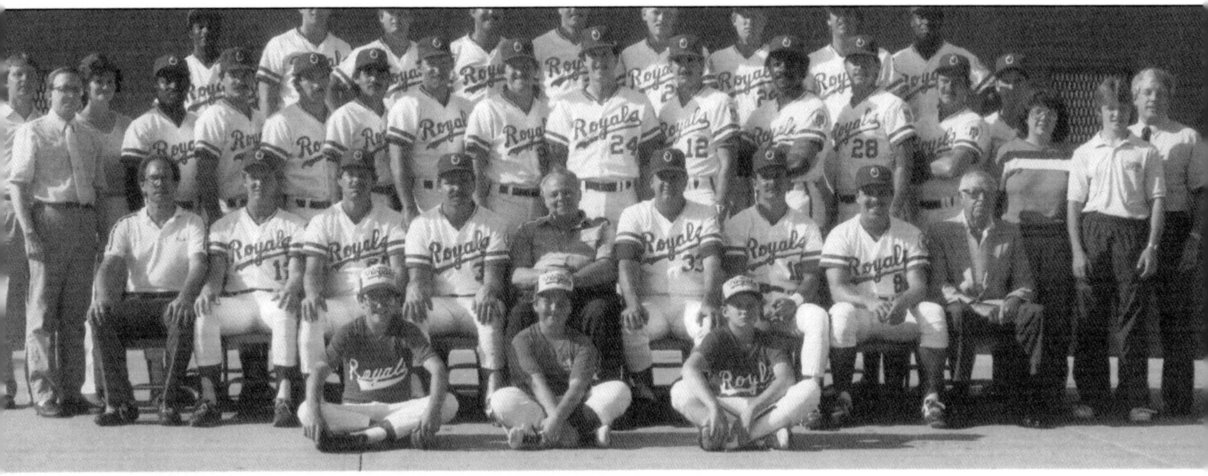

1985 OMAHA ROYALS

CLASS TRIPLE A · AMERICAN ASSOCIATION

Back Row Standing (Left to Right) Mike Cole (OF), Bob Hegman (INF), Rondin Johnson (INF), Jim Scranton (INF), Bill Pecota (INF), Mike Kingery (OF), Pat Putnam (INF), Steve Farr (P), Butch Davis (OF).

Middle Row Standing (Left to Right) Terry Wendlandt (Ass't. General Manager), Matt Bassett (Business Manager), Sue Nicholson (Bookkeeper), Lester Strode (P), Mike Kinnunen (P), Roger Hansen (C), Tony Ferreira (P), Rene Martin (P), Al Hargesheimer (P), Mike Griffin (P), Brian Poldberg (C), Rich Murray (INF), Mark Huismann (P), Ken Baker (OF), Marty Wilkerson (INF), Cindy Kiger (Secretary), Mark Van Ryckeghem (Office Ass't.), Bill Gorman (General Manager).

Middle Row Sitting (Left to Right) Nick Swartz (Trainer), David Cone (P), Buster Keeton (P), Rich Dubee (Coach), Gus Cherry (Owner), Gene Lamont (Manager), Dave Leeper (OF), Russ Stephans (C), Dr. Frank Iwersen (Team Physician).

Front Row Sitting (Left to Right) Bat Boys: Pete MacNaughton, Doug Rosenthal, Joe Truscott.

COMPLIMENTS OF THE OMAHA ROYALS

Despite a fourth place finish, the 1985 Royals under Gene Lamont fielded Steve Farr, with his league leading ERA of 2.02, and Mark Huismann, the American Association Pitcher of the Year. (Courtesy of Gary Kastrick, Project Omaha.)

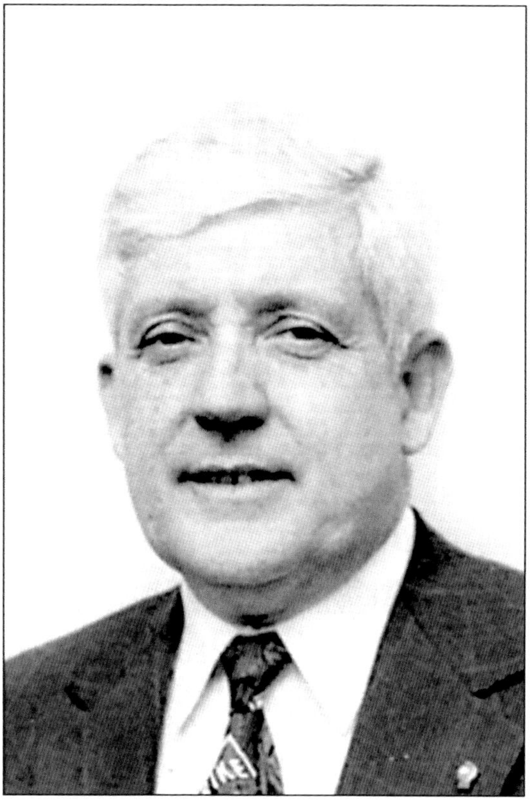

Bill Gorman became the Omaha Royals' general manager in 1971, shepherding the AAA franchise for over 30 years. Gorman was a steady presence in the front office as the franchise itself survived (and thrived) through the three vastly different ownership arrangements that included the parent club Kansas City Royals, businessman Gus Cherry, and the limited partnership of Union Pacific, Warren Buffett, and Walter Scott. Gorman was also visible to the fans, often standing in the main concourse before and after games. As a member of the Omaha community, Gorman was active in the downtown Rotary Club. During Gorman's tenure, George Brett passed through the line-up, making the American Association All-Star team in 1973. Mark Huismann won the AA Pitcher of the Year award in 1985, and the Royals joined the Pacific Coast League in 1998. In the years under Kansas City Royals ownership, Omaha was the site of a once-a-season exhibition game between the parent club and the Omaha Royals farm club. (Courtesy of the Omaha Royals.)

(*Opposite*) The 1993 season marked the 25th anniversary of Royals baseball in Omaha. It was a season opening that included a new playing field at Rosenblatt Stadium, renovated dugouts, photo decks, the stadium-view club, and updated concession areas. To mark 25 years, fans were asked to vote for members of an Omaha Royals-Omaha World-Herald 25th year anniversary All-Star team. Results included Buddy Biancalana (ss), George Brett (3b), Steve Busby (p), Jerry Cram(relief pitcher), Mark Huismann (relief pitcher), Clint Hurdle (of), Charlie Leibrandt (p), Dennis Leonard (p), Jack McKeon (manager), Russ Morman (designated hitter), Bill Pecota (utility player), Paul Splittorff (p), Gary Thurman (of), John Wathan (c), Frank White (2b), Willie Wilson (of). For pitcher Steve Busby, his 1972 debut with the Omaha Royals under Jack McKeon was his second time in Omaha; Busby pitched for the University of Southern California team that won three College World Series championships at Rosenblatt Stadium. Busby himself pitched the USC Trojans' championship game over Southern Illinois in the 1971 CWS. Jerry Cram played on the first Omaha team in 1969 and went on to coach Royals' pitchers. (Courtesy of the Omaha Royals.)

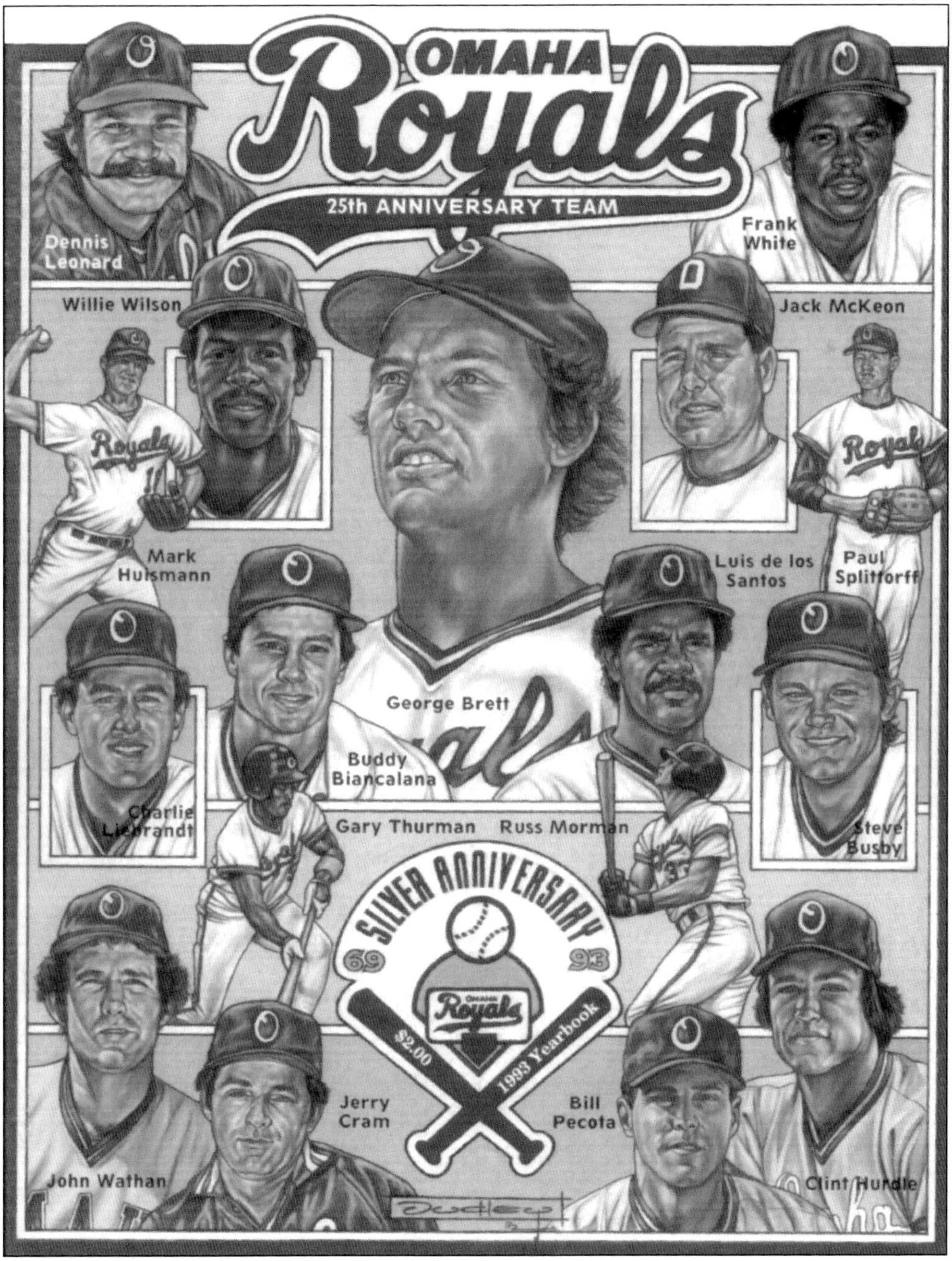
OMAHA
Royals
25th ANNIVERSARY TEAM
Dennis Leonard
Frank White
Willie Wilson
Jack McKeon
Mark Huismann
Luis de los Santos
Paul Splittorff
George Brett
Buddy Biancalana
Charlie Leibrandt
Gary Thurman
Russ Morman
Steve Busby
SILVER ANNIVERSARY
69
93
Royals
$2.00
1993 Yearbook
Jerry Cram
Bill Pecota
John Wathan
Clint Hurdle

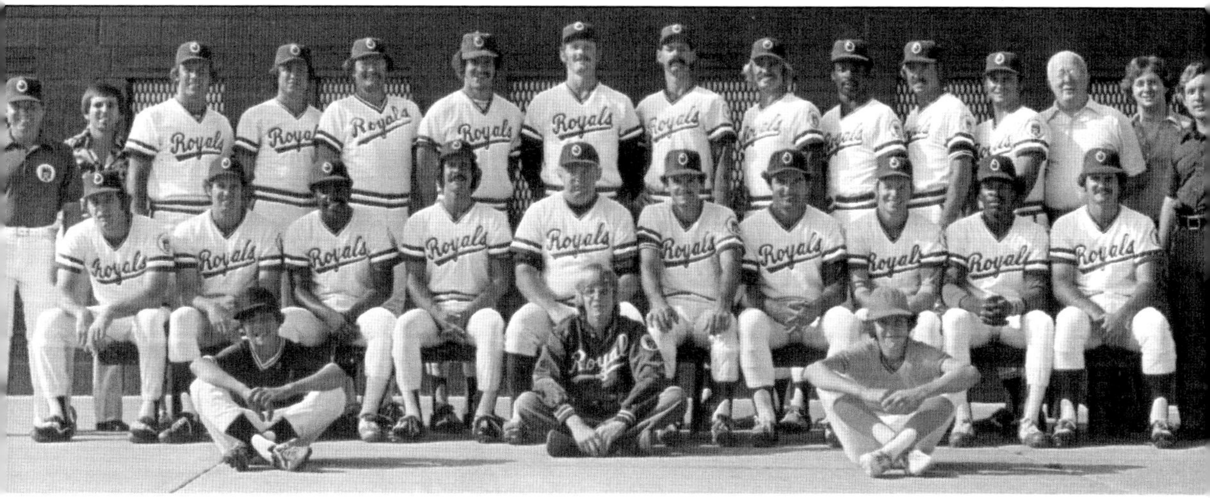

OMAHA
BASEBALL CLUB

1977 AMERICAN ASSOCIATION — CLASS AAA

Front Row: Scott Hill (Batboy), Dale Sorensen (Clubhouse Boy), Tom Herman (Bat Boy)

Second Row: Mickey Cobb (Trainer), Dave Cripe (INF), Ken Melvin (OF), Charlie Beamon (INF), Rudy Kinard (INF), John Sullivan (MGR), Brian Murphy (Player-Coach), Jerry Cram (RHP), Gary Wright (LHP), U. L. Washington (INF), Craig Perkins (C), Bill Gorman (Gen. Mgr.)

Third Row: Ray Alloway (Bus. Mgr.), Dave Hasbach (RHP), Clint Hurdle (OF), Roger Nelson (RHP), Gary Martz (INF), Rich Gale (RHP), Mark Ballinger (RHP), Lynn McKinney (RHP), Willie Wilson (OF), Gary Lance (RHP), Steve Patchin (C), Dr. J. D. Ewing (Team Phy.), Mike Venditte (Adm. Asst.)

OMAHA
BASEBALL CLUB

Under manager John Sullivan, the 1977 club won the American Association Eastern Division title, part of a three year run of division titles that began in 1976 and ended with an unlikely 1978 Western Division championship. The '78 club finished the season with a 66-69 record, but stunned Indianapolis Indians by winning the Western Division series . The 1977 club had the best record in the league behind Willie Wilson's speed on the basepaths, Clint Hurdle's strength at the plate, and the steady play of third baseman Dave Cripe and catcher Craig Perkins. (Courtesy of Gary Kastrick, Project Omaha.)

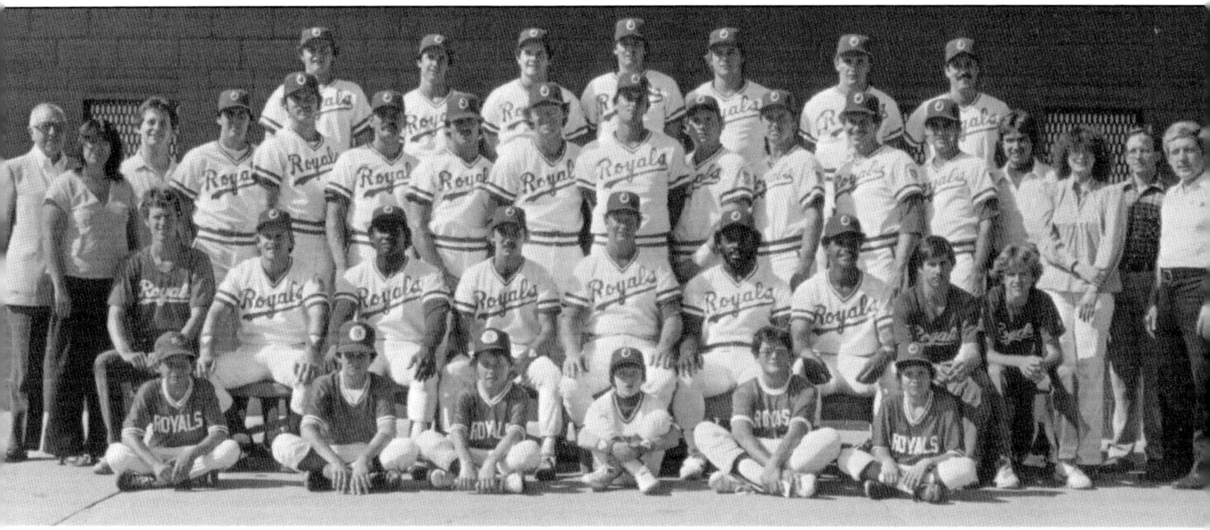

1982 American Association
Western Division Champions

BACK ROW STANDING: (left to right)	Vince Yuhas (P), Buddy Biancalana (INF), Mark Ryal (OF), Bill Kelly (P), Dennis Werth (INF), Duane Dewey (C), Tim Ireland (INF).
MIDDLE ROW STANDING: (left to right)	Dr. Frank Iwersen (Team Physician), Cindy Kiger (Secretary), Mike Venditte (Business Manager), Dan Fischer (P), Jim Wright (P), Greg Keatley (C), Pat Sheridan (OF), Mike Parrott (P), Bob Tufts (P), Ron Johnson (INF), Keith Creel (P), Dave Schuler (P), Frank Wills (P), Paul McGannon (Trainer), Amy D'Ercole (Office Assistant), Matt Bassett (Adm. Ass't.), Bill Gorman (General Manager)
MIDDLE ROW SITTING: (left to right)	Rick English (Clubhouse Manager), Jeff Cox (INF), Bombo Rivera (OF), Kelly Heath (INF), Joe Sparks (Field Manager), Darryl Motley (OF), Luis Silverio (OF), Sam DeGeorge (Home Clubhouse), Rob English (Visitors Clubhouse).
FRONT ROW SITTING: (left to right)	Batboys: Wil Gorman, Jason Bosiljevac, Jeff Jaworski, Rodney Sparks, Mike Truscott, Don DeGeorge

The 1982 club, under the guidance of manager Joe Sparks and the 166-hit season of first baseman Ron Johnson, captured the American Association West Division title from Felipe Alou's Wichita Aeros. Crowd favorite Bombo Rivera hit 27 homeruns in the season, which helped give Omaha its second Western Division title in two years. (Courtesy of Gary Kastrick, Project Omaha.)

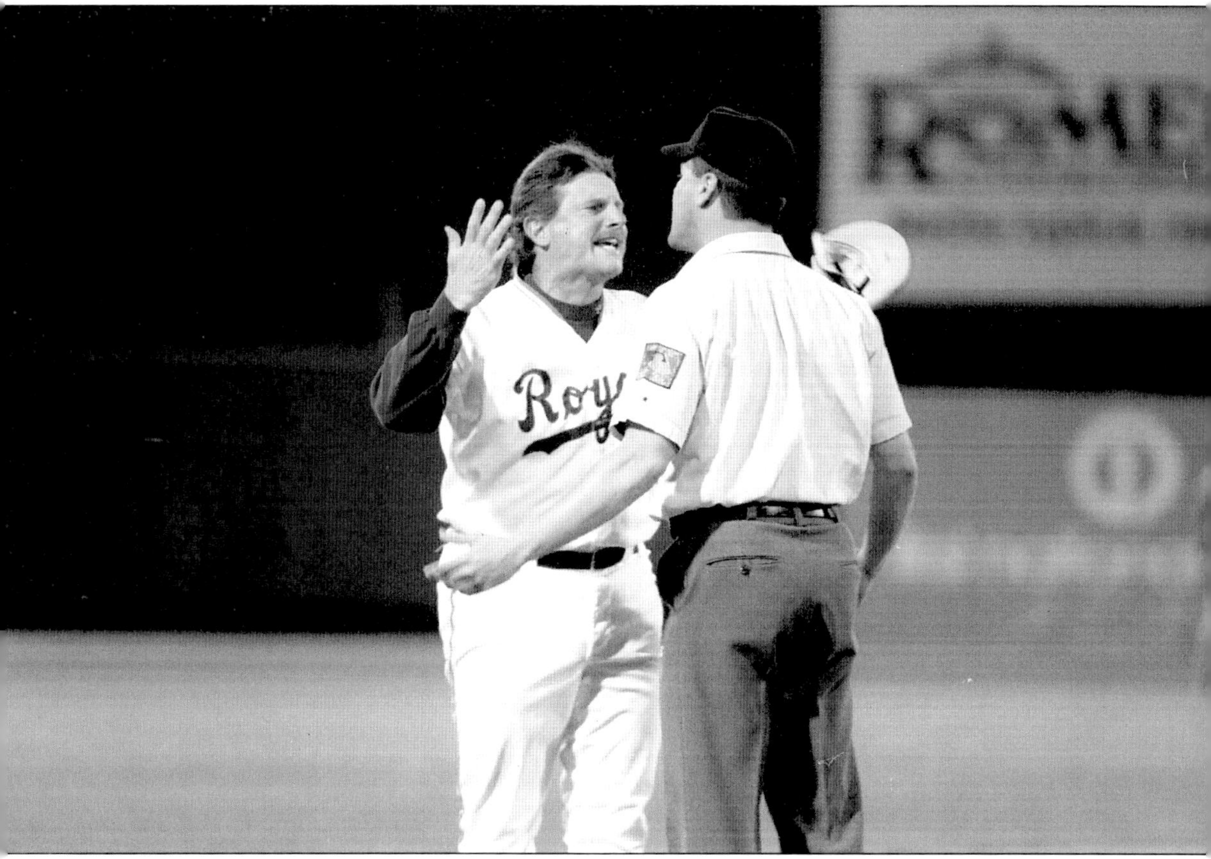

Jeff Cox has issues with the umpire. "Watch our smoke," was the catch phrase around the clubhouse when Cox managed the Omaha Royals through the 1992 and 1993 seasons, following eight managerial seasons with clubs that included the Cincinnati Reds' rookie league club in Billings, Montana, the Pittsburgh Pirates' Short A and A clubs in Watertown and Augusta, and Kansas City's Southern League AA affiliate in Memphis. Towards the end of his playing career, Cox played in 71 games for the 1982 Royals and 53 games in 1983.The Royals under Jeff Cox did not see post-season Octobers, but never suffered for boredom. Fans remember Cox for his charges from the dugout, often arguing his case with the umpires, paying fines and serving suspensions later.

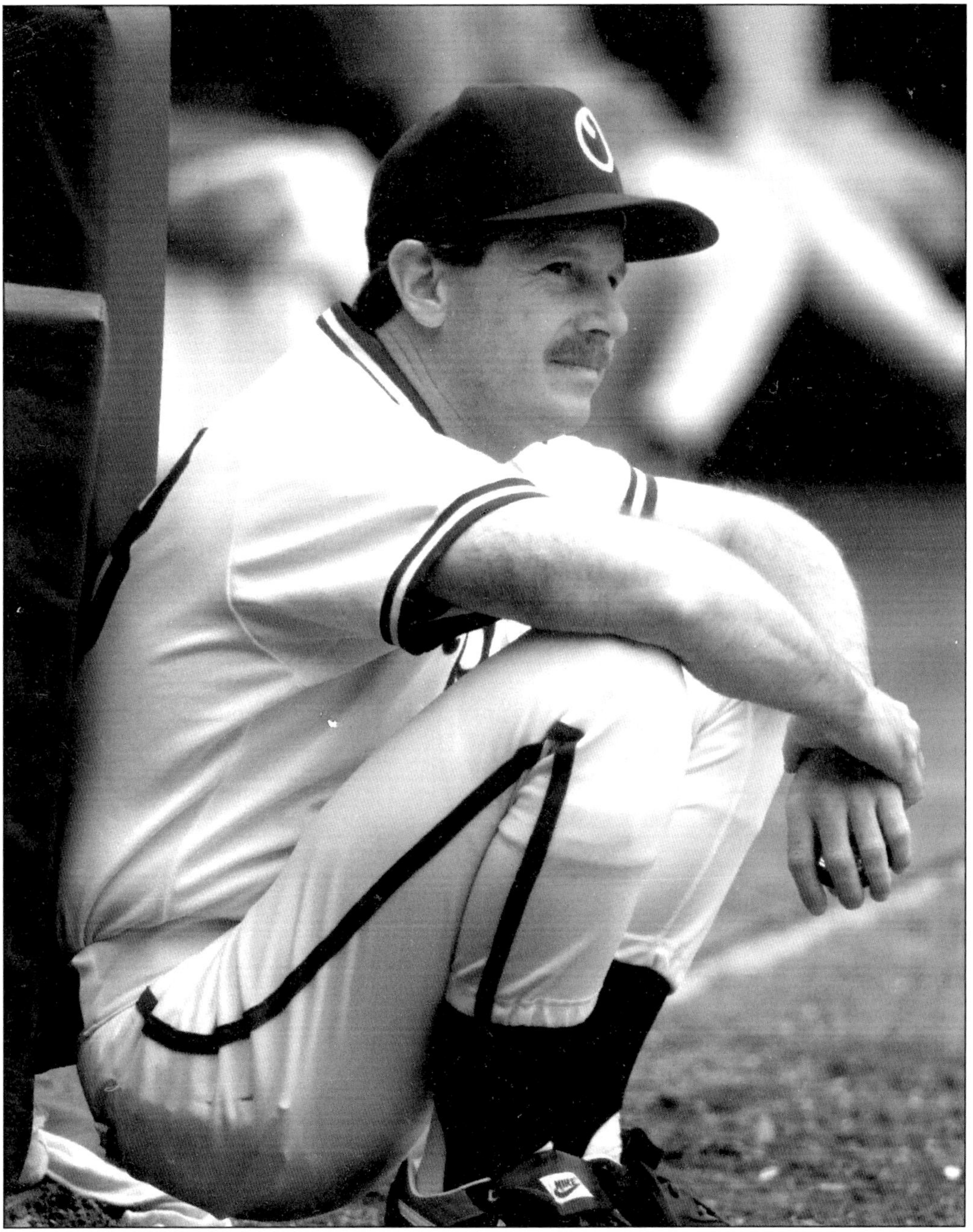

Members of the press covering the Royals during Cox's years often found the manager practically living at Rosenblatt Stadium. Royals' teams of the 1990s saw the sale of the club from Gus Cherry to Union Pacific Railroad, Warren Buffett, and Walter Scott and the 1998 disbanding of the American Association, resulting in Omaha becoming part of the 16-member Pacific Coast League. In 1998, the Royals' Jeremy Giambi won the PCL batting title and Rookie of the Year, while Chris Hatcher enjoyed a "dream season" that included Chris Hatcher Day at Rosenblatt. Hatcher set new club records for homeruns, RBIs, and total bases. (Courtesy Omaha Royals.)

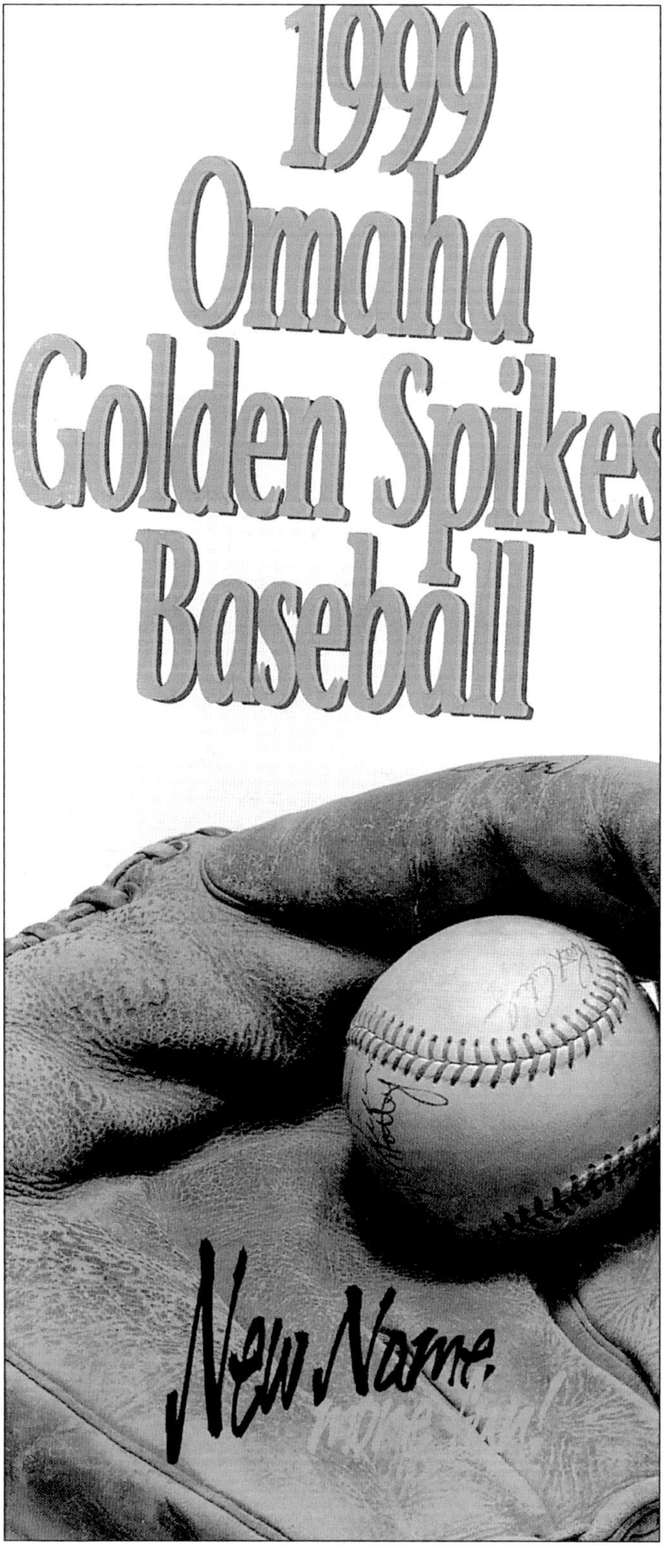

The 1999 season marked the first for a new name, logo, and colors, and 31st for the years the Kansas City Triple A franchise has played in Omaha's Rosenblatt Stadium. In the franchise's 30 seasons, the club has won 11 division championships and 4 league championships. On August 30, 1998, the Omaha AAA club announced the results of fan voting, with the Golden Spikes being the new team name of choice over the Outlaws, Pioneers, and River Kings. The public cast over 2,500 votes, with a pre-game ceremony held at Rosenblatt on August 31 to announce the new name and a new era. Four skydivers dropped to the field bearing a banner with the new name, a moniker significant for its recognition of Omaha's development as a regional rail system center. Responding to local concerns over the name change, Tom Shatel of the OWH mused on the spirit of minor league baseball, offering to the people of Omaha that, "Minor league baseball is supposed to be fun, with a fun name, something signature about the town. And there is nothing more fun than a day or night out at the Blatt, where you and your kids or friends can kick back and enjoy one of the best bargains and best ballparks around. The name may change. But don't let that keep you away. Different name, same great game." Only the different name and new era lasted all of one season. By 2000, the AAA club was renamed the Royals. (Courtesy of the Omaha Royals.)

Here is the familiar layout of Rosemblatt during the Golden Spikes' brief stay in Omaha.

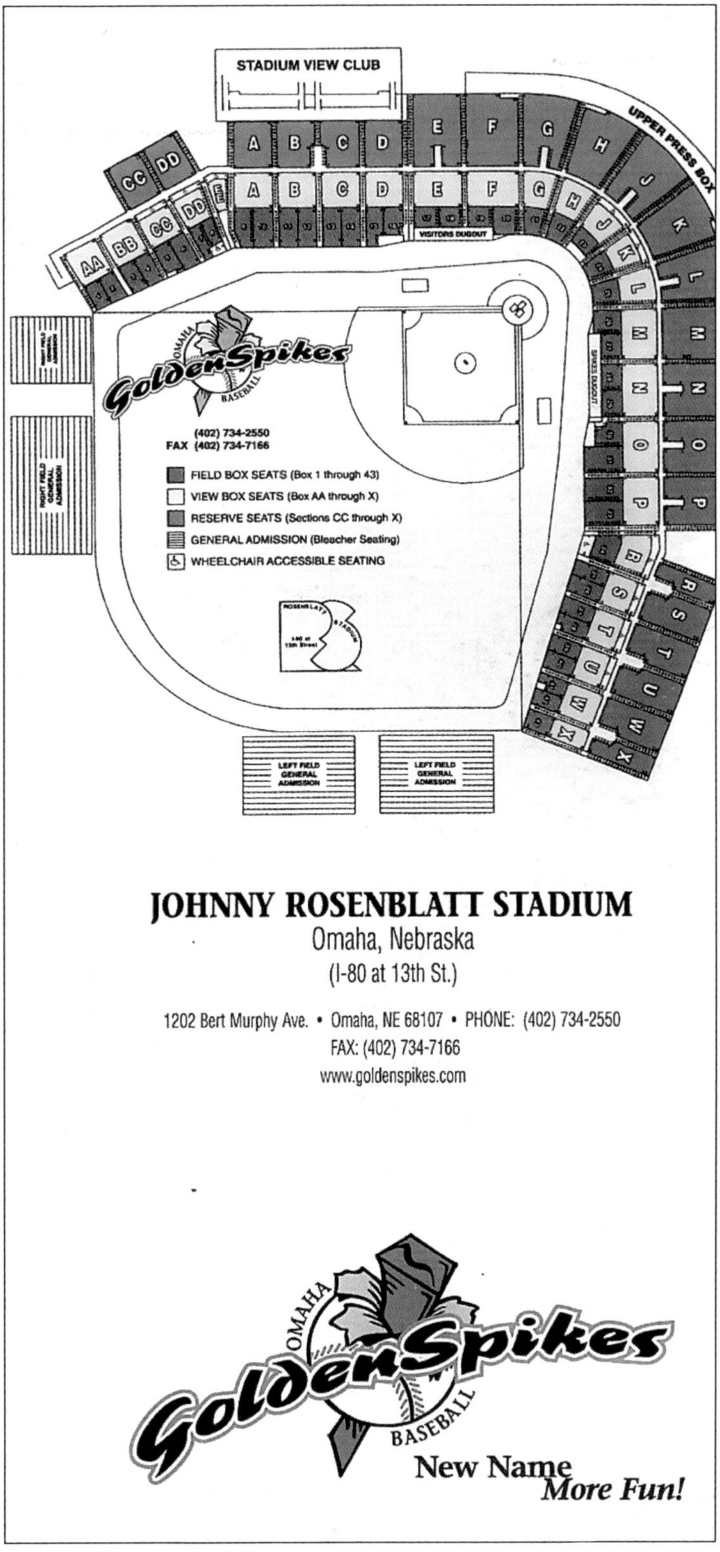

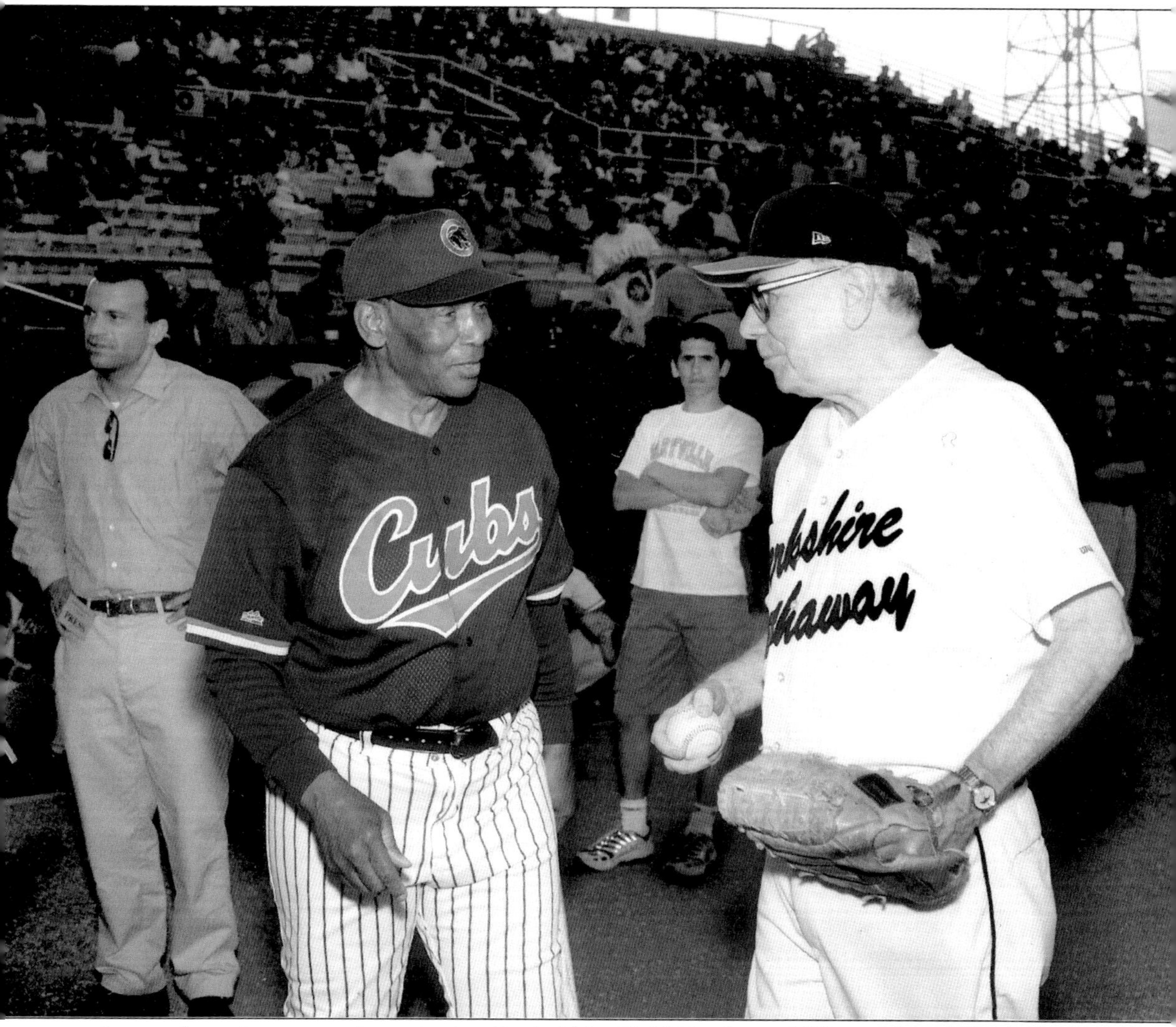

Icons of consistency and continuity, Ernie "Mr. Cub" Banks and Warren "the Whip" Buffett have teamed up for several annual Berkshire-Hathaway shareholders' nights at Rosenblatt Stadium, with Buffett, part-owner of the Royals since 1991, tossing out the opening ball and then participating in batting contests with Banks. Of the first such contest in 1999, Banks explained to Christopher Edmonds, president of Resources Dynamics, "With Warren on the mound, I feel like Hank Aaron, Babe Ruth, Sammy Sosa, and Mark McGuire all wrapped up in one." To which Buffett responded, "I throw a mean premature sinker, the kind that bounces halfway to the plate. Bring your shovel."Banks played his entire 19 season career for the Chicago Cubs, 19 seasons under one mayor, Richard J. Daley, one owner, P.K. Wrigley, and in one ballpark, Wrigley Field. Banks and Gene Baker became the first African Americans to play with the Cubs, with the Cubs signing Banks for two thousand dollars a year from the Kansas City Monarchs of the Negro Leagues where he had played for one and one-half years. (Courtesy of the Omaha Royals.)

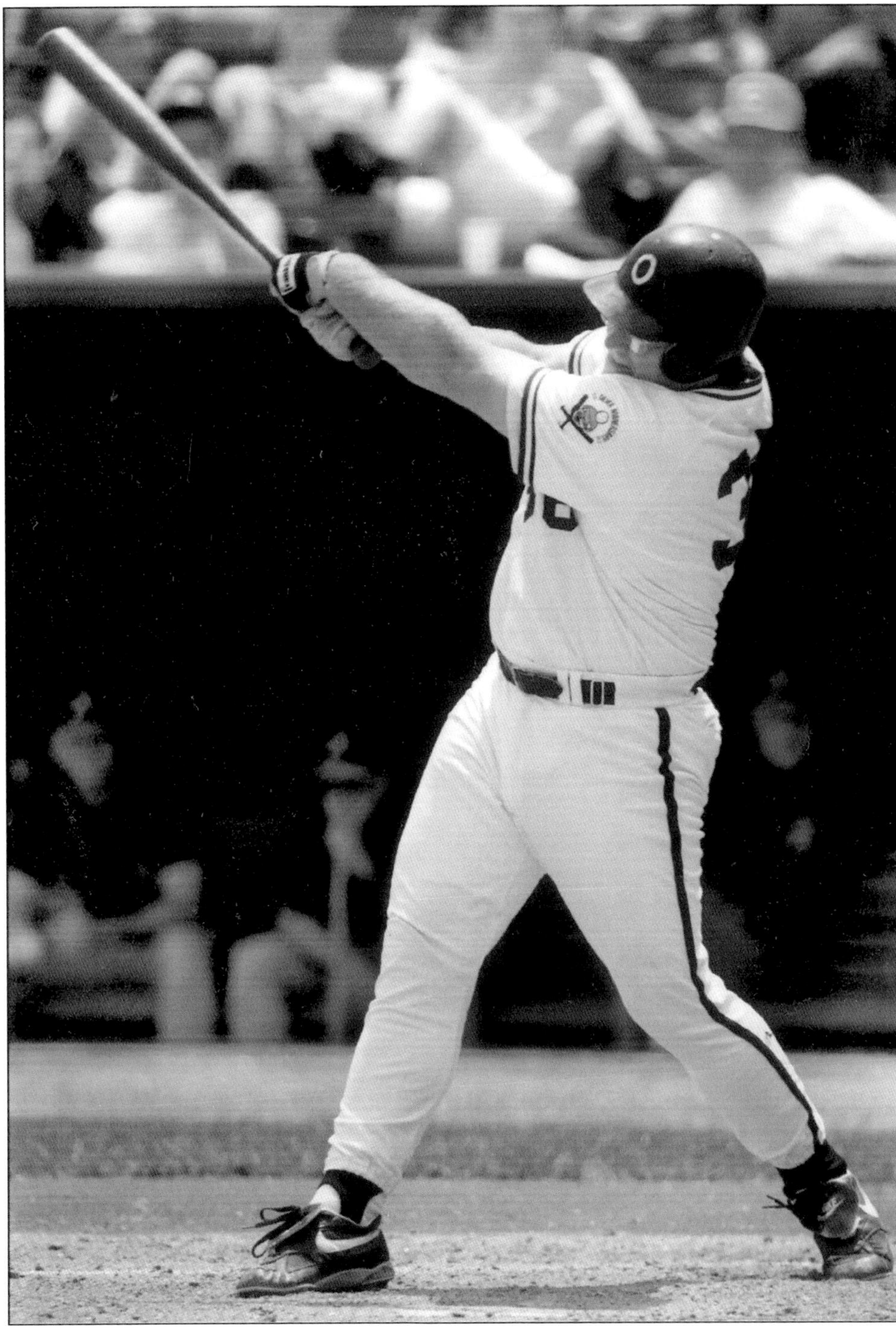

Bob "The Hammer" Hamelin played first base in the Kansas City Royals' organization, earning Rookie of the Year honors in the strike-shortened 1994 season. Before coming over to the Omaha and Kansas City Royals, Hamelin played for the Alaska Goldpanners. In the early 90s, Hamelin was a player recognized at Rosenblatt for a good eye and far reach with the bat, often taking pitches over the outfield fences. (Courtesy of the Omaha Royals.)

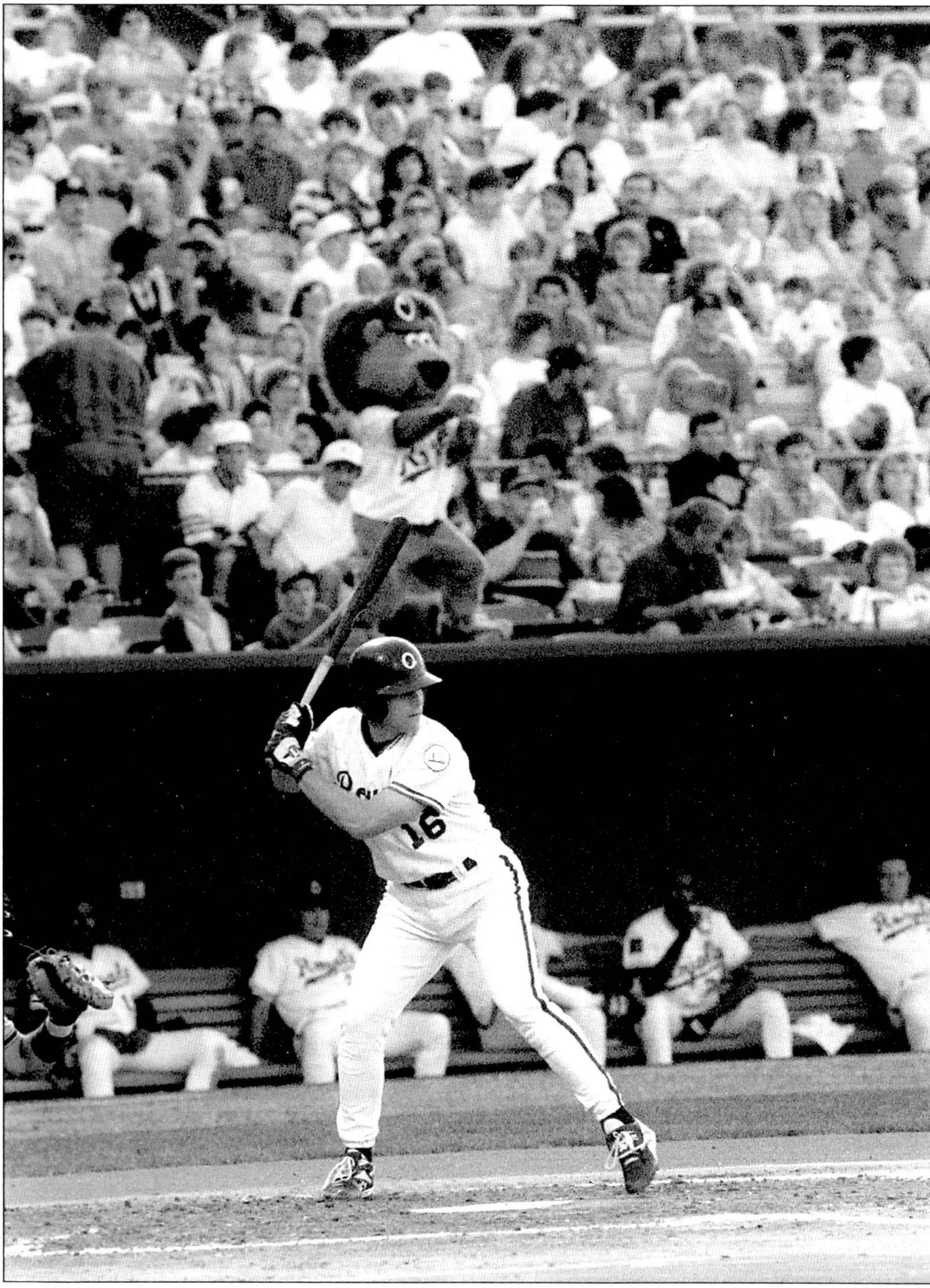

Joe Randa, beginning his fifth season (2004) for the Kansas City Royals, watches the hot corner, or third base, the position for which George Brett earned his defensive marks for Hall of Fame status. In 1994, when Bob Hamelin was having his Rookie of the Year season with Kansas City, Randa was a top Omaha prospect hopeful for a late-season promotion to the Kansas City roster. A strike-shortened season put that debut off for another year.

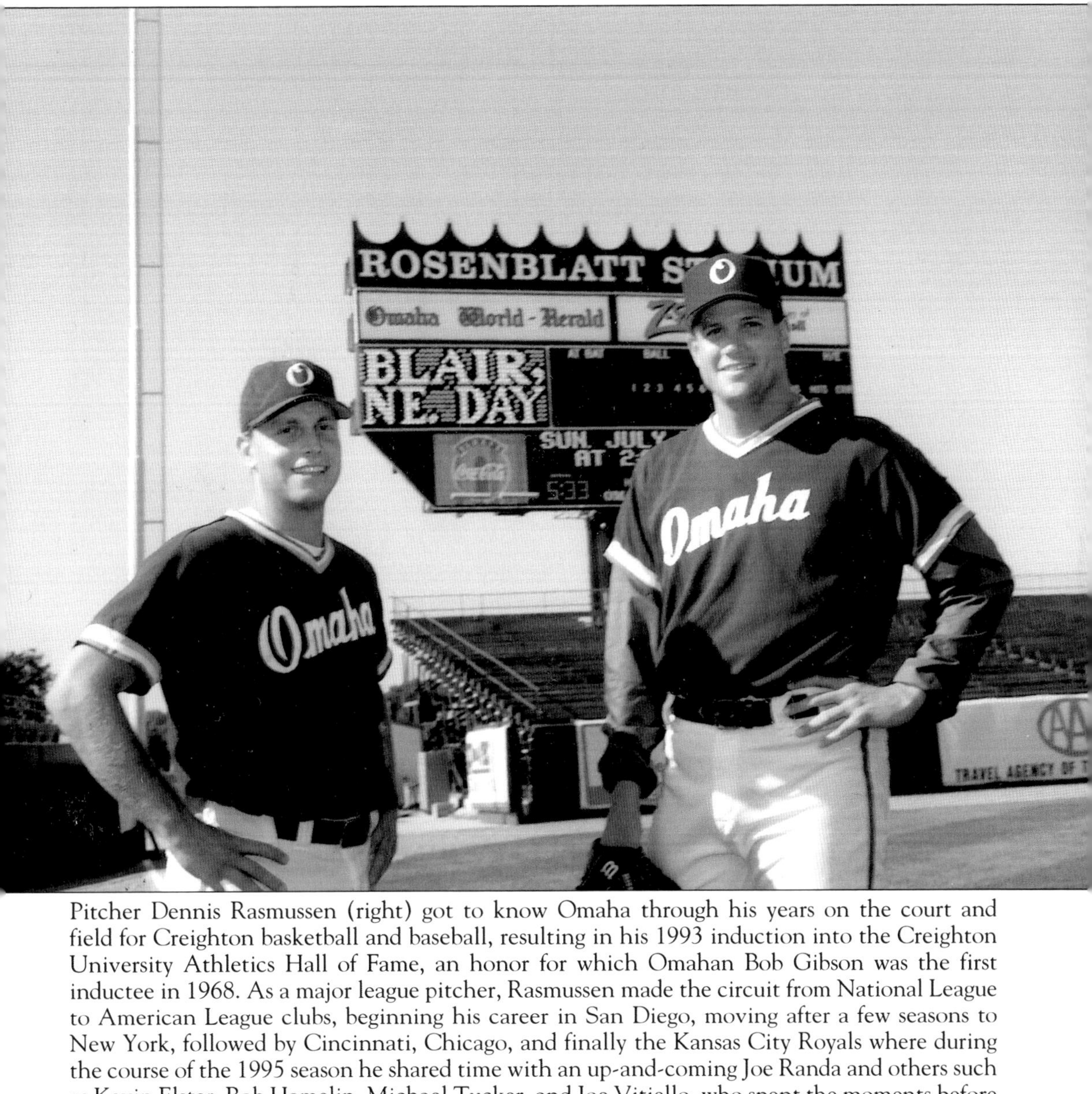

Pitcher Dennis Rasmussen (right) got to know Omaha through his years on the court and field for Creighton basketball and baseball, resulting in his 1993 induction into the Creighton University Athletics Hall of Fame, an honor for which Omahan Bob Gibson was the first inductee in 1968. As a major league pitcher, Rasmussen made the circuit from National League to American League clubs, beginning his career in San Diego, moving after a few seasons to New York, followed by Cincinnati, Chicago, and finally the Kansas City Royals where during the course of the 1995 season he shared time with an up-and-coming Joe Randa and others such as Kevin Elster, Bob Hamelin, Michael Tucker, and Joe Vitiello, who spent the moments before their official break into the majors swapping caps and playing hard for whichever team needed them, the Omaha or Kansas City club. Rasmussen spent part of the 1992 season in Omaha, pitching in 13 games. (Courtesy of the Omaha Royals.)

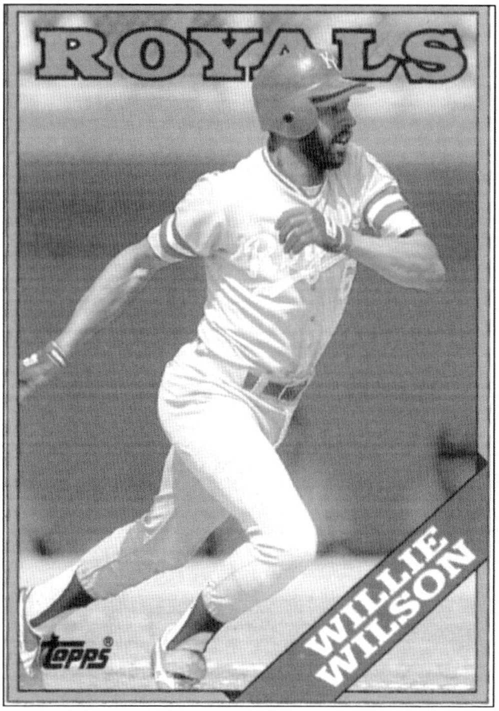

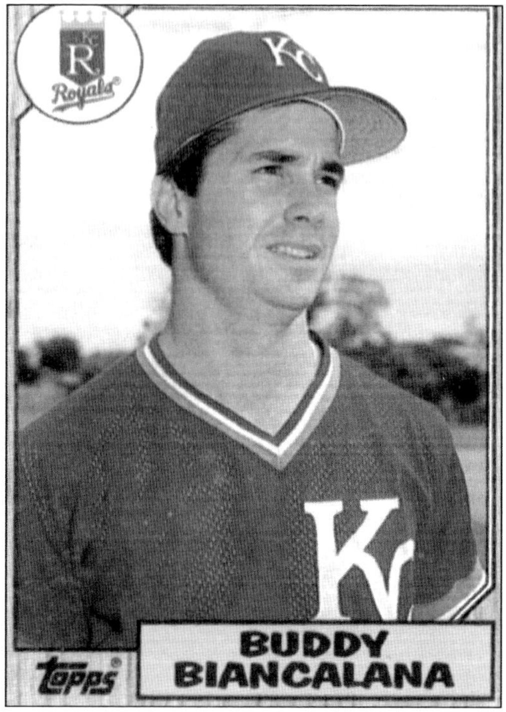

Right: Omaha's PA announcer rolled the name, drawing out each syllable..."at shortstop, Buddy Beeee-anc-alana." In Omaha for parts of five seasons, Buddy Biancalana brought magic to the shortstop spot, eventually garnering him the votes of Omaha fans for a spot on the 25th Anniversary All-Star team. Playing for a major league spot in the early 1980s, Biancalana returned to Omaha for the 1987–1988 seasons fighting back problems and trying to find his way back to a major league roster. While with Omaha in 1988, Biancalana contributed to a Royals team that won the 1988 American Association West Division title, the organization's first since 1982, Biancalana's first season with the club.
Left: Willie Wilson ran through Omaha in 1977, literally, breaking a 56-year old American Association record for stolen bases with 74. While in Omaha, playing for manager John Sullivan, Wilson learned to switch-hit, a skill that combined with speed, made Wilson a natural, invaluable major league prospect. Also while in Omaha, Wilson moved from the catcher's spot to the outfield. A single, pivotal learning season in Omaha set Wilson up for a 17 plus season major league career.

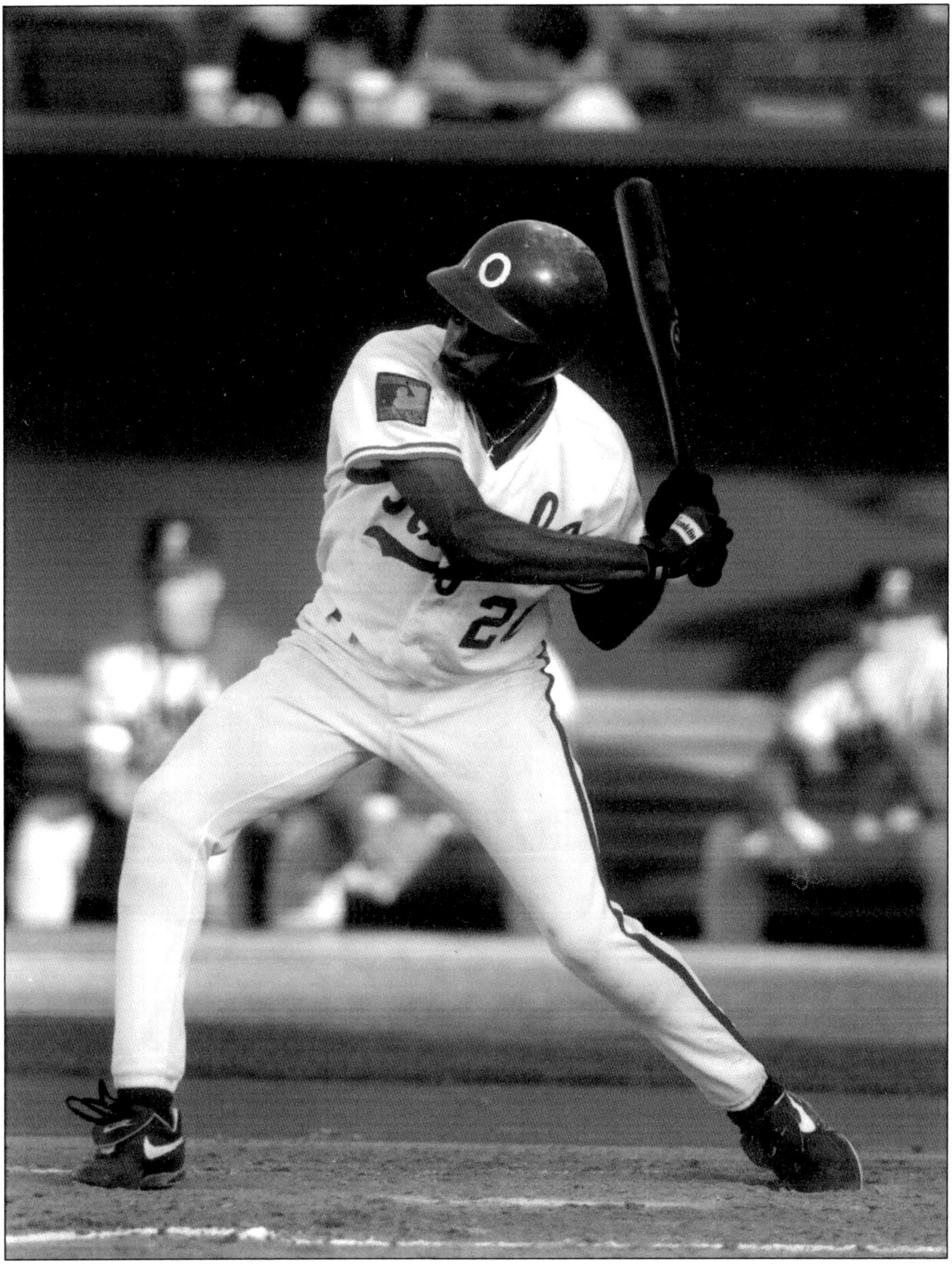

Before a major league career that has taken him from Kansas City to Atlanta to Cincinnati and back to Kansas City, and San Francisco, Michael Tucker stopped in Omaha. Before his mid-90s stint on the Omaha Royals' outfield, Tucker played for Longwood College in Virginia where he earned NCAA Division II Player of the Year and Baseball America's Small College Player of the Year awards in 1992. Also in 1992, Tucker led the United States Olympic baseball team in steals with 28. (Courtesy of the Omaha Royals.)

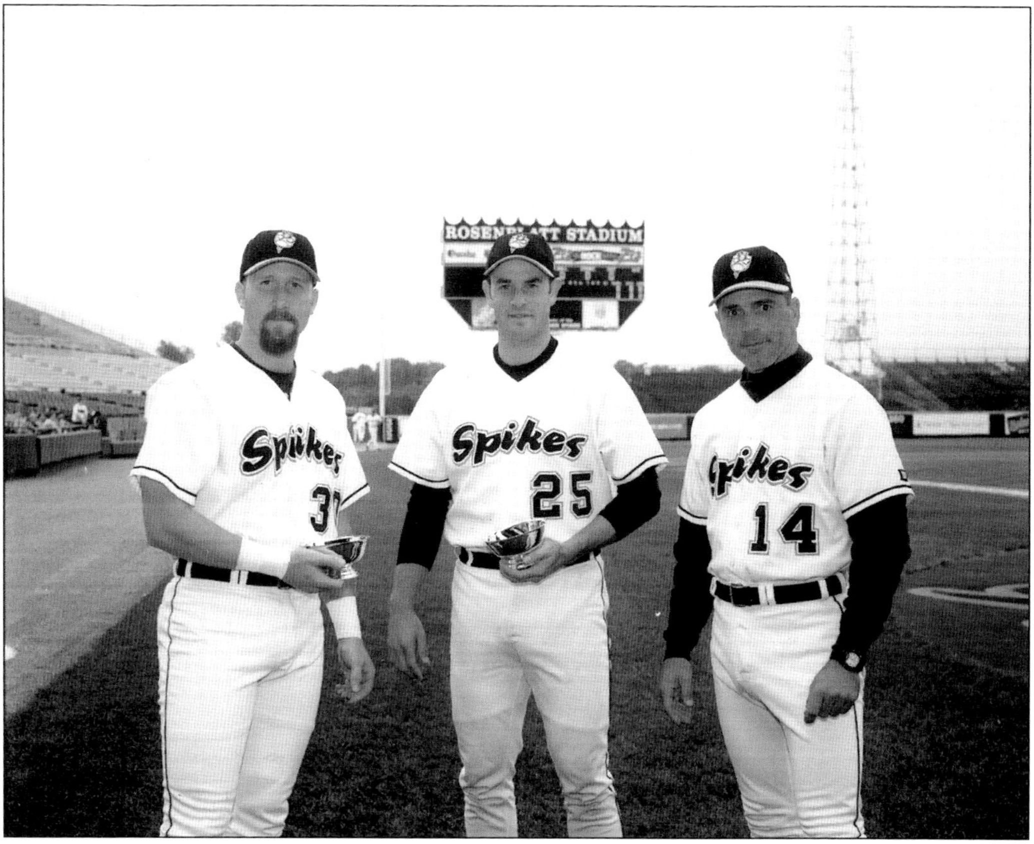
ROSENBLATT STADIUM
Spikes
25
Spikes
14

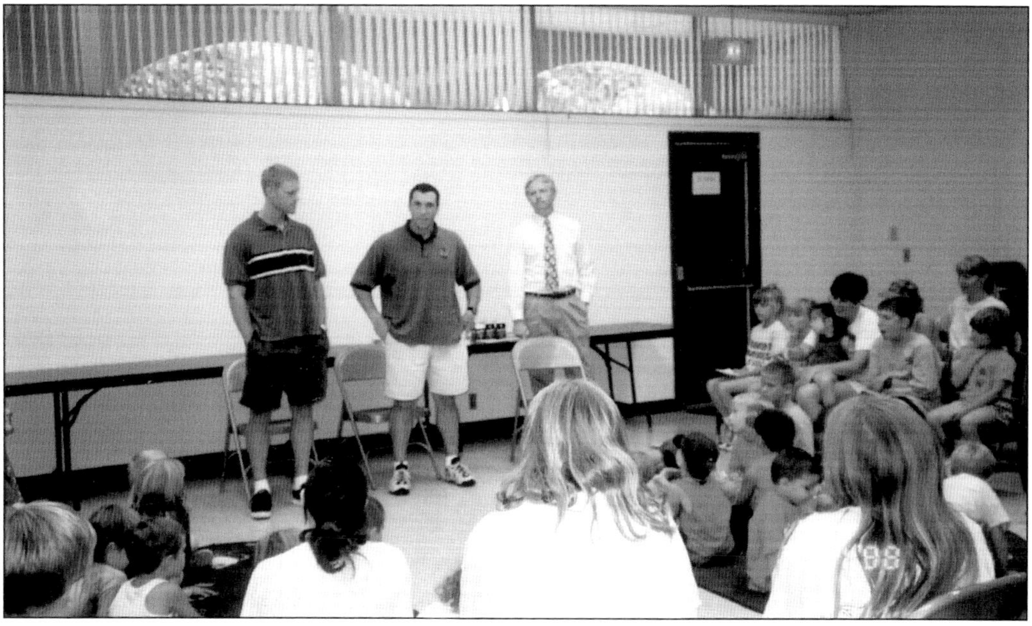

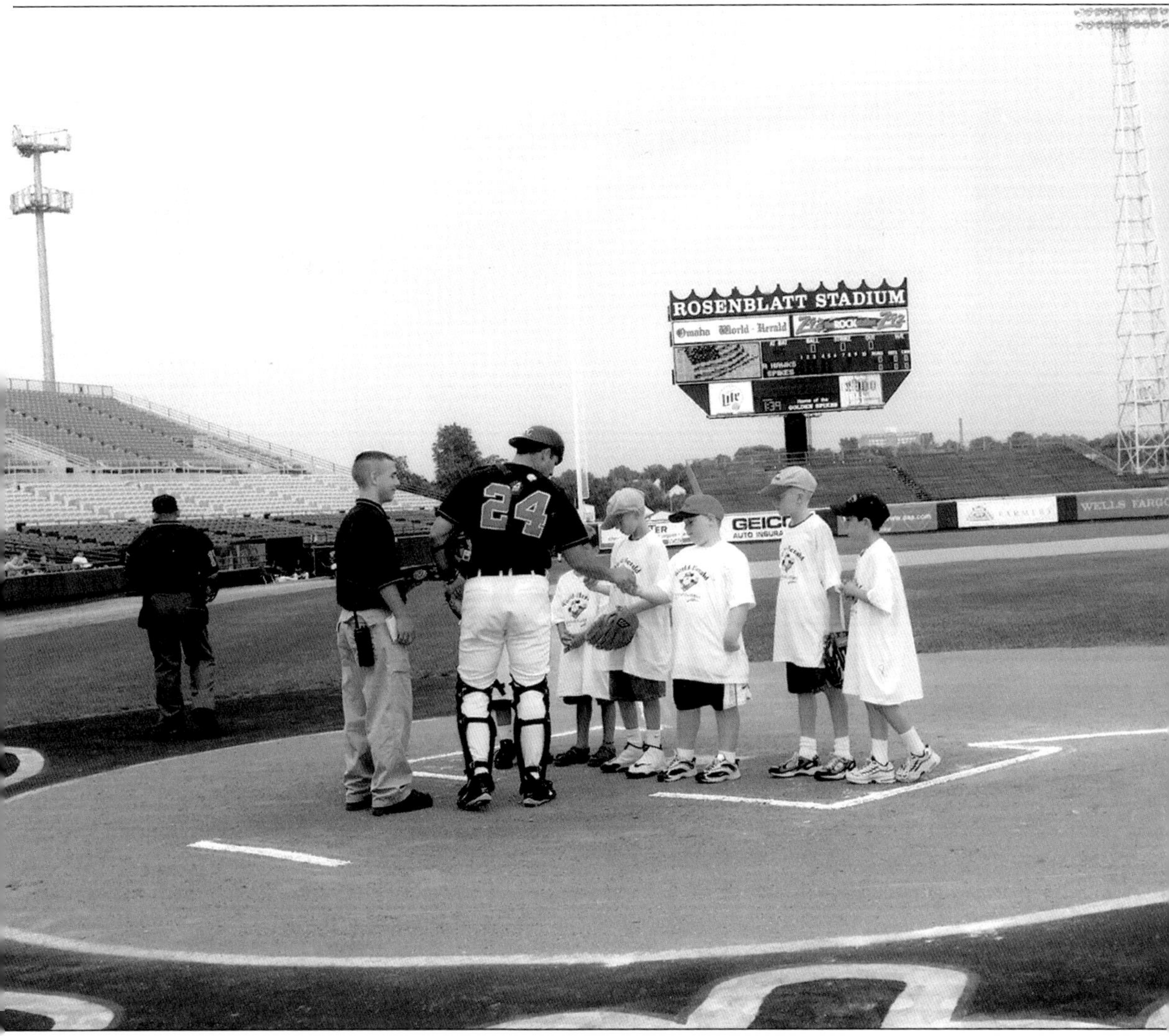

Be they Spikes or Royals, Omaha ballplayers participate in activities to strengthen community ties. Community outreach sends Omaha ballplayers to Omaha schools *(opposite, bottom)*, while welcoming Omaha's children to the mound before a game *(above)*. (Courtesy of the Omaha Royals.)

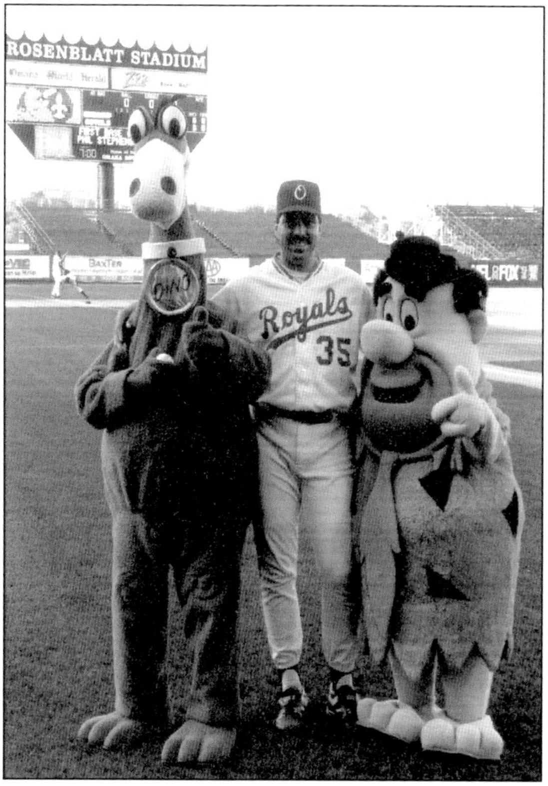

(Photos courtesy of the Omaha Royals.)

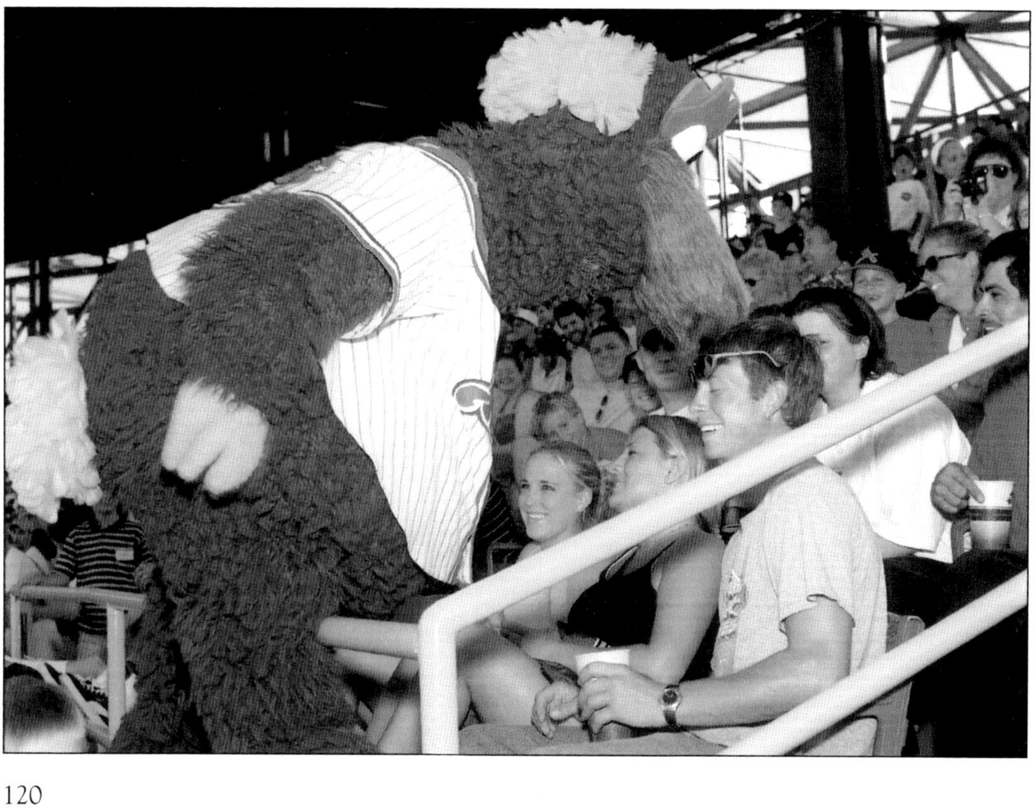

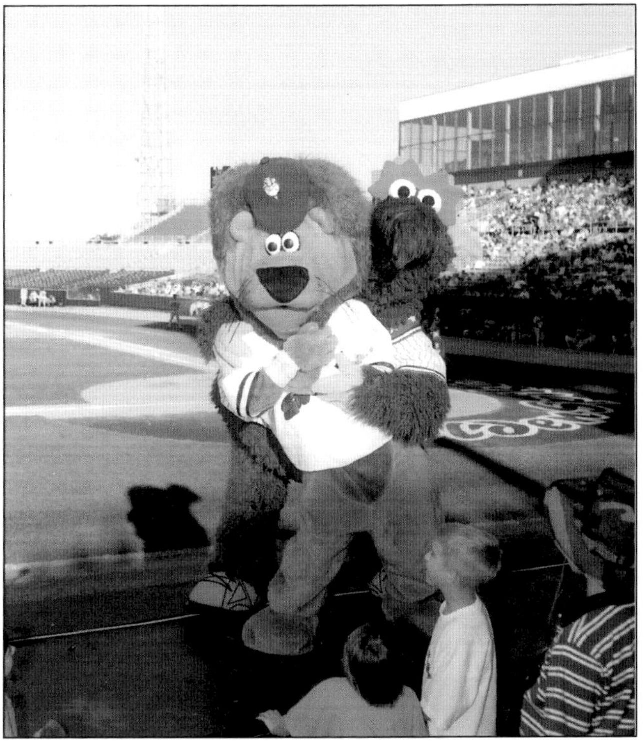

Mascots contribute to memories of summer nights at Rosenblatt Stadium. The visiting Philly Phanatic, seen here, holds Omaha's Casey for a camera mug. (Courtesy of the Omaha Royals.)

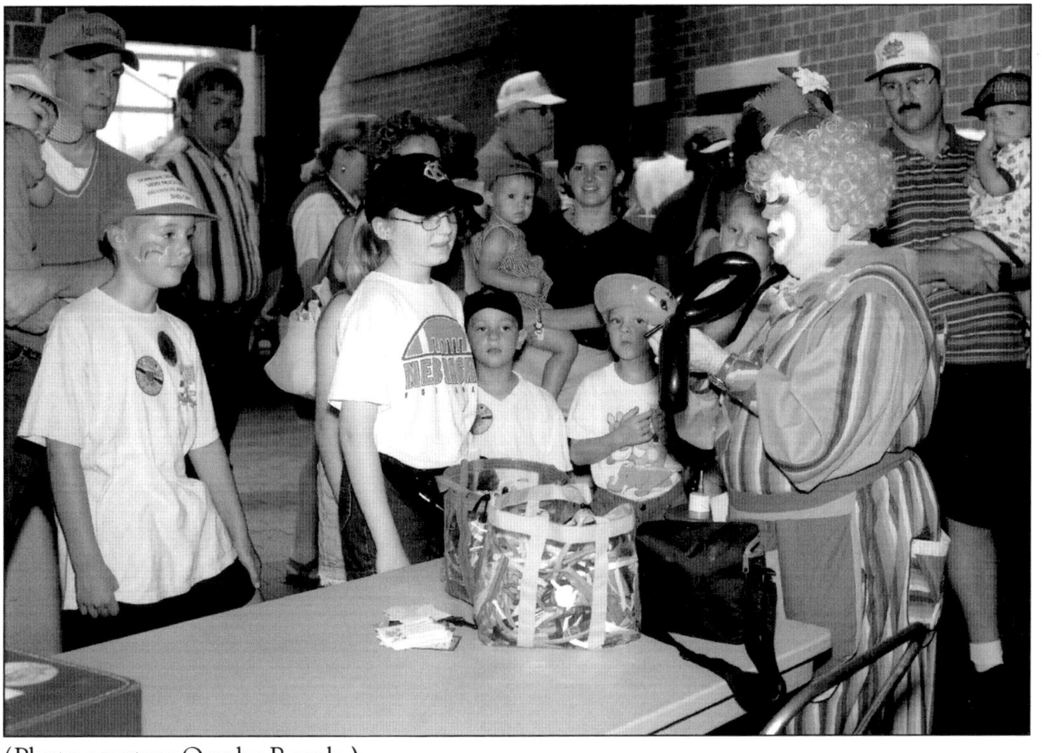

(Photo courtesy Omaha Royals.)

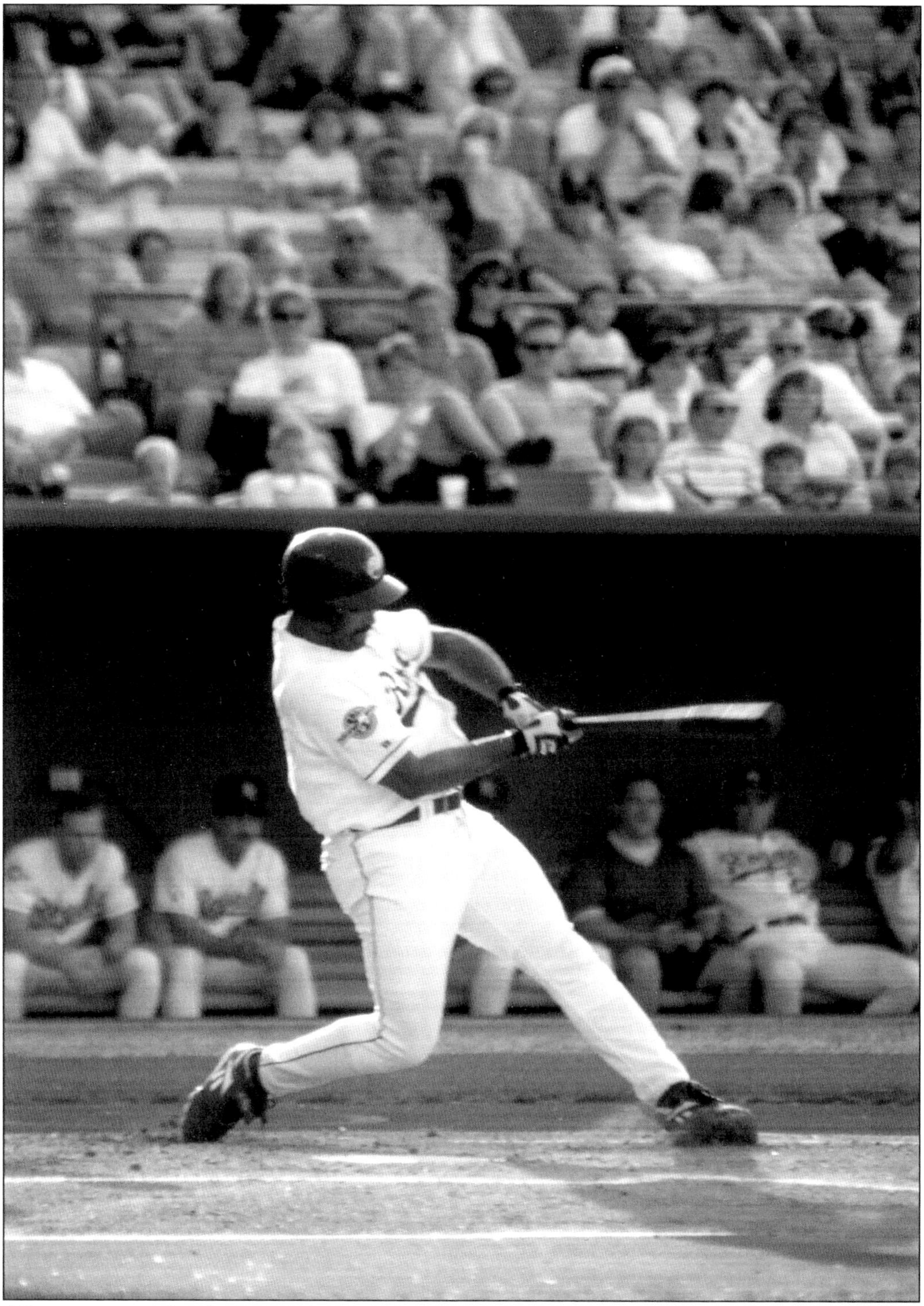

(Photo courtesy Omaha Royals.)

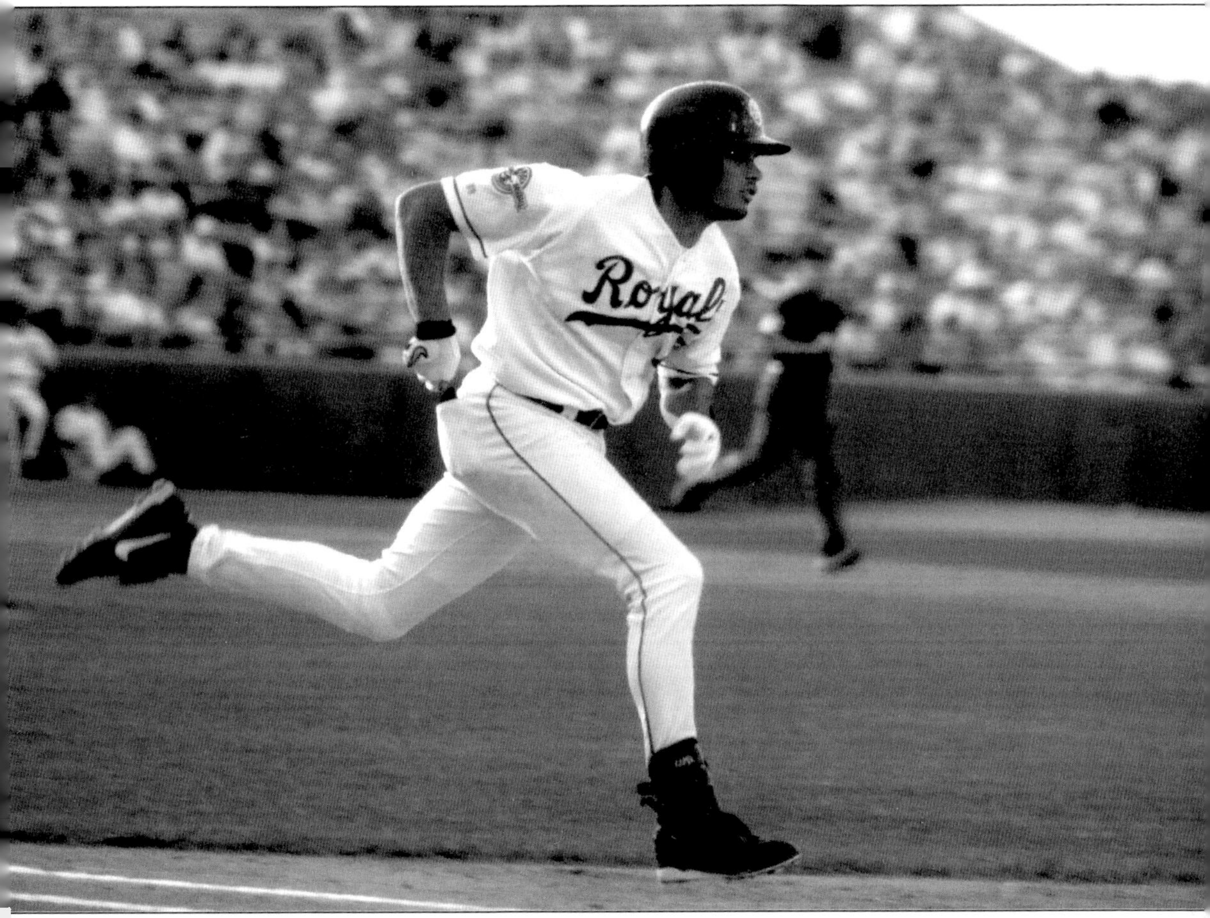

Minor league baseball fans seek out a seat in the grandstands of their local park as much for the experience as for the players on the field. Accepted is the fact of transition, that players on a triple AAA team are on their way up and out to an available spot on a major league roster, on their way back from seasons in the Show, in a rehabilitation stage following an injury, or even giving the game one final swing of the bat before retirement. Rarely do the players stay, season after season, becoming as comfortable a presence as Ernie Banks in Chicago or Cal Ripken in Baltimore. But they do become, ever so briefly, fan favorites. Baseball fans went to Rosenblatt to see Bucky Dent in his brief managerial stint with the Royals, and Dave "Rags" Righetti in the twilight of his pitching career. A minor league fixture of the early 1980s, Bombo Rivera could cull a slow, swelling roar from the crowd at Rosenblatt with each at-bat; whether he struck out or took a pitch to the far corners for extra bases (which he did with 27 homeruns in 1982), Bombo connected with fans. For the minor league fan, it is not so much the winning team that pulls one to the park. The draw is being there, watching, and later, sometimes years later, being able to recount seeing a 19-year-old George Brett take his first minor league swings or Jeff Conine on his way up through Baseball City, Memphis, and Omaha, finally landing on the 2003 World Series winning Florida Marlins roster. The boon is in being there for the beginning, middle, and end, watching paths cross and marking time by the box scores. (Courtesy of the Omaha Royals.)

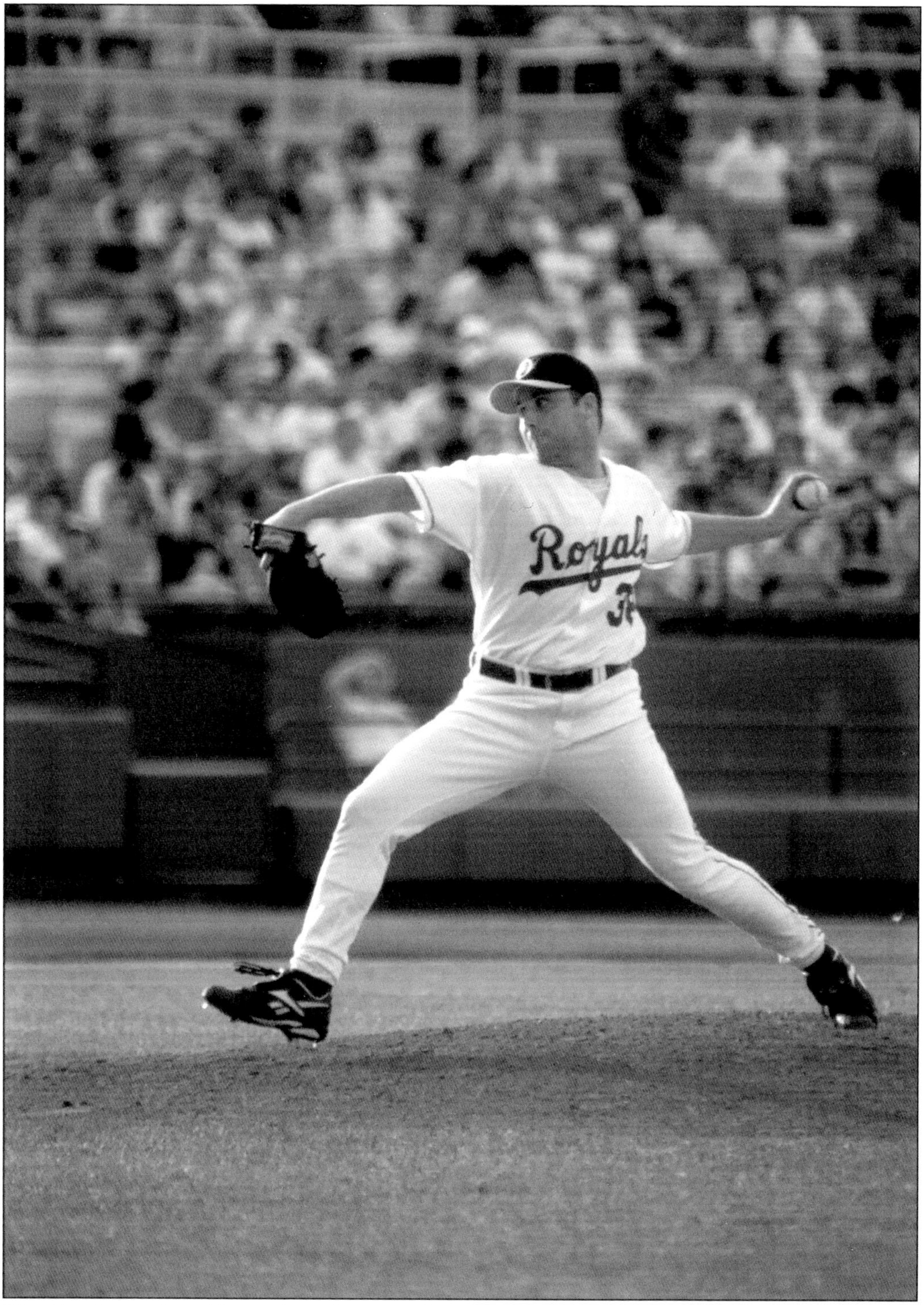

This Omaha pitcher delivers from the mound against the backdrop of Royals faithful. Rosenblatt Stadium in its 2004 form accommodated 23,145, making it one of the larger ballparks in the Pacific Coast League.

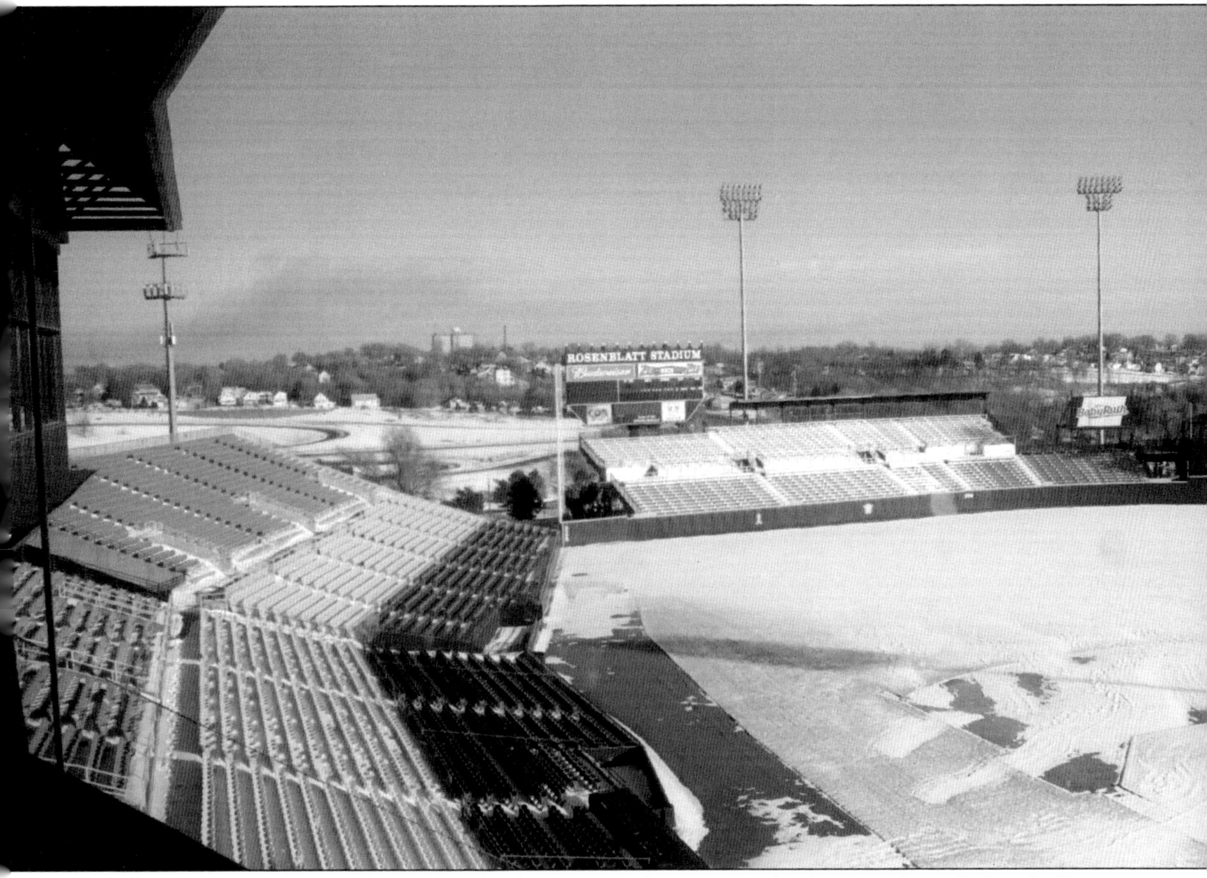

Rosenblatt Stadium in Winter, at rest before another run with the Royals and the College World Series. A glimpse at the interstate beyond left field suggests the view from the stadium-on-a-hill, reminding fans that Omaha is not flat. (Courtesy of Devon M. Niebling.)

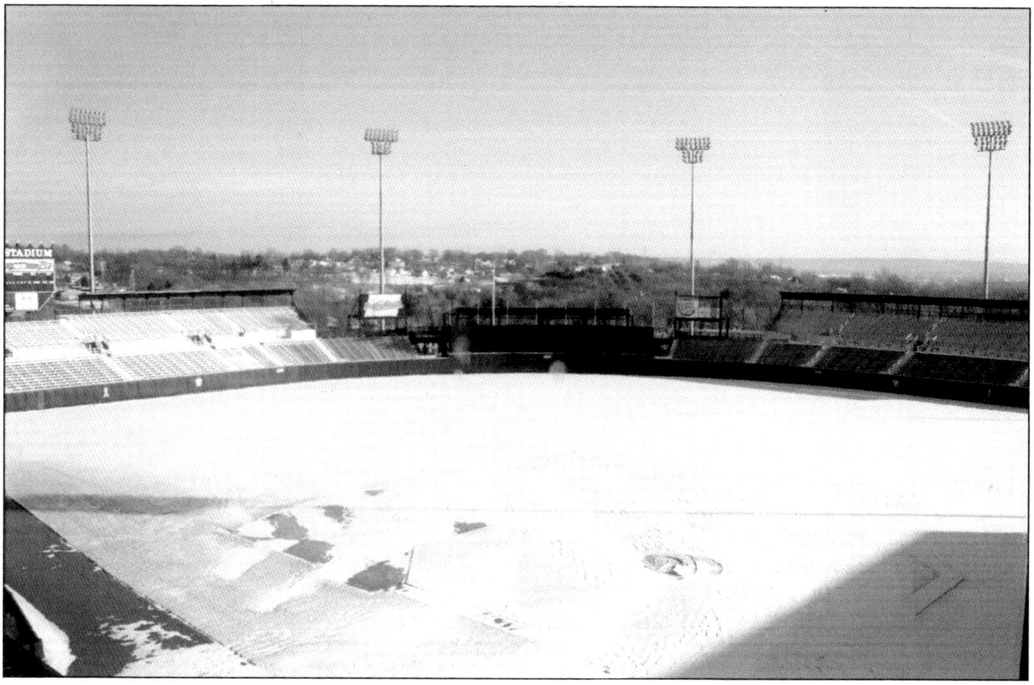

A ballfield in Winter is quiet, haunted by sounds of summers past. This view from the pressbox captures the sheer expanse of the field itself. (Courtesy of Devon M. Niebling.)

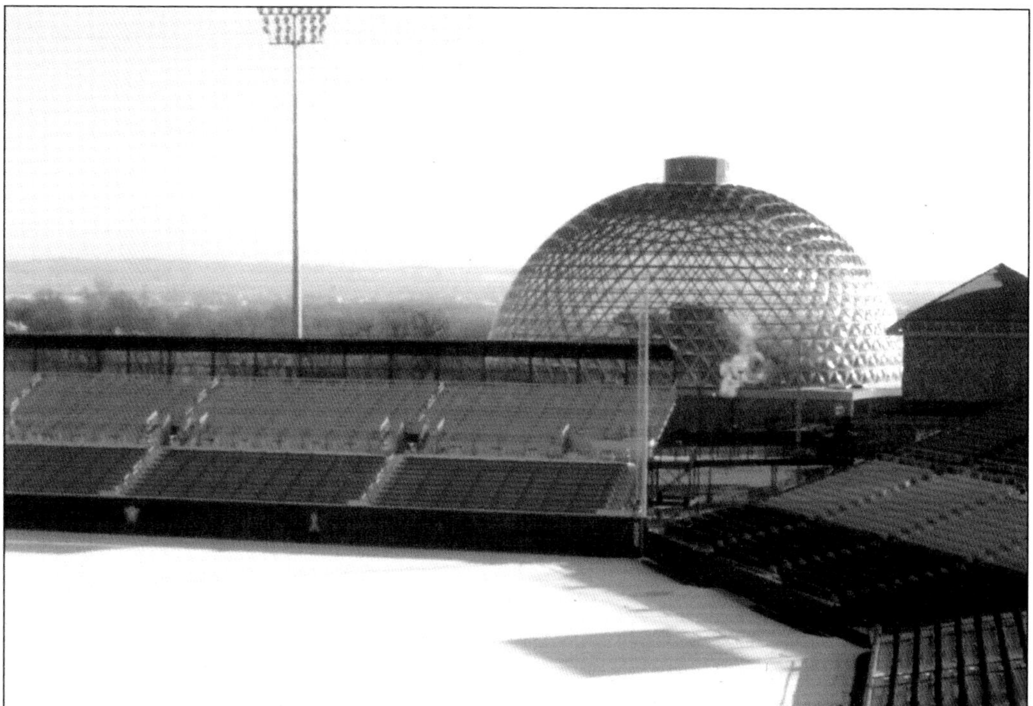

Henry Doorly Zoo's Desert Dome catches the light of a stark winter morning in Omaha. (Courtesy of Devon M. Niebling).

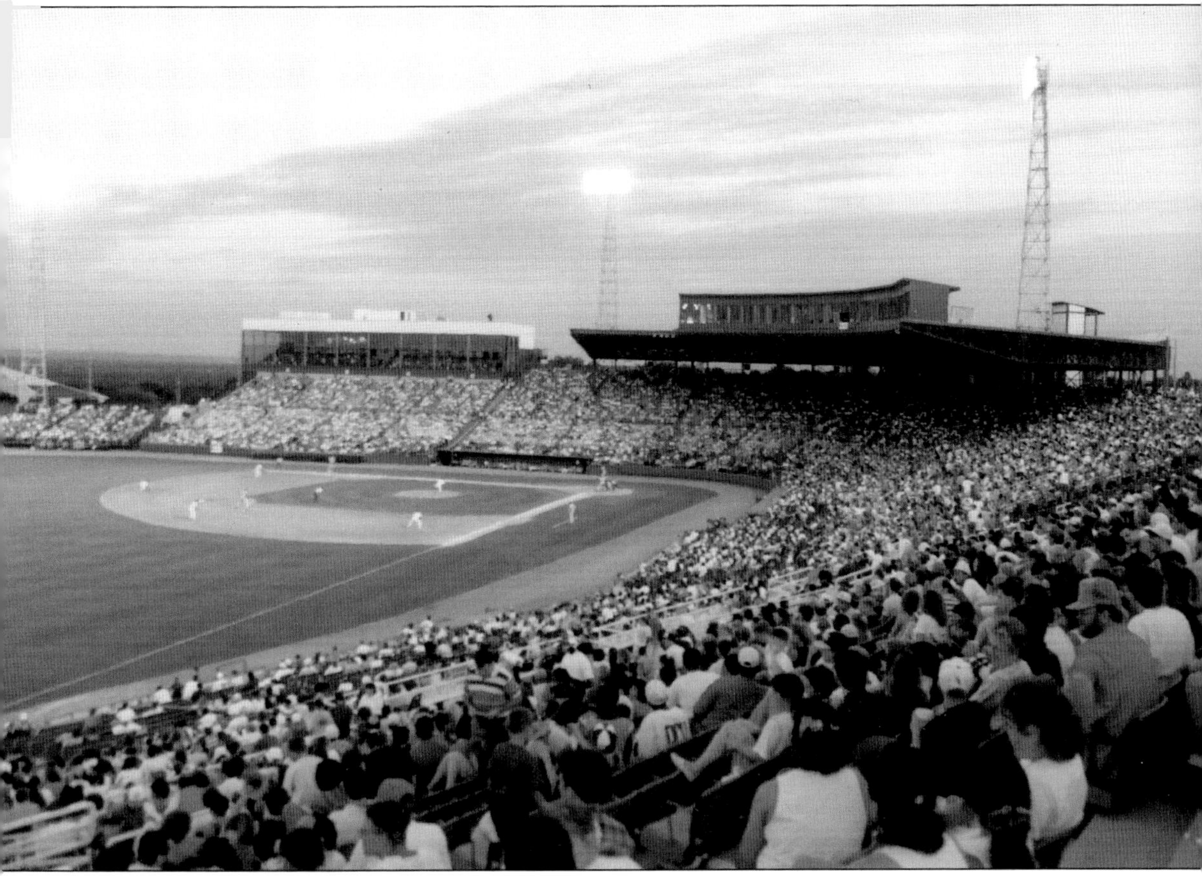

The cycle of seasons brings new faces, logo changes, and new playing fields, but the rhythm of the dance toward home is the same. The steady, precise pursuit of the fundamentals; the connection of bat on ball, running the bases, scooping grounders, following a fly from bat to sky to glove, and sending the ball 90 feet from mound to home on the strength of muscle, bone, and nerve. (Courtesy of the Omaha Royals.)

Special Thanks

The authors would like to note and thank the following sources.
Bahr Vermeer & Haecker, Architects LTD.
Bruce, Janet. *The Kansas City Monarchs: Champions of Black Baseball.* Lawrence, Kansas: University Press of Kansas, 1985.
Bozell & Jacobs
College World Series Omaha
Douglas County Historical Society and Museum
Durham Western Heritage Museum
Federal Writers' Project Papers, University of Nebraska at Omaha Archives
Freeland, John Harrison. *The History of Professional Baseball in Omaha.* M.A. Thesis University of Nebraska at Omaha, 1964.
Louie M's
Madden, W. C. and Patrick J. Stewart. *The Western League: A Baseball History, 1885 through 1999.* Jefferson, North Carolina: McFarland & Company, Inc., 2002.
Metro Area Transit
Nebraska State Historical Society
Omaha Bee
Omaha Print
Omaha Royals
Omaha World-Herald
O'Neal, Bill. *The American Association: A Baseball History 1902–1991.* Austin: Eakin Press, 1991.
Piccolo Pete's
Project Omaha at South High School
The Sporting News
Union Pacific Railroad Museum
University of Nebraska at Omaha